BRECHT AND IONESCO

BRECHT AND IONESCO
COMMITMENT IN CONTEXT

Julian H. Wulbern

University of Illinois Press / URBANA, CHICAGO, LONDON

ACKNOWLEDGMENTS

THIS WORK could never have taken the form it has without work "in the field," in the theaters and archives of Europe. I am particularly grateful to Frau Helene Weigel, director of the Berliner Ensemble, for her hospitality in admitting me to the active work of the Ensemble and allowing me the run of its archives. I am equally thankful for the friendliness, warmth, and openness of the members of the Ensemble, especially Werner Hecht, Manfred Wekwerth, Joachim Tenschert, Wolf Kaiser, and Felicitas Ritsch, to name but a few, whose comments and advice provided an insight into Brecht's work that could not have been gained otherwise. And to Dagmar Schneider, curator of the Brecht-Archiv, must go my special thanks for her interest and cooperation. No less is my debt to the personnel of the National Theatre at the Old Vic and the London Academy of Music and Dramatic Art for their courtesy and hospitality in welcoming my work there. I must similarly express my profound gratitude for the interest and candor of Eugène Ionesco, who interrupted his creative work to grant a mere graduate student a few hours of his valuable time and again provided insights that could have been gained in no other way.

But most of all I am indebted to my advisers at Northwestern University, Professor Walter B. Scott, Jr., of the School of Speech and Drama, and Herbert Heckmann, of the Department of German, who supervised the dissertation out of which this book grew. Without their apparently infinite patience, deep interest, good judgment, humanity, and inspiration, this work could not have been written.

CONTENTS

CHAPTER ONE / *Introduction*

ON JULY 28, 1965, I was present at a meeting of the Brecht Brigade of the Berliner Ensemble held in the Ensemble's rehearsal theater on Bertolt Brecht-Platz in East Berlin, for the purpose of preparing its members for their forthcoming guest performances at London's National Theatre at the Old Vic. Concerned chiefly with western understanding and criticism of the works of Bertolt Brecht, this meeting was devoted to readings, lectures, and discussions by members of the Ensemble of interpretations of Brecht's works by such English-speaking critics as John Willett and Martin Esslin.[1] But the most stimulating presentation of the afternoon was a reading by Ekkehard

---

[1] Werner Hecht, author of *Brechts Weg zum epischen Theater* (Berlin: Henschel Verlag, 1962), presented a critical review of John Willett's *The Theatre of Bertolt Brecht* (London: Methuen, 1959) and Martin Esslin's *Brecht: The Man and His Work* (Garden City, N. Y.: Doubleday Anchor Books, 1960). Hecht dismissed Willett's book as superficial and misleading (after reading a few excerpts, he commented, "Das ist doch Quatsch!"), but he saw Esslin's work as "dangerous" because it attempted to "save Brecht for the West" and because it was taken as authoritative.

Schall of selected passages critical of Brecht from *Argument gegen Argument,* the newly published German translation of Eugène Ionesco's *Notes et contre-notes.* This reading constituted the first direct contact with Ionesco for most of the members of the Ensemble, for, like most western authors, Ionesco remains unpublished in the East Zone; Schall's copy of *Argument gegen Argument* had been purchased in West Berlin and spirited through the Friedrichstraße checkpoint the previous day.

At any rate, Ionesco's criticism of Brecht's politically didactic theater was taken seriously as representative of western thought concerning Brecht by most of those present, and considerable effort was devoted to seeking means of justifying such polemically engaged drama in the eyes of western audiences and critics. The one significant person who failed to accord Ionesco's views such respect was Brecht's widow, Helene Weigel, the director of the Ensemble. It was her feeling that Ionesco was so driven by his hatred for Marxism that his criticism could be dismissed as too poorly informed and too highly subjective to be taken seriously. Other members of the Ensemble rejected this line of thought as too subjective in its own defensiveness to be tenable; particularly, the composer Paul Dessau, long a collaborator of Brecht's, felt that Ionesco represented a valid trend in modern theater, a freeing of the drama from the shackles of socialist didacticism, and that his criticism of Brecht ought to be given due consideration. Nevertheless, Frau Weigel's reaction struck me as quite perceptive, for my own reading of *Notes et contre-notes* had long led me to suspect that Ionesco had had little direct experience with or deep perception of Brecht's works.

The kindness and frankness of M. Ionesco himself removed this observation from the realm of conjecture, for, in an interview in his Paris home on September 11, 1965, arranged through the good offices of his agent, Mme. Rosica Colin, I was able to question him directly concerning the source of his impressions of Brecht. He admitted quite openly that his direct experience of Brecht's works was limited, since he neither read nor spoke German. He had seen a few of the plays in French, such as *Three Penny Opera, The Caucasian Chalk Circle, The Exception and the Rule,* and *A Man's a Man,* and he had seen the Berliner Ensemble's production in German of *Mother Courage* during the Paris International Theatre Festival in the summer of 1954. He had never read any of Brecht's theoretical writings; his criticism of such theoretical concepts as the *Verfremdungseffekt* was based entirely on his own reaction to the French Marxist writers such as Bernard Dort and René Wintzen[2] who had sought to introduce Brecht's works to the French theater public. Singularly unabashed by these admissions of ignorance, M. Ionesco persisted in his vehement criticism of Brecht, and, when I attempted to suggest that there might be more to Brecht than *Verfremdung* in the interest of Marxism, that indeed his own theatrical practices bore some external resemblance to those of Brecht, he grew visibly impatient. At this juncture it seemed prudent to change the subject.

In essence, then, Ionesco's severe criticism of Brecht does not draw upon direct experience of representative plays, but is rather based entirely upon his rejection of Brecht's avowed commitment to Marxism and his use of the theater to serve political ends. Indeed, so great is Ionesco's clearly stated antipathy to polemic theater in general, so strong is his sense of the ultimate absurdity of political action, that he could scarcely be expected to take a sympathetic or even an objective view of Brecht the poet. The political attitudes of the two stand in such violent and unequivocal opposition that they inevitably preclude any possibility of mutual understanding, as can be seen in the reaction of Frau Weigel, who refused to take Ionesco seriously either as a critic or as a playwright.[3] No reproach of either person is intended here, such as is implied by Reinhold Grimm, who

---

[2] Cf. Bernard Dort, *Lecture de Brecht* (Paris: Éditions du Seuil, 1960), and René Wintzen, *Bertolt Brecht* (Paris: Éditions Pierre Seghers, 1954).

[3] Throughout the reading of Ionesco's criticism, Frau Weigel was scornfully derisive, and she closed the discussion following the reading by remarking, "Wir können leicht gegen solche Meinungen stossen. Übrigens glauben viele, die Ionesco-Welle ist vorbei."

takes Ionesco to task for a regrettably false evaluation of Brecht's works.[4] It must simply be realized that there is no possibility that either could be receptive to the other, so great is the mutual exclusiveness of their beliefs. As a matter of fact, so wide is the void that separates the two that it is even difficult to find critics or interpreters of their dramas who are capable of taking an objective view of the works of both. There is a tendency among such critics to identify, as Grimm has done, with a single point of view and, as a consequence, to be blind to the merits of the other playwright. For example, aligning themselves with Grimm on the side of Brecht are such critics as Kenneth Tynan (the current literary director of England's National Theatre, whose set-to with Ionesco has become a celebrated feud), Bernard Dort, Werner Hecht, and John Willett, while on the other hand such writers as Richard Coe, Renée Saurel, Jacques Lemarchand, and Pierre-Aimé Touchard have opted for Ionesco. Indeed, of all the writers who have dealt with both Brecht and Ionesco, only Martin Esslin has been able to treat the two with equal sympathy and perceptivity. Hence much that has been written in comparison of the two has been so colored by the particular allegiance of the critic involved that no reliably objective comparative interpretation of their works has emerged.

Yet, in spite of the vast political distance which separates the two, a very real similarity exists between them which constantly finds expression in their works. Indeed, the differences which distinguish the two may be understood largely as the consequence of Brecht's imposition of a Communist discipline upon his creative self and of Ionesco's absolute rejection of any such external discipline. But even in Brecht's case this discipline remained less than perfect, for glimpses of a basically existential outlook can be seen throughout his works, and a similar existential concern continually occupies Ionesco. They share a common view of the incapacity of man to control his own destiny, as may be seen in the essentially passive and neg-

---

[4] Reinhold Grimm, "Brecht, Ionesco, und das moderne Theater," *German Life and Letters* 13 (April 1960): 224.

ative traits which recur continually in the protagonists of their plays. Both express as well, though in vastly different ways, a sense of frustration with regard to the capacity of language to convey the condition of man in the modern world. Robert Brustein has accurately observed that Brecht is in essence morbid, sensual, anarchical, and pessimistic,[5] and the same observation may certainly be made concerning Ionesco.

It is also striking that the two followed a parallel pattern of development in their early and middle writings, both dramatic and theoretical. Having started as theatrical renegades, both gradually evolved toward a more conventional mode of theater, although they were to go different ways in their mature works, Brecht toward more nearly traditional drama and Ionesco toward the anti-theater of his early works. Martin Esslin, in both his book on Brecht and his highly seminal work, *The Theatre of the Absurd*, has made much of such similarities, even going so far as to term Brecht a precursor of the absurd theatrical movement of the fifties. But in so doing, he draws his inferences largely from Brecht's very early works, such as *Baal* and *In the Jungle of the Cities*, and fragments such as *The Wedding* and *The Elephant Calf*, and he generally considers relatively superficial resemblances between the technical details of these works and those of Ionesco's early works, such as *The Bald Soprano* and *Jacques, or the Submission*.[6] While it will readily be admitted that such similarities do exist, particularly among the early works of both men, it is nevertheless equally clear and considerably more significant that their more mature works, though based upon similar insights into the human condition, are markedly dissimilar in both dramatic form and thematic content.

In short, while Brecht and Ionesco both perceive the world about them in remarkably similar ways, their perceptions are, especially in their middle and late works, couched in dramas which differ pro-

[5] Robert Brustein, *The Theatre of Revolt* (Boston: Little, Brown, 1962), p. 232.
[6] Esslin, *Brecht*, p. 243, and Esslin, *The Theatre of the Absurd* (Garden City, N. Y.: Doubleday Anchor Books, 1961), pp. 271–274.

foundly in both form and philosophic statement. These differences arise partly out of the particular form of engagement with which each became identified: Brecht's overt commitment to Communism and Ionesco's unequivocal rejection of any form of political commitment. But they arise as well out of the particular role which each felt the theater could play, not only with respect to its capacity to express his own perception of the world, but also with respect to its capacity to change the world thus perceived. Brecht, on the one hand, saw the theater as an instrument for the effectuation of social change (and thus he stands firmly rooted in the German tradition extending back to the *Jesuitendrama* of the late sixteenth century, the tradition of the theater as an institution for moral education), while Ionesco persists to this day in his insistence that theater can only be theater (and thus he stands rooted in the French tradition of *l'art pour l'art*). Hence the preliminary phases of this study will be devoted first to an investigation of the attitude of each playwright with regard to engagement and then to an examination of the dramatic theories of each, in order to clarify their expressed purposes in writing.

But ultimately much more goes into the creation of a work of literature, particularly of a drama, than didactic or polemic intention, and the basic question posed by this study, to what extent political commitment or lack thereof influences drama, must ultimately be answered in terms of the works themselves. As it happens, both Brecht and Ionesco wrote, at approximately the middle of their respective careers, works in which they expressed their exclusively political concerns. These two works, *The Measures Taken* and *Rhinoceros*, will be analyzed in detail in order to determine to what extent they are limited by the intentions of their authors and whether they may be taken as exclusively polemic or whether they achieve a greater degree of universality than the playwrights foresaw. And yet more important, neither Brecht nor Ionesco remained long exclusively dedicated to polemic drama, for the bulk of the later works of each is motivated by much more fundamentally human concerns than political didacticism. Of these more mature works, Brecht's *The Life of Galileo* and Ionesco's *Exit the King* will be taken as representative and subjected to detailed scrutiny in order to elaborate both the essential similarity of insight into the consequences of human action from which they issue and the striking dissimilarity they evidence in dramatic form and thematic statement. In the process, it will be suggested that Ionesco's categorical distrust of all *théâtre engagé* is ill-founded, that in fact political engagement can in some cases and did in the case of Brecht exert a positive influence in conditioning the creative act.

CHAPTER TWO / *The Problem of Engagement*

> Whoever fights for Communism
> Has of all virtues only one:
> That he fights for Communism.
>
> BRECHT[1]

> It is true that I have chosen a different
> engagement; it was an anti-engagement.
>
> IONESCO[2]

To SUGGEST that the significance of a work of literature may be the direct outgrowth of the political ideology held by its author is absurd, for the process of literary creation is far too complex to permit such simplification. To reduce a work of literary art to statement of a given doctrine is to do violence to that which distinguishes it as art, the uniqueness of its form. One has but to experience the intellectual

---

[1] Bertolt Brecht, *Die Maßnahme,* in *Stücke 4* (Frankfurt am Main: Suhrkamp Verlag, 1962), p. 266.

[2] Eugène Ionesco, "Journal," quoted in *Arts* (16 March 1966), p. 16.

contortions indulged in by, say, the Marxist school of critics (of which Ernst Schumacher's voluminous and "scholarly" study of Brecht's early works is an excellent example)[3] to sense that they impose upon the literature criteria which have nothing at all to do with literary merit. On the other hand, political commitment is distinctly a significant factor in the complex set of attitudes that determines a creative artist's perception of the world, and it plays an important role in conditioning his expression of that perception. Such is the case in the matter of the two playwrights under consideration, Brecht and Ionesco. Each responded in his own way to political and social conditions existing in his own country and in the world at a decisive time in his career—conditions which were strikingly analogous—and the resultant forms of engagement exerted, and for Ionesco continue to exert, considerable influence in shaping both the content and the form of their dramas. What is at issue here is the nature of the political intentions of each; it will be left to a later chapter to show that these intentions are not consistently carried out in their dramas.

Ionesco's attitude toward politics will serve as the point of departure, if only because he is the more unequivocal of the two in expressing his views, although this is not to suggest that his is ultimately the less complicated philosophy. As he makes quite clear in the epigraph of this chapter, he does consider himself engaged, but his is a negative engagement, a passionate disavowal of any form of political commitment. This anti-engagement has given many of his critics and interpreters no little trouble, for they have repeatedly tried to force from the plays political or social statements that coincide with their own views, statements which Ionesco insists are not there at all, at least not in his intention. Typical of such critics is Kenneth Tynan: having welcomed the successful introduction of Ionesco's works in England in the middle fifties, Tynan in 1958 turned on his erstwhile protegé with a vigorous attack which initiated

[3] Cf. Ernst Schumacher, *Die dramatischen Versuche Bertolt Brechts, 1918–1933* (Berlin: Rütten und Loening, 1955).

what is still referred to as "The London Controversy." In a review of a London production of *The Chairs*, he castigated Ionesco for his lack of any positive statement: "M. Ionesco certainly offers 'an escape from realism': but an escape into what? A blind alley, perhaps, adorned with *tachiste* murals. Or a self-imposed vacuum, wherein the author ominously bids us observe the absence of air. Or, best of all, a funfair ride on a ghost train, all skulls and hooting waxworks, from which we emerge into a far more intimidating clamour of diurnal reality. M. Ionesco's theatre is pungent and exciting, but it remains a diversion. It is not on the main road, and we do him no good, nor the theatre at large, to pretend that it is."[4]

Tynan's sense of frustration at a drama which offers him no answers or solutions to the plight of man is too strong to be missed, and he must hence be defended against those who criticize him for his misunderstanding of Ionesco,[5] for his frustration stems from a very accurate perception of the play's portent. But in the end he makes a demand of the new theater (not, it must be noted, of Ionesco himself) which Ionesco has no intention of meeting, as his reply to Tynan makes perfectly clear:

> M. Tynan reports that I have been called, with my approval, a sort of "messiah" of the theater. This is doubly inaccurate, for on the one hand, I have no taste for messiahs, and on the other, I don't believe that the calling of the artist or the dramatist is directed toward the messianic. I have the distinct impression that it is M. Tynan who is seeking messiahs. To bring a message to mankind, to want to direct the course of the world, or to save it, is the affair of founders of religions, of moralists or politicians—who, parenthetically, do a rotten job of it, as we know only too well. A dramatist restricts himself to writing plays in which he offers witness, not a didactic message—per-

---

[4] Kenneth Tynan, "Ionesco: Man of Destiny?" *The Observer* (22 June 1958). Reprinted in Eugène Ionesco, *Notes and Counter-Notes*, Donald Watson, trans. (New York: Grove Press, 1964), pp. 88–89.

[5] Cf. George Wellwarth, *The Theater of Protest and Paradox* (New York: New York University Press, 1964), p. 52.

sonal, emotional witness to his anguish and the anguish of others, or, more rarely, to his happiness. Or he expresses his tragic or comic sentiments on life.

A work of art has nothing to do with doctrines. I have already written elsewhere that a work of art which is only ideological, and nothing else, is useless, tautological, inferior to the doctrine which it expresses; it could be better expressed in the language of demonstration and debate. An ideological play is nothing other than the vulgarization of an ideology. In my opinion, a work of art has a system of expression which is its own, its own means of direct apprehension of reality.[6]

Having thus disposed of ideology in the theater, Ionesco proceeds to attack ideology in general:

That [attitude of Tynan's] is what would constrict the "main road," what would reduce by a considerable degree the various levels of reality, and limit the field open to experiment in artistic creation. I believe that what separates us from each other is politics, which raises barriers between men and always adds up to misunderstanding.

If I may speak paradoxically, I would say that true society, the authentic human community, is extrasocial—it is a broader and deeper society which is revealed in the common anxieties, the desires, the secret nostalgia of all of us. The history of the world is governed by this nostalgia and these anxieties, which political activity can only reflect, and which it reflects quite imperfectly. No society has ever been able to abolish human sadness; no political system can free us from the pain of life, the fear of death, or our thirst for the absolute. It is the human condition that determines the social condition, not the contrary.[7]

What Ionesco perceives as the human condition which governs the social condition, his basic concern, is more properly the subject of

[6] Eugène Ionesco, "Le role du dramaturge," *Notes et contre-notes* (Paris: Gallimard, 1962), p. 72. Originally published in an English translation by Donald Watson in *The Observer* (29 June 1958). The version cited here is my own translation of Ionesco's original French. Except as otherwise noted, all translations are my own.

[7] Ionesco, *Notes et contre-notes*, p. 73.

another chapter; what is significant here is his attitude toward ideologies in general. They are to him not the forces which unite men to solve common problems, but rather the forces which divide men into opposing camps, creating conflicts, misery, and disaster. As such, all ideologies, all pat sets of slogans, all sets of ideas which can be capitalized, are anathema to him.

In his role as the predominant anti-Establishment literary critic in England, Tynan was predictably irked by Ionesco's reply; his rebuttal the following week reiterated his demand that the dramatist make some sort of statement, some sort of choice:

> As I read the piece, I felt at first bewilderment, next admiration, and finally regret. Bewilderment at his assumption that I wanted drama to be forced to echo a particular political creed, when all I want is for drama to realize that it is a *part* of politics, in the sense that every human activity, even buying a pack of cigarettes, has social and political repercussions. Then, admiration: no one could help admiring the sincerity and skill with which, last Sunday, M. Ionesco marshaled prose for his purposes. And ultimately, regret: regret that a man so capable of stating a positive attitude toward art should deny that there was any positive attitude worth taking toward life. Or even (which is crucial) that there was an umbilical connection between the two.[8]

And this demand was echoed a week later, as Orson Welles joined what was becoming a generalized literary fray:

> Can the artist evade politics? He should certainly avoid polemics. Directing the course of the world, writes M. Ionesco, 'is the business of the founders of religions, of the moralists or the politicians.' An artist's every word is an expression of a social attitude; and I cannot agree with M. Ionesco that these expressions are always less original than political speeches or pamphlets. An artist must confirm the values of his society; or he must challenge them. . . . Under the present circumstances, the call to abandon ship is not merely unpractical: it is a cry

[8] Kenneth Tynan, "Ionesco and the Phantom," *The Observer* (6 July 1958); and *Notes and Counter-Notes*, p. 95.

of panic. If we are doomed indeed, let M. Ionesco go down fighting with the rest of us. He should at least have the courage of our platitudes.[9]

That Ionesco not only lacked "the courage of our platitudes," but was in fact engaged actively in attacking those very platitudes, was made abundantly clear in his second reply to Tynan:

To renew the language is to renew the conception, the vision of the world. Revolution consists of changing the mentality. Each new artistic expression represents an enrichment which corresponds to a spiritual need, a broadening of the limits of known reality: it is a gamble, an adventure; it cannot be simply an imitation of a classified ideology; it cannot serve a truth other than its own (for when such a truth has been uttered, it is already out of date). Any work that answers this need may appear absurd at the outset, for it conveys that which has never yet been conveyed in this way. And since its expression, its structure, its internal logic is everything, it is its expression which ought to be examined. One should look to its reasoning to see whether the conclusion proceeds logically from its assumptions, for it is a construction which appears (and *only* appears) to be independent, to stand by itself—just as a play, for example, is a construction which ought to be described in order to check its internal unity. The assumptions of any reasoning are, of course, determined by other reasoning, which itself is again only a construction.

I don't believe there is any contradiction between creation and cognition, for the structures of the mind are very likely reflections of universal structures.[10]

That *The Observer* purchased but decided not to publish this last rebuttal by Ionesco was probably merciful,[11] for it brought to an early end a squabble between two opposing camps that could not under

---

[9] Orson Welles, "The Artist and the Critic," *The Observer* (13 July 1958); and *Notes and Counter-Notes*, p. 100.

[10] Ionesco, *Notes et contre-notes*, p. 85.

[11] The text of this reply was purchased by *The Observer* but withheld from publication. It first appeared in French in *Cahiers des saisons* 15 (Winter 1959): 265.

any circumstances come to agreement, nor even see any merit in the viewpoints of their adversaries, however politely they may have addressed each other. What the controversy did accomplish was to bring to public light a viewpoint which Ionesco had long held and which he continues to hold tenaciously to this day. As early as 1955 he wrote an article entitled "My Plays Do Not Claim to Save the World,"[12] and in pages of his journal published recently in *Arts* on the occasion of the premiere of his latest work, *Hunger and Thirst*, he recounts the following anecdote:

> At an international convention of theater people, an orator at the podium expressed his indignation that dramatists were not writing plays about the famine in India. My friend P. A. Touchard rose to say that the victims of famine needed to be given bread, not plays about bread. The orator and numerous partisans were indignant at the intervention of Touchard. They would rather kill, rather let the suffering starve than renounce the fanaticism of their propagandas.
>
> And there you have the crime, the obstinacy, the universal stupidity, the daily bread of our world: idiotic murderers who have become idiots because they have been dehumanized, desensitized.[13]

This sense of dehumanization, of being rendered insensitive, is characteristic of his reaction to any political ideology. In short, he appears to hold the same view of ideologies that is expressed by Lionel Trilling: "But to call ourselves the people of the idea is to flatter ourselves. We are rather the people of ideology, which is a very different thing. Ideology is not the product of thought; it is the habit or the ritual of showing respect for certain formulas to which, for various reasons having to do with emotional safety, we have very strong ties of whose meaning and consequences we have no clear understanding."[14]

And the essence of these strong ties relating to our emotional

[12] Eugène Ionesco, "Mes pièces ne prétendent pas sauver le monde," *L'Express* (15 October 1955), p. 34.

[13] Ionesco, "Journal," quoted in *Arts* (16 March 1966), p. 16.

[14] Lionel Trilling, *The Liberal Imagination* (Garden City, N. Y.: Doubleday Anchor Books, 1953), p. 277.

safety, as Ionesco sees them, is inhuman and dehumanizing. But even worse, ideologies are commonly used to mask the aggressiveness and hatred that man employs against man, as Ionesco points out in one of his most forceful essays:

It seems to me that in our time and at all times religions and ideologies have never been anything but alibis, masks, pretexts for the will to kill, for the destructive instinct, for the deep hatred of man for man; people have killed in the name of the Order, against the Order, in the name of God, against God, in the name of the fatherland, to depose an evil order, to liberate themselves from God, to free others, to punish the evil in the name of the race, to stabilize the world, for the well-being of humanity, for glory, or because they had to live by snatching their bread from the hands of others: everywhere there have been massacres and torture in the name of love and of charity. In the name of social justice! The saviors of mankind have founded inquisitions, invented concentration camps, built crematory ovens, established tyrannies. The guardians of society have built jails, the enemies of society have murdered: I even believe the jails appeared before the crimes.

I will be saying nothing new if I assert that I fear those who desire ardently the well-being or happiness of mankind. When I see a do-gooder, I take flight as if I'd seen a madman armed with a dagger. "You have to choose," they tell us today. "You have to choose the lesser of evils. It is better to move with the times." But where are the times going? I believe this is a new deception, a new ideological justification of the same permanent murderous impulse; for thus we "commit ourselves," and we have a more subtle reason to compromise or to join this or that party of murderers. That is the latest of hypocrisies of the most recent mystification. We have noted it well: he who dares not to hate is banished by society: he becomes a traitor, a pariah.[15]

Such unequivocal rejection of any form whatsoever of political ideology is so characteristic of Ionesco that pages could be filled with quotations just as vehement as the one cited above; there are scores of such passages in *Notes et contre-notes* alone. But it is time here

---

[15] Ionesco, *Notes et contre-notes*, pp. 138–139.

to take a different tack, to seek deeper roots for Ionesco's distrust of political ideologies and the solutions they propose to untangle the dilemma of humanity. Fundamental to his apolitical disposition, there is an undercurrent of discomfort, of malaise or apprehension toward life in society, which runs through both his critical writings and his dramas; this current comes most clearly to expression in his second rebuttal to Kenneth Tynan, in a passage attacking a criticism by Philip Toynbee:

> On the other hand, I am a little astonished at the astonishment of M. Philip Toynbee at the idea that a man can be impaired in his movements by society or by the air that he breathes. I feel that it is quite difficult to breathe and to live; I feel, too, that it is possible for a man not to be a social animal. The child has a great deal of trouble conforming to society; he resists it and adapts himself to it with difficulty—teachers will know what I am talking about here. And if he adapts himself to it with difficulty, it is because there is something in human nature which has to evade society or be alienated by it. And once man conforms to society, he doesn't handle it well. Social life, life with "the others" has been depicted for us by Sartre himself (whom M. Toynbee will certainly permit me to quote) in his play *No Exit*. Hell is society, hell is "the others." And didn't Dostoievski say that it was impossible to live more than a few days with anyone without beginning to detest him? And doesn't the hero of [Brecht's] *Mann ist Mann* lose his soul and his name, and even his individuality, in joining the collective irresponsibility of uniforms?[16]

In perceiving thus the perplexity of the social role man is forced to play, in sensing that there is something inherent in humanity that struggles to escape social determinism, Ionesco here gives vent to one of his most basic apprehensions, that felt toward the conformity forced by any society upon its individual members. The real danger that he sees in this conformity is that it dehumanizes the individual

16 *Ibid.*, pp. 88–89.

by seeking to efface the traits which distinguish him from the rest of the herd, the traits which form the essence of his humanity. In short, Ionesco despises and fears any force which tends to lump humanity into an amorphous mass or class. And yet he may at times seem guilty of tending to overgeneralize, of indulging in the same sort of classification of humanity for which he castigates his critics and politically oriented writers in general. He admits quite freely that his feelings concerning the bourgeois are highly ambivalent, as may be seen in the following notation from his journal:

> Today, of course, we have finally succeeded in "demystifying" racism, and we realize that the noble ideals of war were simply economic in nature. What would we do if we didn't have the bourgeois to kill and the petit-bourgeois to ridicule? And the petit-bourgeois is no myth, he is not a decoy; he cannot be demystified, because he has already been unmasked. How could one invent a more extraordinary scapegoat? He is there before us, right at hand; you have only to take your pick. Before, alas, not everyone was a Jew or a Negro. You had to hunt for your Jew or Negro. Today, however, anybody can be accused of being a bourgeois or a petit-bourgeois if his ideas aren't exactly those which you would wish or if he displeases you: petit-bourgeois, asocial, reactionary, bourgeois mentality—these are the new insults, the new ways of pillorying. And the accusers are, more often than not, themselves petit-bourgeois gone mad. For example: X and Z are typical petits-bourgeoises, tinged by Marxist readings—for I, too, believe in the petit-bourgeois, and hate him.[17]

Thus fundamentally, although he realizes that he is falling into the same sort of stereotyped thought of which he is suspicious in polemic works of art, it is disgust for and even fear of the bourgeois which motivate Ionesco. Yet this fear and disgust are consistent with his apolitical bent, for it is precisely the bourgeois spirit of conformity as it is manipulated by what he calls the "tyranny of political regimes"

[17] *Ibid.*, p. 216.

that he sees as dehumanizing. It was this demagogic influence of propagandistic art that he singled out for his criticism in a lecture given at the Sorbonne in March of 1960:

> But we know quite well that when religions speak of salvation of the soul, they are thinking above all of hell, where they are sure all souls that rebel against salvation must go; we know as well that when one speaks of education, one turns up very quickly with re-education, and we all know what that means. The pedants of all camps, the educators and the re-educators, the propagandists of whatever beliefs, the theologians and the politicians—all these constitute, in the final analysis, the oppressive forces against which the artist must struggle. I have found it necessary to assert on several occasions that two dangers menace the life of the spirit and of the theater in particular: the mental sclerosis of the bourgeoisie on the one hand, and the tyrannies of regimes and political movements on the other—that is, the bourgeois of all opposing camps. By the bourgeois I mean conformity from above, from below, from left, from right, bourgeois irreality as well as socialist irreality, systems of worn-out conventions. Often, alas, the worst bourgeois are the anti-bourgeois bourgeois. I wonder if art might not be that liberation, that reapprenticeship to a freedom of mind to which we have been dehabituated, which we have forgotten, but whose absence impairs those who believe themselves free without being so (being deterred by their prejudice) as well as those who don't believe they are or can be free.[18]

This last passage is certainly not without an ironic edge quite typical of Ionesco, for he deliberately suggests that he may be among those worst bourgeois who are often the anti-bourgeois bourgeois. Nevertheless, he *is* unequivocally anti-bourgeois in his critical writings, and even more so in his plays, which abound in pathetically bourgeois figures, either complacent in their snug little niches in life or struggling futilely to preserve an order which threatens to destroy them.

[18] *Ibid.*, p. 63.

Hence Ionesco is an engaged dramatist to the extent that he is critical of society and of the Establishment and to the extent that he attacks violently the current political attitudes which have bred hostilities among men by dividing them into opposing factions. Yet in thus attacking extant ideologies, he refuses to provide, as even favorable critics suggest he should, an alternative ideology, as witness his reply to a review of *Rhinoceros* by Walter Kerr:

> If I were to ask M. Walter Kerr, the critic of the *New York Herald Tribune*, to define for me his personal philosophy, he would be very embarrassed. And yet it is precisely his job, not mine, to find the solution, his job, that of the other critics, and especially that of my audience. Personally, I'm fed up with the intellectuals who for thirty years have done nothing but propagate rhinoceritis and who do nothing but sustain philosophically the collective hysterias that periodically engulf whole nations. Wasn't it the intellectuals who invented Nazism? If I set one ready-made ideology against other ready-made ideologies which are cluttering our minds, I would only be countering one system of rhinoceritic slogans with another.[19]

But if he does not propose to counter one system of rhinoceritic slogans with another, one might ask, what does he propose? His answer, given further along in the same article, is eloquent: "It strikes me as ridiculous to demand of a dramatist a Bible, a way to salvation; it is ridiculous to think for everyone and to give everyone a pat philosophy. The dramatist poses questions. In their leisure, in their solitude, the people must think about these questions and grope for their own solutions in utter freedom. An impractical solution found by oneself is infinitely more valuable than a ready-made ideology which prevents one from thinking."[20] The key words in this passage are leisure and solitude, for Ionesco has no intention of enflaming the masses in favor of this or that new order; on the contrary, his view of humanity is best perceived in contemplation and solitude *after* the

19 *Ibid.*, p. 187.
20 *Ibid.*

experience of one of his plays, for the condition of man is a complex one which cannot be remedied by a ready-made or a made-to-order ideology. And again solitude is important, for it is, in Ionesco's view, the ultimate state of man in modern society: "One of the great critics of New York complains that, after having destroyed one conformity and having put nothing in its place, I left him and the audience in a void. That is just what I intended to do. It is this void out of which a free man must extricate himself alone, by his own strength, not by that of others."[21] Ilis is thus not the sort of *l'art pur* criticized so eloquently by Sartre as being out of place in this age; Ionesco is engaged in trying to portray the absurdity of a world divided among ideologies incompatible with one another. Yet he refuses either to choose sides or to commit himself to a new ideology, which he justly fears would be equally incompatible with those already existing. What he seeks to convey is the utter solitude and the fragile mortality of the man who has the courage to regard himself as an individual at the mercy of the machinery of modern society. In this respect he is neither purely negative in his criticism, nor, as Tynan seems to suggest, purely passive; he does not sit with his fingers in his ears awaiting the blast, but is rather crying the alarm as loudly as he can.

At this juncture it is necessary to examine to some extent the actual world to which Ionesco reacted in choosing a posture of nonalignment. And, while I do not propose to deal with the historical background in any depth, it is nevertheless striking how analogous the social and political conditions in postwar France in 1945, to which Ionesco reacted, were to those in postwar Germany in 1918, to which Brecht reacted. In the first place, both countries emerged as defeated nations, for although France was a member of the victorious allied powers in 1945, the stigma of defeat in 1940 and subsequent German occupation constituted a blot on her national pride and served further to divide already dissident forces. Both countries were dependent upon external sources for their continued existence; Germany lay at the mercy of the allies, and France was dependent

[21] *Ibid.*

on foreign aid to reestablish her demolished economy and war-ravaged industry. In both countries the old regime had been discredited, and no new order seemed likely to come into being to restore balance to the system. Rather, both fell prey to dissident factionalism, and nothing resembling an integration of national interests or spirit could be established to unify the divisive elements; one political crisis followed another to foil all attempts to create stability. Both countries had saddled themselves with governmental systems fundamentally ill-equipped to deal with the exigencies at hand; in France the Fourth Republic had been modeled on the moribund and static Third Republic, and in Germany the Weimar Republic could be regarded as little more than an idealistic attempt to impose democratic institutions upon a nation unprepared to handle them. Economic and social crises plagued the struggling bureaucracies, and the middle class, the bourgeoisie, was gripped by political disillusionment and torpor. Above this general chaos hovered the specter of war and its consequent deprivation, degradation, and suffering, accentuated in both countries by the presence of the army as a powerful and dissident political force.

There were, of course, differences, particularly in the ways in which the situations developed in the two nations. Whereas Germany had lost its foreign possessions as a consequence of World War I, France after World War II became engaged in a series of long, bloody, expensive, senseless, and eventually futile struggles in attempting to preserve her colonial empire and thereby squandered her already depleted economic and human resources. In addition, France in the postwar years existed in an age which stood in the shadow of the malevolence and genocide perpetrated by Hitler, which seemed to stress the malignant side of human nature, and in the shadow of the atomic and hydrogen bombs, which underscored man's power to do evil. Even the hopeful developments of the postwar years, the establishment of the European Economic Community, the ultimate resolution of colonial affairs, and the advent of a semblance of economic and political stability with de Gaulle's accession to power, were tainted by precariously negative aspects, and the world at large was repeatedly threatened by the confrontations and "brinksmanship" of what passed for diplomacy in the cold war. It was, in short, a situation which seemed to be beyond the influence of the individual being, even though he might align himself with a political party. As Stanley Hoffman has observed: "The problems of economic and social change were handled by the bureaucracy rather than by Parliament; what came before the nation's representatives were the incidents and crises in the process—budgetary or taxation problems, claims by special interests. In those cases, French parties, as in the thirties, tended to behave more like pressure groups and to defend the interests of their principal voters. Their incapacity for defining coherent policy resulted in multiple cabinet crises and undermined the parliamentary system once again."[22] But even more fundamental to the breakdown of political efficacy in postwar France was what Hoffman has aptly termed "political lag":

> The most obvious paradox is the political lag. Social change remains behind economic change; political change is even further behind. Social and international changes affect but slowly the political system, and seem indeed more affected by *it*. Observers who have noticed the solidarity of French regimes in such misdemeanors as centralization, keeping the public out, and treating the voters like children, want to *donner la parole au peuple* instead, at last. But at present *le peuple* tends to speak the only language it knows, the language in which it has been trained by this solidarity of regimes, the language of delegating decisions to others, of intransigence and discord, and of lingering nostalgia for a fundamental unity, which can be reached only at the level of feelings and dreams or at the cost of ambiguity. In a substantive sense France is not yet a political community, not because of merciless clashes of values (there are fewer than before) but because of this common language.[23]

[22] Stanley Hoffman, "The French Political Community," *In Search of France* (Cambridge: Harvard University Press, 1963), p. 25.
[23] *Ibid.*, p. 106.

Again and again, in speaking of the French who have thus long felt alienated from the political system, Hoffman expresses the same sense of disorder, of inability to communicate, that pervades Ionesco's critical writings and dramas. Yet even had there been no such alienation between the Frenchman and his government, it is unlikely that Ionesco could have become politically committed, for he is fundamentally apolitical. As Richard Coe has accurately perceived:

> . . . Problems of political and social organisation, concerning as they do almost exclusively the conscious and material aspects of existence, can rarely be of more than marginal interest, and in fact may dangerously obscure the real issues at stake. On the other hand, the "horror" of existence and the universal eminence of death, above all the universal awareness of the *fear* of death, are specifically linked with certain definite political combinations in the modern world, and, consequently, these combinations are never negligible. To put the same conclusion in another form: if it is true that Ionesco has roundly condemned both Sartre and Brecht and all "committed" literature, it is no less true that he could never have written the plays for which he is known, if indeed he had written at all, were it not for Hitler and Hiroshima.[24]

The situation in Germany in 1918, on the other hand, developed in a different direction. Whereas factionalism in France defied any sort of political integration, there tended in Germany to be a drift among the politically active toward alignment with either the extreme left or the extreme right, with the bulk of the bourgeoisie remaining politically inert in the middle. By the late twenties there were only two activist political forces, the Communist Party on the one hand and the National Socialists and their imitators on the other; the specter of militant nationalism had been revived. Confronted with this choice, Brecht chose Communism, representing as it purported to a supra-national anti-war movement directed against both

[24] Richard Coe, *Eugene Ionesco* (Edinburgh: Evergreen Pilot Books, 1961), pp. 79–80.

the militant chauvinists at the opposite extreme and the politically moribund bourgeoisie.

Any account of Brecht's commitment to Communism must contend with certain difficulties. In the first place, Brecht was an extremely complex personality whose utterances and actions were, more often than not, contradictory. Even if the temptation to oversimplify him can be successfully resisted, there remains the danger that somewhere in the process of analyzing his works and his politics, the process of dissecting him and trying to patch him back together again, some elements of the whole Brecht are almost certain to be lost or obscured. Another significant difficulty lies in the fact that very few of Brecht's own writings on the subject of his political conversion have been published; most remain in his *Nachlaß* in the Brecht-Archiv in East Berlin, which jealously guards not only the rights of publication, but even access to the documents. As a consequence, one is forced to rely largely upon what others have said about the man and his politics. But herein lies the greatest difficulty of all, for so polemic are Brechtian criticism and biography, so inextricably entangled are politics and aesthetics, that it is often difficult to discern the real Brecht from the viewpoint of the particular critic or biographer involved. Generally speaking, western critics, even those of leftist inclination, are reluctant to let Brecht be both a genuine Communist and a significant artist. They seek either to dilute his political commitment to the East and thus "save him for the West," as Frau Weigel claims both Esslin and Willet have done, or they question the validity of his art, as Otto Mann, Friedrich Luft, and Ionesco have done. In the East, on the other hand, the tendency is either to make Brecht such a doctrinaire party-liner that his plays must be distorted almost beyond recognition in the process of interpretation or to take him to task for not being familiar enough with party teaching and practice, as does the study by Ernst Schumacher already alluded to. It should be made clear at the outset that this study will seek to present a more integrated view, for there is no inherent contradiction between commitment to Marxism and devotion to art, provided that the artist is talented, honest, and cunning enough to couch his perception of the truth in terms which have some appeal to the regime.

Brecht's earliest writings reflect no political commitment whatsoever; indeed, they bear striking resemblance in both form and theme to Ionesco's dramas. However, they also bear the seeds of what was later to condition his turn to Communism. One of the attitudes which clearly manifests itself in the early plays, poems, and critical writings is his abhorrence of war, which can be traced as far back as an essay written in 1915, when Brecht was a seventeen-year-old student at the Augsburg Gymnasium. Assigned to write on the theme "Dulce et decorum est pro patria mori," he responded thus: "The saying that it is sweet and honorable to die for one's country can only be evaluated as propaganda. The leaving of life is never easy, either in bed or on the battlefield, least of all certainly for young men in the full bloom of their years. Only hollow-heads can carry vanity so far as to believe in an easy leap through the darkness of the last hour. When the grim reaper approaches them in person, they take their shields on their backs and flee, just like the emperor's chubby jester at Philippi who thought up this proverb."[25] But his biographers are justifiably unanimous in tracing the extreme fervor of his later pacifist disposition to his direct experience of the war as a medical orderly during the closing months of World War I. Brecht recounted his own views of this experience years later to Sergei Tretiakov: "As a boy I was mobilized in the war and placed in a hospital. I dressed wounds, applied iodine, gave enemas, performed blood transfusions. If the doctor told me: 'Amputate a leg, Brecht,' I would answer: 'Yes, your excellency,' and cut off the leg. If I was told: 'Make a trepanning,' I opened the man's skull and tinkered with his brains. I saw how they patched people up in order to ship them back to the front as soon as possible."[26]

[25] Marianne Kesting, *Bertolt Brecht in Selbstzeugnissen und Bilddokumenten* (Hamburg: Rohwolt Verlag, 1959), p. 14.
[26] Sergei Tretiakov, "Bert Brecht" (Trans. anon.), *International Literature*

The bitterness with which the young poet felt this experience is reflected even more clearly in his ballad *Legende vom toten Soldaten*,
composed during those hectic days just before Germany's collapse.
In this poem he tells how, in the *fifth* year of the war, the Kaiser has
a dead soldier dug up, declared fit for service, and marched off to
war again. The tone is unmistakably acrid:

> And because the soldier stinks of rot,
> A priest limps on ahead,
> And swings a censor over him
> So that he cannot stink.
>
> . . . .
>
> A gentleman in a morning-coat went on ahead
> With a starched shirt.
> He was, of course, as a German
> Conscious of his duty.
>
> . . . .
>
> The stars are not always there,
> There comes a red dawning,
> Yet the soldier, as he has been trained,
> Goes on to a hero's death.[27]

The second of the three verses cited here indicates another of Brecht's
early *bêtes noires*; the bourgeois patriot aware of his duty was already
a frequent target of his critical thrusts. But while the elements of
his later Marxist leanings were already apparent, it was still too early
for them to take coherent form, even though an opportunity for
political activism arose when he was elected to the Soldiers' Council
by his co-workers in the hospital at the end of the war. He later explained his inability to rise to the occasion as follows:

(Moscow), May 1937, p. 62. Reprinted in Peter Demetz, ed., *Brecht: A Collection
of Critical Essays* (Englewood Cliffs, N. J.: Prentice-Hall, 1962), p. 18.

[27] Bertolt Brecht, *Gedichte 1* (Frankfurt am Main: Suhrkamp Verlag, 1964), pp.
136–140.

At that time I was representative on an enlisted men's council in a field hospital in Augsburg, and at that I had taken the job only at the urgent insistence of a few friends who claimed to have an interest in the matter. (As it turned out, however, I could never have changed the state so that it would have been good for them.) All of us suffered a lack of political conviction, and I especially suffered my old lack of capacity for enthusiasm. In brief, I was scarcely different from the rest of the soldiers, who were certainly fed up with war, but were in no condition to think politically. Thus I don't particularly like to think about it.[28]

Three important elements conditioning his immediate postwar works are touched upon here: his inability to think politically, his lack of capacity for enthusiasm in any cause (a weakness which he never succeeded in overcoming), and his satiety with war.

The piece in which all three of these elements emerge most clearly is *Drums in the Night*, set against the background of the Spartakus uprising in Berlin in 1918. Kragler, a soldier just returning from four years of captivity, finds his former fiancée now engaged to a war profiteer and himself rejected by her and her parents. In despair he is about to join the ranks of the left-wing revolutionary Spartakus movement, with which Brecht actually had considerable sympathy, when at the crucial moment Anna, his fiancée, finds him and confesses her love for him. Kragler's political disengagement could not be more strikingly put, as he chooses the comfort of the marriage bed over a hero's death in the name of the revolution:

My body should rot in the gutter for the sake of your pie in the sky? Are you drunk? I've had it up to here! It's just ordinary theater. This is the stage, and that's a paper moon, and behind it is the chopping block—only that is real. They've left the drums behind. The half-Spartacus, or the Power of Love! The Bloodbath in Fleet Street, or

---

[28] Werner Hecht, *Brechts Weg zum epischen Theater* (Berlin: Henschel Verlag, 1962), p. 8.

let every man save his own skin! Either with your shield or without it. The pipes are skirling, the poor are dying in Fleet Street, the houses are falling on them, gray dawn is breaking, they're lying like drowned cats on the pavement. I'm a pig, and the pig goes home! I'll put on a fresh shirt, I still have my skin, I'll take off my tunic and polish my boots. The shouting will all be over tomorrow morning, but I'll lie in bed and screw so that I won't die out! Don't gape so romantically! You madmen! You cutthroats! You bloodthirsty cowards, you! Drunkenness and screwing! Now comes the bed, the big, white, wide bed! Come![29]

This ending, which places Kragler approximately where Ionesco was to place Bérenger in his *Rhinoceros* thirty years later, firmly against involvement, was later a source of considerable embarrassment to the committed Brecht. In 1954, six years after his return to East Berlin, he wrote the following apology, which amounts to a recantation of Kragler's defection:

Of my first works, the play *Drums in the Night* is the most hybrid. The resistance of a convention that ought to be rejected led here almost to the rejection of a great social resistance. The "normal," that is, conventional development of the plot would either have returned the girl to the soldier coming back from the war, who has joined the revolution because she has taken a new lover, or would have denied her to him altogether, in either case allowing him to remain revolutionary. In *Drums in the Night* the soldier Kragler gets his girl back, even if she's a bit shopworn, and turns his back on the revolution. This seems now to be the most shopworn of all possible solutions, the more so since the approval of the playwright can be inferred.

I see now that my contradictory nature—I suppress the urge to insert the word "youthful," since I hope I have it undiminished yet today—led me close to the limits of the absurd.[30]

In thus linking the exaggeration of his eternal spirit of contradiction (*Widerspruchsgeist*) with the concept of the absurd, Brecht gives

[29] Brecht, *Stücke 1*, pp. 203–204.
[30] *Ibid.*, p. 5.

us a clue as to why Martin Esslin has found so much in common with the early Brecht and the French absurdist movement of the 1950s. For in this drama, as in other early works and fragments, Brecht expressed such contradiction in concrete terms, so that the form of the play corresponded to its absurd content, as is always the case with genuinely absurd theater. It was not enough that Brecht flouted theatrical tradition in the construction of the play, for example; such tradition was actually concretely destroyed as Kragler ripped down the makeshift scenery to expose the bare mechanism of the stage behind it, and thus Brecht anticipated what he was later to term *Verfremdungseffekte* in the physical destruction of theatrical illusion. Yet such observations are more properly the concern of the next chapter; what is at issue here is not dramatic form, but political commitment, and even more revealing, in the context of the play itself, is Brecht's later rationalization of Kragler's self-seeking cowardice in his explanation of why the piece was not rewritten to conform with his later ideals: "Certainly I couldn't do much. The figure of the soldier Kragler, the petit-bourgeois, couldn't be touched. Even the relative justification of his attitude had to be retained. Even today the proletariat still has more understanding of the petit-bourgeois who defends his own interests, even when they are the most wretched and even when they are defended against the proletariat, than of those who conform out of romanticism or out of mischief."[31] In thus characterizing Kragler as a *Kleinbürger*, a petit-bourgeois, Brecht does considerable violence to his own play. This piece must be taken as utterly anti-bourgeois, for the bourgeoisie are brilliantly lampooned in the figures of Herr and Frau Balicke, Anna's parents, as well as in that of the war profiteer Murk, her new fiancé. But to dismiss Kragler as an irremediable *Kleinbürger* is to overlook the fact that he is the only thoroughly genuine—and noble —figure in the entire play, and no amount of political rationale can change that fact.

Hence Brecht was, as he has admitted, in no condition to think

[31] *Ibid.*, p. 7.

politically, and he remained in this condition for a number of years thereafter, as he recognized in his 1954 commentary upon *Mann ist Mann*, completed in 1925:

> I turned to the reading of the comedy *A Man's a Man* with particular apprehension. Here again I had portrayed a socially negative hero not without sympathy. The problem of the play is the false, bad collective (that of the mob) and its seductive power, the same collective that was at that time being recruited by Hitler and his backers, exploiting the inarticulate demands of the petit-bourgeois against the historically mature, genuinely social collective of the workers. Two versions existed, the 1928 production by the Berlin *Volksbühne*, and the one staged in 1931 in the Berlin *Staatstheater*. I felt that the original version, in which Galy Gay conquers the mountain fortress of Sir El Dchowr, ought to be revived. In 1931 I had ended the work after the assembly scene, since I saw no possibility of showing the growth of the hero within the collective in a negative light.[32]

Thus the committed writer concerning his early uncommitted works: he mercilessly attacks everything in each of them (for *Baal, In the Jungle of the Cities*, and *Life of Edward II of England* also come under his fire) that does not conform with his later mode of thought, and yet—and this is important for an understanding of Brecht's nature—he allows them to be reprinted and played without significant changes.

Brecht's political sympathies had always lain with the oppressed, the poor, and the exploited, and he had spared no effort in attacking and caricaturing the oppressors, the rich, and the exploiters, as well as the complacent German *Spießbürger*, conditioned, through his spirit of conformity, to political and social passivity except in his own interests. Indeed, virtually the only things that held Brecht back from active political commitment were his cynicism, which he had already referred to as his lack of capacity for enthusiasm, and his inability to think "politically," that is, to think in terms of positive

[32] *Ibid.*, pp.14–15.

political engagement. But the deeply ingrained negative attitudes described here form the point of departure for his conversion to Marxism, and it should come as no surprise that, once exposed to Marxist dialectic, with its rational, intellectual approach to solution of the world's problems, he became fascinated with it. He encountered Marx, as he put it, through a sort of occupational accident:

> For a certain play I needed the wheat market of Chicago as a background. I thought I would be able to gather the necessary knowledge quickly by interviewing a few specialists and men of practical experience. But it turned out otherwise. Nobody—neither noted economists nor businessmen—I traveled from Berlin clear to Vienna to interview a broker who had worked all his life in the Chicago market—nobody could explain to my satisfaction the machinations of the wheat market. I got the impression that these machinations were utterly inexplicable, which is to say not comprehensible to the reason, which is further to say simply irrational. The way in which the grain of the world was distributed was absolutely inconceivable. From every viewpoint save that of a few speculators, the grain market was a vast swamp. The planned drama was not written; instead I began to read Marx, and then, for the first time, I *read* Marx. Then my own practical experiences and random observations really began to come to life.[33]

But here Brecht does not claim to have become a systematic Marxist doctrinaire, and it is dubious that he could have been, for fascination and enthusiasm are far from identical, and his old political cynicism continued to hold him back. Yet while he had by no means become an avowed Communist, the intellectual appeal exerted upon him by the writings of Marx can scarcely be overstated. Particularly as a dramatist of what he then considered to be the dawn of a new age for both mankind and drama, he was so taken with the rationalism of dialectic materialism that he even went so far, in a fragment written late in 1926, as to term Marx "the only spectator for my pieces": "When I read Marx's *Das Kapital,* I understood my plays.

[33] Hecht, *Brechts Weg,* p. 77.

It must be understood that I desire widespread distribution of this book. Naturally I didn't discover that I had written a whole pile of Marxist plays without knowing it, but this Marx was the only audience for my plays that I had ever seen; for just these plays should interest a man with such interests, not because of their intelligence, but because of his; they would have made food for his thought."[34] Hence the appeal of Marxism was double-edged; on the one hand, it appeared to him to be rational and pragmatic and, on the other, humanistic, for it seemed to offer relief from the human misery and exploitation he saw at every hand.

A valuable clue to the nature of Brecht's perception of the possibilities of Marxism is provided by Fritz Sternberg (to whom Brecht dedicated the first edition of *Mann ist Mann* with the epigraph: "Meinem ersten Lehrer"[35]), in his account of Brecht's quest for understanding of Marxism:

> At that time I was giving courses in which I was attempting to analyze certain relationships between Marxism and other humanistic disciplines. Brecht participated in these courses for a while, but then gave them up—and we were agreed that this was best. Systematic thought just didn't suit him. Hence whenever a certain theme was being analyzed by a large group, discussion with him wasn't very fruitful. On the other hand, discussion with Brecht alone could be highly productive. I once told him, "You don't think in straight lines, but in leaps. You think in associations which nobody else would think of."[36]

But even this thinking in jumps and associations, Sternberg hastens to admit, had its positive side: "Brecht was uncommonly inquisitive and could ask penetrating questions. Often in the course of an evening it was striking how much he had learned in a few hours. Sometimes in questioning, sometimes in reflecting, something would

[34] Bertolt Brecht, *Schriften zum Theater 1* (Frankfurt am Main: Suhrkamp Verlag, 1963), p. 181.
[35] Fritz Sternberg, *Der Dichter und die Ratio* (Göttingen: Sachse und Pohl Verlag, 1963), p. 12.
[36] *Ibid.*

explode in him, and he would say quite new, original things. Thus many an evening which had begun with Brecht wanting to learn certain very specific things from me would become very fruitful for me, for in the middle of an explanation he could formulate views which were quite new to me and which forced me to think things out anew."[37]

Hence initiation into and fascination with Marxism are not to be taken as synonymous with commitment thereto. Brecht remained critical of Marxism until it became obvious that, as a result of the deepening economic crisis in 1929, the National Socialists were steadily gaining power. As Sternberg reports, his attitude toward the Communists at that time was conditioned by his perception of the motivation of the middle classes, the bourgeois:

> As the economic crisis intensified our discussions occurred more frequently for a while. Brecht saw quite clearly that the Nazis were gaining ground and that the position of the Left was deteriorating. We were not in agreement as to all of the factors that had led to this development. At that time Brecht held a stance much too uncritical of the Communist Party of Germany for my taste, although he was not a member of the party. But apart from quite significant differences of opinion about concrete political questions, we were still agreed that a considerable portion of the German middle class—shaken by the following inflation in which a great number had lost their fortunes, shaken by the great economic crisis, which hit Germany harder than the other countries of Europe—could and would most likely fall prey to the propaganda of the National Socialists.[38]

Yet Brecht had by no means become entirely uncritical of the dealings of the Communist Party of Germany; he insisted upon his right to think for himself and to apply criticism where he felt it was necessary. Sternberg illustrates Brecht's sense of independence by describing a political discussion held one night in 1929 with the Russian

[37] *Ibid.*
[38] *Ibid.*, p. 18.

Sergei Tretiakov, in which the agricultural collectivization then in progress in the Soviet Union was sharply criticized:

> Tretiakov, who had at first taken active part in the conversation, was growing more and more monosyllabic. But finally he turned to Brecht and burst out, "Where have you brought me? These are enemies of the Party, enemies of the Soviet Union!" Brecht replied, "How so? All we are doing—and it seems to me that we have every right to do so—is criticizing Stalin's collectivization policy." And when Tretiakov then began to quote some speech of Stalin's, Brecht interrupted him and declared, "Sternberg is right. The true Marxist is not interested in what statesmen say about their policies, but in what they do."[39]

Nevertheless, Brecht was inclined to the political left, and he did not really feel that the other leftist party, the Social Democrats, presented an effective alternative. But still he remained uncommitted between the two until May Day, 1929, when the Social Democrat commissioner of police of Berlin forbade any sort of political demonstration by the German workers in order to avoid conflict between the two leftist factions. The Social Democrats largely abided by the ban, but the Communists sought to demonstrate in small groups and were badgered and finally fired upon by the police. Brecht watched one such demonstration from the apartment of Sternberg, who describes his reaction thus:

> What he saw was how the demonstrators were being split up and harried by the police. As far as we could tell, these people were unarmed. The police fired repeatedly. At first we thought they were just warning shots fired in the air. Then we saw that some of the demonstrators were falling and were later carried away on stretchers. As nearly as I can remember, there were on that day over twenty dead among the demonstrators in Berlin. When Brecht heard the shots and saw that people were being hit, he grew paler than I had ever seen him before in my life. I believe this experience figured no little in what drove him more and more strongly toward Communism.[40]

[39] *Ibid.*, p. 23.
[40] *Ibid.*, p. 25.

Taken in the context of Brecht's bitterness over the senseless human sacrifice he had experienced during the war, Sternberg's account of the emotional impetus applied by the experience of this act of brutality gains considerable force, and Werner Hecht, one of Brecht's chief eastern interpreters, shares the view that it was one of the strong motivating factors in Brecht's turn to Communism.[41] Such a process of radicalization is certainly familiar to many American liberals who witnessed the suppression of demonstrations during the Democratic Convention in Chicago in 1968.

There were, however, other factors contributing to Brecht's conversion, chief among which was the nature of the political turmoil that gripped Germany in the late twenties and early thirties. It was, as Sternberg points out, a time when one *had* to make a choice:

> To oversimplify matters, today, when employers are scrambling for kids just graduating from school, when the demand for qualified workers in every field is greater than the supply, conditions are right for the development of apolitical tendencies. Then, on the other hand, hundreds of thousands of youngsters went from the schoolroom into unemployment, so that a sociological gap developed that forced men to commit themselves politically. There was a general feeling that something new had to happen in the state and in society, for conditions were getting more and more unbearable, and the tensions in the political atmosphere were growing stronger and stronger. This sociological gap was in essence diametrically opposed to what we take for granted today. Brecht felt this in his entire being.[42]

Nor was the external political situation the only motivating factor; Brecht's biographers all agree that he felt an inner need to overcome the cynicism which had produced the anarchical attitudes and tortured confessional works of his youth. Sternberg cites this need for some sort of external discipline, some form of positive engagement, as a strong motivational force in Brecht's turn to Communism:

[41] Hecht, *Brechts Weg*, p. 81.
[42] Sternberg, *Der Dichter*, p. 30.

His sympathies went out to the Communist Party. He was not uncritical, but held the view that its errors were correctible. I often told Brecht in those years that he was too gullible. The German Communist Party, whose back still bore the scars of the factional struggles of the Russian Bolshevist Party, was, as far as I was concerned, not a positive factor in German political life, but rather a very decisively negative one. It seemed to me that Brecht's sympathy for the Communists stemmed from the fact that—especially after his somewhat anarchical past—he wanted to and had to identify positively with something.[43]

Whatever the direct cause and exact moment of his turn to Communism, it can be placed quite positively before the time when Brecht began to write his *Lehrstücke*, which are clearly Marxist in their didactic portent. These plays, *The Baden Didactic Play on Acquiescence, He Who Says Yes, He Who Says No*, and *The Measures Taken*, constantly turn upon the theme of *Einverständnis*, a German word rich in connotations conveyed by no equivalent single English word. *Einverständnis*, for Brecht, implies first an understanding of the problem faced in all its ramifications, then seeing that there is but one possible solution, and finally embracing this solution, being cognizant of, but nevertheless accepting, its inherent dangers. These plays thus reflect the nature of Brecht's conversion to Communism; as Sternberg has pointed out, it represented to Brecht the only possible solution to the problems Germany faced at the time, and he finally embraced the party and dedicated his subsequent work to furthering its causes.

Yet it is ironic that the very plays in which he first sought to serve a positive didactic purpose were not looked upon with favor by the party, for the *Lehrstücke* mentioned above, as well as the subsequent works *Rise and Fall of the City of Mahagonny, The Mother*, and *St. Joan of the Stockyards*, all fell prey to violent critical attacks in the party press. Indeed, *The Measures Taken*, written as a conscious song of praise to the party and its salutary disciplinary effect, was

[43] *Ibid.*, pp. 22–23.

scathingly denounced for painting a false picture of the party, as well as for being a piece of petit-bourgeois formalism, and Brecht was urged to abandon such abstract and intellectualized theater, to take as his model the new "socialist realism."[44]

When Hitler came to power in January, 1933, Brecht became a *persona non grata* as a Communist, and a month later, the day after the burning of the Reichstag, he left Germany, not to return until after the war. And he chose to emigrate not to Soviet Russia, as might have been expected of a Communist forced to leave Germany, but by way of Prague and Vienna to Zürich, later to continue to Denmark, Finland, and finally clear across Russia to embark in Vladivostok for the west coast of the United States, where he spent the last seven years of his exile. Why he elected not to go to the Soviet Union is indicated by Sternberg:

> Brecht's positive assessment of Russia certainly did not extend to Russian art. Here Brecht couldn't be deceived. He had been in Russia and had seen the low ebb of literature and art there with his own eyes. At the beginning of the Thirties a series of Russian plays had been brought to Berlin, and the director who was supposed to stage them had showed them to Brecht. Brecht knew for certain that they were cheap commercial stuff, plays without class. He was convinced that this was no coincidence. He felt that the level of Russian art could not be expected to rise significantly in the foreseeable future. As I have already said, in the first phase of his emigration he had gone to Vienna, and from there on to Denmark. When we discussed our situation then, he wasn't even remotely considering emigration to Russia. Incidentally, Brecht's rejection of the literary and particularly the dramatic works that reached the west from Russia was by no means one-sided. The official spokesmen of the Soviet Union rejected Brecht just as they had Picasso.[45]

It takes very little digging into the background of Soviet literature

[44] Martin Esslin, *Brecht: The Man and His Work* (Garden City, N. Y.: Doubleday Anchor Books, 1960), pp. 154–157.
[45] Sternberg, *Der Dichter*, p. 30.

at that time to see why Brecht took such a dim view of the possibilities for creative art in Russia. As early as 1928, under the aegis of the first five-year plan, the writers of the Soviet Union had been organized into the Russian Association of Proletarian Writers (RAPP) and instructed by "social commands" to concern themselves with matters affecting the welfare of the socialist state. Such writers as Mayakovsky (for whose plays, produced by Meyerhold in Berlin, Brecht had expressed his admiration) were criticized for their "formalism" (any obtrusive experimentation in literary technique) and pressured to conform to the "new trend" in literature; indeed, earlier works by Mayakovsky, such as *The Bedbug* and *The Bathhouse* were suppressed as anti-proletarian. Other writers, such as Pilnyak and Zamyatin, were denounced for publishing forbidden works abroad. But even this censorship was mild in comparison with what was to come, for in 1932 RAPP was dissolved by order of the Central Committee and replaced by the Union of Soviet Writers, responsible directly to Stalin, who in the same year instructed these writers to become "engineers of human souls."[46] And at the First Congress of Soviet Writers in Moscow in 1934, the doctrine of "socialist realism" was formally adopted as the credo of the Union: "Socialist realism is the basic method of Soviet literature and literary criticism. It demands of the artist the truthful, historically concrete representation of reality in its revolutionary development. Moreover, the truthfulness and historical concreteness of the artistic representation of reality must be linked with the task of ideological transformation and education of workers in the spirit of socialism."[47]

There can be no doubt that Brecht was, at the time of his emigration, a convinced Marxist, nor can there be any doubt concerning the purpose to which he devoted the rest of his writing: to propagate the doctrines of Marx. On the other hand, he had no intention

---

[46] Jürgen Rühle, *Literatur und Revolution* (Munich: Knaur Verlag, 1963), pp. 559–561.

[47] Abram Tertz [pseud.], *On Socialist Realism* (New York: Pantheon Books, 1960), p. 24.

of becoming a party hack, cranking out slick little plays depicting noble peasants and workers cooperating to build a glorious future. The theater was his life, and for him theater was unthinkable without experimentation. But just such experimentation was then being denounced in Russia as formalism, so there was obviously no chance for him there. Despite his *Einverständnis* with the ends of Marxism, he saw clearly that the means currently in vogue were likely neither to reach those ends nor to stimulate art in the theater, so he opted for emigration in a series of neutral countries.

Motivated by the dilemma in which he found himself, Brecht wrote in 1934 a pamphlet entitled "Five Difficulties in Writing the Truth," ostensibly for underground distribution in Nazi Germany, to indicate possible means for dissemination of the truth under the totalitarian regime of the Fascists. But the methods suggested by this document are applicable under any form of totalitarianism, and it is hence of great significance for an understanding of all his subsequent works, as well as of most of his subsequent actions. He introduces the essay by listing the five difficulties of ("requisite virtues for" would probably be a better term) writing the truth:

> Whoever wants to combat lies and ignorance and write the truth today has at least five difficulties to overcome. He must have the *courage* [*Mut*] to write the truth, even though it is suppressed everywhere; the *wit* [*Klugheit*] to recognize it, though it is obscured everywhere; the *know-how* [*Kunst*] to make it useful as a weapon; the *judgment* [*Urteil*] to select those in whose hands it will be useful; and the *cunning* [*List*] to propagate it among them. These difficulties are great for those who write under Fascism, but they also exist for those who have emigrated or have been expelled, and even for those who write in countries where civil liberties still exist.[48]

It is significant, first, that he points out that these difficulties exist not only for those who wish to write the truth under a Fascist regime, but even for those who write in countries where civil liberties pre-

---

[48] Brecht, *Versuche 9* (Frankfurt am Main: Suhrkamp Verlag, 1949), p. 85.

vail, for he thus invites extension of the policies which he suggests to, for example, Russia. But it is also significant that he holds the quality of *cunning* (*List*) until last and that he devotes half of the essay to this quality, for it is one of his most characteristic traits.

Yet it is just this quality of cunning, of craftiness, that makes it difficult for a westerner, raised in a tradition that pays a good deal of lip service to forthright honesty, to approach Brecht. We are exposed from birth to innumerable proverbs, folk tales, and religious parables in praise of honesty, and, while we may perceive intellectually that there is much about life that is dishonest, we traditionally expect honesty of our artists. If a man has a perception of some truth, we expect him to assert that truth forthrightly; while we may permit him to speak enigmatically, we do not expect him to hedge or to becloud the truth. But we cannot expect such forthrightness of Brecht, for it is simply not a part of his nature. This is not to say that he was willfully untruthful, for he was deeply concerned with truth, as witness his abandonment of his distorted picture of American capitalist society once he had experienced that society directly.[49] But he recognized that, in order to disseminate the truth and stay alive in these times, the artist must be cunning, must express the truth in devious ways, especially if he works within the framework of a regime which holds some truths to be disruptive or even destructive. That this assessment of his times was correct is statistically supported by the number of distinguished writers who have perished at the hands of totalitarian regimes in this century because they refused to remain silent with the truth or were not cunning enough in their portrayal thereof.[50] Indeed, that Brecht wrote and produced his plays when and where he did and survived may be considered something of a miracle, and this miracle is the result of his innate cunning.

[49] Cf. Barbara Glaubert, "Bertolt Brechts Amerikabild in drei seiner Stücke," Master's thesis (Boulder: University of Colorado, August 1961).

[50] Cf. the dedication page of Rühle, *Literatur*, which lists 78 documented instances of writers who thus perished.

To return to his essay, the examples he cites of *List* applied in the literature of the past are significant to an understanding of his own methodology. He cites, for example, Lenin and Voltaire:

Lenin, threatened by the Czar's police, wanted to expose the exploitation and suppression of the island of Sachalin by the Russian bourgeoisie. He used Japan instead of Russia and Korea instead of Sachalin. The methods of the Japanese bourgeoisie reminded all of his readers of those of their Russian counterparts in Sachalin, but the piece was not suppressed, since Japan was an enemy of Russia. Much which may not be said in Germany about Germany may be said about Austria.

There are many kinds of cunning by which the oppressive state may be deceived. Voltaire combated the belief of the church in miracles by writing a gallant poem about the Maid of Orleans. He described the miracles which doubtless must have come to pass in order for Joan to have remained a virgin in an army, at the court, *and* among the monks.[51]

Here he describes one of his own favorite techniques, transposition of time, place, and institution. To cite but one example, in *The Life of Galileo* the specific institution under attack is the inquisition of the Roman Catholic Church during the sixteenth century in Italy, a politically safe target for a Communist writer. But the abuses attacked, the systematic suppression of truth, are the abuses of any totalitarian regime, including Nazi Germany, the Soviet Union, *and* the German Democratic Republic.

Brecht's interpretation of Jonathan Swift's *A Modest Proposal* serves even better to reveal the sort of cunning he continually practiced in his own personal and political life:

Jonathan Swift suggested in a pamphlet that the children of the poor be slaughtered and sold as meat, so that conditions in the country would improve. He drew up precise figures which proved that much could be saved if people were not held back by moral horror.

[51] Brecht, *Versuche 9*, p. 91.

Swift played dumb. He defended a way of thought abhorrent to him with a great deal of fire and thoroughness, applying that mode of thought to a matter in which its meanness was made apparent to everybody. Everybody could be smarter, or at least more humane, than Swift, especially those who had never before tested certain viewpoints for the consequences which resulted from them.

Propaganda for thought in any field is useful to the cause of the oppressed. Such propaganda is necessary. Thought is held in low repute among governments which serve the cause of exploitation.[52]

The technique of playing dumb was a familiar one to Brecht, who had used it in his school days to get a failing mark in French raised. Where a classmate had attempted to correct some of his own mistakes on an exam and had been caught, Brecht marked as mistakes perfectly correct passages on his own paper and humbly asked his teacher what was wrong with them; embarrassed at his own apparent carelessness, the teacher hastened to change the grade.[53] This sort of cunning stupidity was just as typical of one of Brecht's favorite literary characters, the hero of Jaroslav Hasek's *The Good Soldier Schweyk*, which he had helped Erwin Piscator to stage as a drama in 1927. The basic element of Schweyk's behavior may be simply described as blind and stupid obedience to superiors regardless of the consequences; he gives the impression of trying to please, but in effect causes chaos because he carries out each order to the ultimate absurdity of its last letter. Brecht later wrote a play, *Schweyk in the Second World War*, and he continually practiced "Schweykism" himself; no better instance could be cited than his purposely confusing testimony before the House Un-American Activities Committee in 1947, which caused him to be complimented by the committee chairman for his exemplary cooperation as a witness.[54] This technique was certainly influenced by his association with the Munich

[52] *Ibid.*, p. 93.

[53] Herbert Ihering, "Der Volksdramatiker" in Peter Huchel, ed., *Sinn und Form: Sonderheft Bertolt Brecht* (Berlin: Rütten und Loening, 1949), p. 5.

[54] This testimony appears in Demetz, *Brecht*, pp. 30–42.

cabaret comedian Karl Valentin, whose satiric sketches abound in Teutonic obsequiousness, and it is manifested as well in many of his stories of Herr Keuner, his fictitious *alter ego*. It is a particularly effective device under any totalitarian institution.

Yet this cunning was for Brecht much more than simply a means of survival; it was an integral and organic part of his dialectical mode of thought, of his creative technique:

> The dependence of each thing upon many other things which are constantly in flux is a thought dangerous to dictatorships, and it can crop up in many forms without attracting much attention or offering the police an opening. A complete exposition of all the conditions and processes encountered by a man who opens a tobacco shop can strike a telling blow at dictatorships. The governments which visit misery on the masses must prevent people from thinking of the government as a source of misery. They speak much of fate; it, not they, must be blamed for all want. Whoever seeks for the cause of want is arrested before he singles out the government. But it is possible to counter talk about fate in general; it can be shown that man's fate is brought on by other men.[55]

The reference to the person who opens a tobacco shop is certainly prophetic of his *The Good Woman of Setzuan*, but again it is *The Life of Galileo* that provides the most striking example of the effect wrought by this dialectic technique. To see this play in East Berlin is almost a terrifying experience; as the action progresses and the audience is made aware of the parallels that exist between their situation and that of Galileo, the tension actually becomes palpable. Among all his plays it is certainly the most dangerous to the regime, and the fact that it is still played (it was, in fact, scheduled for a new production by the Berliner Ensemble during the 1965–66 season) is further tribute to Brecht's cunning.

This same quality of *List* plays no small role in Brecht's recommitment to Communism after the war, a phenomenon which western

[55] Brecht, *Versuche 9*, pp. 94–95.

interpreters of his works generally find difficult to explain. It is difficult to explain because it was an outgrowth of a number of intricately interrelated motivational factors, no one of which can satisfactorily explicate his choice. But if all of these factors are considered, the choice must seem inevitable. In the first place, the choice was limited, for, as has already been observed, Brecht's life was the theater, and it had to be German-speaking theater, for he recognized the difficulty of translating his language, as witness his two-year collaboration with Charles Laughton on the translation of *The Life of Galileo*.[56] And the choice determined thus was narrowed still further, for, while Brecht had applied for an entrance visa into West Germany on his return to Europe in 1948, his application was ignored by the military government of the allied powers.[57] This *de facto* denial left only three German-speaking countries from which to choose, Austria, Switzerland, and the Russian-occupied East Zone of Germany. One of his numerous Keuner stories expresses his inclination: "Mr. K. preferred City B to City A. 'In City A,' he said, 'I am loved, but in City B they are friendly to me. In City A I was used, but in City B they needed me. In City A I was invited to the table, but in City B they invited me into the kitchen.' "[58] In short, while he was welcomed in Switzerland and would later be granted Austrian citizenship, he felt needed in East Germany, and when the "invitation into the kitchen" finally came in August, 1948, taking the form of an invitation to direct a production of his *Mother Courage* in the prestigious Deutsches Theater, he could scarcely resist the temptation. Out of the success of this production grew his appointment as general director of the newly founded Berliner Ensemble, with its own theater, the old Theater am Schiffbauerdamm, and his decision to cast his lot with the regime of the German Democratic Republic seemed a natural consequence.

[56] Cf. Bertolt Brecht, *Aufbau einer Rolle: Laughtons Galilei* (Berlin: Henschel Verlag, 1962), pp. 9–12.

[57] Kesting, *Bertolt Brecht*, p. 160.

[58] Brecht, *Prosa 2* (Frankfurt am Main: Suhrkamp Verlag, 1965), pp. 120–121.

Yet much has been made of the ways in which Brecht hedged his commitment to the East after the war. Having originally entered the Zone on a Czechoslovakian passport issued in Prague, both Brecht and his wife, Helene Weigel, applied for Austrian citizenship, which was granted them on April 12, 1950.[59] And in 1949 he entered a contract with Suhrkamp Verlag of Frankfurt am Main, which granted that West German publishing house sole rights to print his works, with the result that even the editions of his works now published in East Germany by the Aufbau Verlag are *Lizensausgaben*; editorial control resides with and royalties are paid to Suhrkamp.[60] Sternberg, among others, has suggested that these manipulations represented doubts on Brecht's part regarding his commitment to Marxism, but it seems quite clear that they were simply a further manifestation of his cunning. Always a realist so far as his personal safety and freedom were concerned, Brecht knew perfectly well what he was getting into in the East Zone, and these measures may be regarded as a form of insurance which rendered him immune to the extreme forms of censorship to which the majority of East German writers are subjected.[61] It might be argued that Brecht's international eminence as a playwright had already granted him some degree of immunity, but it seems obvious that he was taking no chances, for he thereby opened every possible avenue of escape. And the very fact that he never exercised the option he had secured by these measures, even after the most severe of his difficulties with the party and the regime, emphasizes the degree of his commitment to the principles of Marxism, for he had every opportunity to exercise his choice; he remained free to and in fact did travel to the West on frequent occasions, but he always returned to the fold.

It should not, however, thereby be inferred that Brecht remained uncritical of the actions of the party and the regime. Much of the

---

[59] Kesting, *Bertolt Brecht*, p. 160.

[60] A finding of the writer's research in the Brecht-Archiv.

[61] For example, the works of Franz Kafka were not published in the DDR as late as 1965, nor could they be legally imported.

material which would be required to document his disagreement regarding the practices of the government of Walter Ulbricht is, unfortunately, held inaccessible in the Brecht-Archiv and will probably never be made public. Nevertheless, a few shreds of evidence have succeeded in slipping through, thanks largely to Brecht's wide circle of friends in the West, so that a more generalized pattern of opposition may safely be inferred. The occasion for his greatest falling-out with the regime was the workers' uprising in East Berlin on June 17, 1953, on which occasion he wrote a long letter to Ulbricht suggesting revisions in the policies and practices of the regime, which he closed with the following formal declaration, almost a cliché in German epistolary style: "I feel obligated to express to you at this moment my commitment to the Socialist Unity Party of Germany [the official name of the Communist Party of East Germany]. Your Bertolt Brecht."[62] The party saw fit to publish only this last sentence, which it printed as the full text of a telegram, as a sign of Brecht's unflinching support of the regime, thereby touching off a storm of protest in the West that led to a short-lived boycott of his works, as well as to Günter Grass's recent play, *The Plebeians Rehearse the Uprising*, in which Brecht is portrayed as exploiting the rebellious workers to get ideas for his own staging of the revolution scenes in his *Coriolan*. Brecht is reported to have been livid at this spurious telegram, and the next day he fired off the following genuine one: "On the morning of the 17th of June, when it became clear that the demonstrations of the workers were being misused for warlike purposes, I expressed my commitment to the Socialist Unity Party of Germany. I hope, now that the provocators have been isolated and their network of associates destroyed, that the workers, who demonstrated in justifiable dissatisfaction, will not be lumped into the same class as the provocators, and that the so necessary dialogue concerning the errors of both sides will not be prejudiced."[63] For reasons that must be obvious, this telegram was never published

[62] Andre Müller, *Kreuzzug gegen Brecht* (Berlin: Aufbau Verlag, 1962), p. 67.
[63] Kesting, *Bertolt Brecht*, p. 139.

in the East Zone; despite the obsequious tone (cf. Galileo's letter to the Duke of Medici!)[64] and the ominous reference to a network of provocators, the allusion to the justice of the cause of the workers was too critical of the party to be released. But after his death in 1956, the following satirical poem, entitled "The Solution," was found in his *Nachlaß*:

> After the uprising of the 17th of June
> The Secretary of the Writers' Congress had
> Broadsides distributed in the Stalinallee
> In which it was stated that the people
> Had frivolously forfeited the trust of the Government
> And could only regain it by redoubled work.
> Wouldn't it be simpler if the Government
> Dissolved the people and elected another?[65]

And yet, in spite of these and many similar troubles, especially those relating to official interpretation, criticism, and outright censorship of his works, Brecht remained in the East not, as Sternberg would have it, purely out of the desire to keep a good thing going, but because he remained committed to the ideals of Marxism. And fundamental to this commitment was his pathological fear of war; he regarded the establishment of the West German *Bundeswehr* in 1949 with horror as the specter of German militarism reborn, and he rewrote the final scene of *The Resistible Rise of Arturo Ui* to end with the following epilogue:

> But you must learn to see rather than to gape
> And to act rather than to talk on and on.
> Something like that [Ui/Hitler] once nearly ruled the world!
> The people mastered him, yet nevertheless—
> Lest any of us cry triumph too soon—
> The womb is fruitful yet from which that slunk![66]

[64] Brecht, *Stücke 8*, p. 56.
[65] Brecht, *Gedichte 7*, p. 9.
[66] Brecht: *Stücke 9*, p. 365.

His notes to this piece make it quite clear that the still-fertile womb from which the horror of Nazism slunk was the same western capitalism which he continued to identify with militarism, as well as with exploitation of the worker. And the last piece that he brought to the stage, *Coriolan*, which indeed he was preparing for its London premiere at the time of his death in 1956, is equally critical of both the capitalist structure that exploits the worker and the war that deepens his misery.

Thus Brecht was committed to Communism, and he did seek to write polemical theater in its service. It is essentially because of this commitment that Ionesco has attacked him, and it is the didactic aspect of Brechtian theatrical practice, as he understands it, against which Ionesco reacts so violently in many of his critical and theoretical writings, for he clings stubbornly to his contention that politics is the ultimate absurdity of the human condition and that theater can only be theater. The problem remains, however, that intentions have a way of frequently getting lost in the process of creation of a work of art. This process and the relationship between theory and practice of theater will be examined in the subsequent chapters.

CHAPTER THREE / *Dramatic Theory and Engagement*

> The modern theater is the epic theater.
> BRECHT[1]

> The theater can only be theater.
> IONESCO[2]

THERE IS ALWAYS some risk involved in taking dramatic theory as a point of departure for an examination of creative drama, and this risk is especially great in a comparative study of Brecht and Ionesco. In the first place, any such study is bound to seem overweighted in favor of Brecht, if for no other reason than that for over thirty years he was a *Dramaturg* involved actively in the life of the theater; he wrote continuously and copiously concerning theatrical practices in his own works and in those of others (as witness the seven volumes of his *Schriften zum Theater*), and he went through at least four

---

[1] Bertolt Brecht, *Stücke 3* (Frankfurt am Main: Suhrkamp Verlag, 1962), p. 266.
[2] Eugène Ionesco, *Notes et contre-notes* (Paris: Gallimard, 1962), p. 20.

distinct phases of development in his theoretical approach to the drama. Ionesco, on the other hand, has had virtually none of this sort of close association with the theater, and his theoretical writings are consequently more abstract and considerably less voluminous than Brecht's. But an even more basic objection may be raised to such an approach, for in both cases the theoretical writings are almost exclusively an outgrowth of the plays themselves, rather than a stimulus to the plays. Neither Brecht nor Ionesco adopted a programmatic, *a priori* dramatic theory which controlled his creative efforts; on the contrary, the theoretical writings represent an attempt to articulate, to rationalize, to systematize, and even to defend dramas previously written and theatrical practices already introduced, as Ionesco has recognized:

> On the other hand, what I have just said does not constitute a preconceived theory of dramatic art. It did not precede, but rather followed from my own personal experience of the theater. These few ideas are the result of my reflection on my own creations, good or bad; they are after the fact. I don't have any ideas before writing a play. I have them once I have written the play, or while I am not writing at all. I believe that artistic creation is spontaneous. It is for me. And again all that I have said is valid solely for me; but if I might believe I had discovered in myself instinctive and permanent ideas of the objective nature of the theater, had come upon what is the essence of theater, I would be very proud.[3]

And Brecht has made similar admissions that his theoretical writings have grown out of his dramas:

> Many of my writings about the theater are, I must observe, misunderstood. I see this especially in letters and articles which claim to agree with me. Then I feel as a mathematician must feel, if he were to read, "I quite agree with you that two times two is five." I believe certain writings of mine have been misunderstood because I took important things for granted instead of formulating them.

[3] *Ibid.*

Most of these writings, if not all, were written as comments upon my plays, so that the plays would be staged correctly. That gives them a dry, craftsmanlike tone, as if a sculptor were writing about how his statues should be exhibited, in what sort of a place, on what sort of a stand—cold-cut directions. Perhaps the readers expected something about the spirit in which the statues were formed: they must exert the effort to extract that from the remarks.[4]

Yet, even though both playwrights seem to call their theoretical writings into question by such disclaimers, there are nevertheless distinct advantages to be gained from an examination of these theories at the outset. In the first place, both are as well known in this country for their theoretical innovations as for their plays—Brecht for his "epic" theater and Ionesco for his absurdist "anti-theater"— and these innovations are widely misunderstood. Secondly, the dramatic theories of the two are considerably more deeply influenced by their political inclinations than are their plays; frequently their theoretical pronouncements amount to little more than an attempt to square an apparent inconsistency in a play with some element of their political philosophies. But most important, the theories, if correctly grasped, serve as an excellent point of departure from which to approach the plays themselves, to demonstrate that there is, as Ionesco suggests above, considerably more to the process of creating living theater than the application of a given dramatic theory to a given plot or situation.

It would be difficult to find better evidence of the fact that Brecht's theories have been misunderstood than Ionesco's criticism of them. His *Notes et contre-notes* bristles with slighting references to Brecht's didacticism and its negative effect upon the drama, as witness the following passage:

> When, on the other hand, I saw the actor too much the master of his role, outside of his character, dominating it, separating himself

[4] Bertolt Brecht, *Schriften zum Theater 6* (Frankfurt am Main: Suhrkamp Verlag, 1963), p. 183.

from it, as desired by Diderot or Jouvet, or Piscator, or after him Brecht, I was just as displeased. That, too seemed to me to be an inadmissible mixture of the true and the false, for I felt the need of that transformation or transposition of reality which only the artistic imagination can make meaningful, more true, more dense; realistic didacticism can only weight such a transformation down and at the same time impoverishes it to the level of a sub-ideology. I didn't like the actor, the star, who seemed to me anarchic in principle, who dissolved or destroyed to his own advantage the scenic organization, and who drew all attention to himself at the expense of the coherent integration of the elements of the performance. But the dehumanization of the actor as it was practiced by Piscator or by Brecht, that disciple of Piscator, who turned the actor into a simple pawn in a theatrical chess game, a tool without fire, without life, without either participation or individual originality, to the advantage in this case of the production, which in turn drew all attention to itself, I was just as exasperated by this priority of the scenic organization. It gave me the impression of suffocation: to annul the ingenuity of the actor, to kill the actor, is to kill the production.[5]

This criticism represents profound misunderstanding of Brecht's entire approach to the theater, for the actor in the Brechtian theater is neither dehumanized nor denied personal invention or passion; his initiative is by no means smothered, but he is given rather more freedom than is the actor in the traditional naturalistic theater. Indeed, the demands made by Brecht upon the technical versatility of the actor are among the most extreme made by any modern playwright. Yet precisely the sort of misunderstanding of the task of the actor in Brecht's "estranged" theater that Ionesco expresses here is fairly common. Such oversimplification of Brecht's approach to the theater has all too often served as an excuse for inept acting, as, for example, in the 1965 production in London of Brecht's *Mr. Puntilla and His Man Matti*. This production by an English company was roundly panned by the critics, and it prompted Harold Hobson to

---

[5] Ionesco, *Notes et contre-notes*, p. 6.

reflect: "English directors seem to misunderstand Brecht. Because he is a progressive writer, they assume that the reactionary characters in his plays must be absurd. They make them absurd, and stop at that. They create no sense of power or of conflict. Behind the joke the threat is missing."[6]

As Hobson implies, no analysis of Brecht's dramatic theories can be valid which does not at the outset take cognizance of Brecht's respect for and demands upon the actor, for the highly talented, disciplined, and sensitive artist is the basis upon which Brecht's dramatic practice and his success as both a playwright and a *Dramaturg* rest. Indeed, his concern for just such sensitivity, talent, and discipline preceded by far his conversion to Marxism and turn to polemic theater, and it was a concern in which he never relented, the tradition of which is still carried on in current productions by his Berliner Ensemble.

In reading Brecht's earliest published theoretical writings, his reviews for the *Augsburger Volkswille* between 1918 and 1921, one is constantly struck by the depth of his concern for acting technique. In a review of a 1919 production of Henrik Ibsen's *Ghosts*, for example, he takes the performance of even minor roles under scrutiny, praising the "naturalness" of Pastor Manders at one juncture, criticizing Mrs. Alving's lack of depth at another, recognizing the adaptability of the actor playing Engstrand at still another. But what comes through most strongly in this very early review is his praise of isolated moments of the production such as Regina's final exit or Oswald's behavior while inveigling morphine from his mother, moments in which there seemed to develop a delicate harmony between word and action.[7] Such deft touches represented to him the theatrical high points of the production, and his concern for them represents as well an already very highly developed feeling for *das Gestische*, an all but untranslatable term that connotes a unity

[6] Harold Hobson, "Brecht for Grown-ups," *The Times* (London, 19 August 1965).

[7] Brecht, *Schriften zum Theater 1*, pp. 10–11.

between the words uttered by an actor and every other aspect of his acting technique: tone of voice, facial expression, attitude, gesture, posture, and movement.

Certainly other concerns mark Brecht's early reviews, not the least of which is his concern for social justice. But this is never his exclusive concern, as his 1920 reviews of Georg Kaiser's *Gas* and Schiller's *Don Carlos* demonstrate: he praises the former work for its visionary implications and yet condemns the production for its lack of clarity, and despite his reservations about the relevance of Carlos's quest of freedom (he compares Schiller's work unfavorably with Upton Sinclair's *The Jungle*), he takes the production seriously and praises the sureness of individual characterizations.[8] He shows consistent scorn for "culinary" or "commercial" theater (his withering criticism of the 1920 production of Goethe's *Tasso*[9] is matched only by his devastation of the sentimental *Alt Heidelberg*[10]), and his sharpest barbs are directed at actors who fell into the prevalent abuse of playing to the galleries.[11] But time and again his criticism turns upon the concept of *Gestus*, by which individual players achieve the unity and clarity he seeks in productions. It was not long before he articulated the concept, in a 1920 review of a production of August Strindberg's *There Are Crimes and Crimes*:

> The production, carried by two of our most capable actors, was in all respects the best of the season. There was tension there, electricity, and occasionally even Strindberg, where the words became more important than the surroundings. An intellectual will was perceptible in the direction, as well as hard work. Mr. Aicher's Maurice had both intellectual format and inner line. *Gestus* and word achieved a strong rhythmic unity; the performance grew out of and into experience. In the second half of the work, especially in the next-to-last scene, one had the direct impression of great art (I dare to use this strong word!).

[8] *Ibid.*, pp. 14–17.
[9] *Ibid.*, p. 28.
[10] *Ibid.*, p. 30.
[11] *Ibid.*, p. 42.

Here Mrs. Aicher-Simson, who had been almost too simplistic and devoid of nuances in the first scenes, achieved astonishing power of expression, and in the turn-about of the last scene she showed something which too seldom occurs on the stage: simply theater blood and stage instinct.[12]

The concept of *Gestus* cited here as being so necessary for clarity and unity was later formulated more polemically by Brecht in the "bible" of his epic theater, his *Little Organon for the Theater*, thus:

> The realm of attitudes which the characters adopt toward one another we shall call the realm of *Gestus*. Bodily posture, accent, and facial expression are determined by a social *Gestus*: the characters insult, compliment, teach one another, etc. The attitudes adopted by one person toward another even include the apparently quite private ones, like the expression of physical pain in sickness, or of religious feeling. These expressions of *Gestus* are usually complicated and contradictory, so that they cannot be conveyed by a single word, and the actor must be careful not to lose anything by the necessarily heightened portrayal, but try to heighten the whole complex thereby.[13]

Thus it can be seen that Brecht's feeling for *das Gestische*, for the importance of mastery of every nuance of the actor's trade, remained constant throughout his entire career, and yet it is this facet of the man's creative being that is most consistently overlooked by his critics and interpreters. But it was unequivocally the prerequisite point of departure for Brecht's own productions of his plays, for he deemed such technical perfection the *sine qua non* of lucid theater. So important to him were consistency and unity of word and action that he never tired of writing practice scenes for actors, including a number of parallel scenes for classics of the German stage by authors such as Schiller and Shakespeare. His introduction to a series of such scenes is revealing as to his purpose: "The following adaptations of

---

[12] *Ibid.*
[13] Brecht, *Schriften zum Theater 7*, p. 44.

the murder scene from *Macbeth* and the dispute of the queens from *Maria Stuart*, reducing them to a prosaic level, should serve to 'estrange' the classic scenes. For a long time these scenes have not been played on our stages for their thematic content, but rather for the outbursts of temperament made possible by the thematic content. The adaptations recreate the interest in the content, and besides create in the actor a fresh interest in the stylization and the versification of the originals as something special, something extraordinary."[14] Here Brecht makes, as he always made in productions of his own works, an implicit demand that scenes be played organically, for the occurrences depicted rather than as opportunities for outbursts of thespian temperament, but Ionesco patently fails to show comprehension of this demand in his criticism of Brecht.

Not all of Brecht's practice scenes were on quite such a high plane as his parallel scenes for Shakespeare and Schiller. He also recommended the "round" poem as a practice exercise, as in the following example:

A good exercise is the recitation of round poems (*Rundgedichte*) such as:

> A dog went into the kitchen
> And stole an egg from the cook.
> The cook took his cleaver
> And cut the dog in two.
> The other dogs came
> And dug him a grave
> And put on it a headstone
> With the following epitaph:

> A dog went into the kitchen . . .

This eight-liner is to be recited each time as it might be said by a different character in a different situation. The exercise may also be used for learning the fixation of a method of portrayal.[15]

---

[14] Brecht, *Schriften zum Theater 5*, p. 185.
[15] *Ibid.*, p. 208.

And the measure of the success of such training may be seen in the fact that, when Günther Naumann recited this bit of doggerel eight times, with eight hats as props, during a demonstration conducted by the Berliner Ensemble in the London Academy of Musical and Dramatic Art in the summer of 1965, before an audience consisting exclusively of theater people, he brought down the house.[16] This is precisely why, whenever the Ensemble undertakes a tour in the West, it evokes such enthusiastic responses from audiences and critics alike; its minimal standard of acceptance, in the tradition established by Brecht and carried on by his widow, Frau Weigel, is dazzling clarity of portrayal that communicates even with those who do not understand the language. *The Resistible Rise of Arturo Ui* provides a case in point: whoever reads this Brechtian parable depicting Hitler as a small-time Chicago gangster, whether it be in the original version published in *Sinn und Form* in 1957 or in the revised form of *Stücke 9*, must emerge from the experience shaking his head sadly, dismissing it as an impossible piece, as did the Italian critic Fedele d'Amico: "*The Resistible Rise of Arturo Ui* was written in 1941, but it was not produced during Brecht's life. I read the work about two years ago, when the periodical *Sinn und Form* first published it, and—may God forgive me—it seemed to me only a partly successful work, somehow mechanical and even a bit boring. When I then saw the title of the work on a poster of the Berliner Ensemble, with the announcement that it was to be presented again after having been staged at the beginning of this year, I was a long way from having the wish or intention of dashing off to see it."[17] However, the critical response to the actual production of this work by the Berliner Ensemble has been unanimously enthusiastic, as, indeed, was d'Amico's final judgment: "It was not only a magnificent production, such as we have long been accustomed to as the general level of the Berliner Ensemble, but for me it was also a revealing

---

16 The writer attended all such demonstrations and symposia referred to.

17 Fedele d'Amico, "Gangster und Naziismus," *Neues Deutschland* (16 December 1959).

and extraordinarily instructive work with respect to the theatricality and art of Brecht, if not to say straight out that it was absolutely a revelation of theatrical art, and it will always and deservedly be unforgettable to me."[18] And even before London audiences with little command of German, the Berliner Ensemble's tour production of the work in 1965 evoked similar responses, as Jeremy Kingston serves to exemplify in his enthusiastic review:

> Nine years ago this very August Bertolt Brecht's Berliner Ensemble came to London and played their momentous season at the Palace Theatre. The style of those productions worked so powerfully on the imaginations of some of our then lesser-known directors that Brecht's plays have been presented to us off and on ever since. On and, with occasional exception, quickly off. When translated into English his work has generally been less interesting than his promoters make out. Now the Berliner Ensemble has returned to London (National Theatre for three weeks) and whatever reservations I may express about the works themselves, the production given to the two I have seen so far is quite superlative. With a permanent company of over sixty actors to call upon (and up to seven months for rehearsals) this is theatrical entertainment at its dazzling peak. For consistent excellence in production and in performances, for skill in manipulating groups of actors, both simple groups and complicated, quickly moving ones, there are only two other companies in the world that I would bracket with the Berliner Ensemble. These are Karlos Koun's Greek Art Theatre and Giorgio de Lullo's Compagnia dei Giovani.[19]

Brecht was, of course, cognizant of the problems involved in presenting drama to an audience which understood little of the language in which it was played. In his last known writing, an open letter to the Ensemble just two weeks before his death, on the occasion of their first tour to London, he briefly sketched both the problems and his proposed solutions:

[18] *Ibid.*
[19] Jeremy Kingston, untitled review of the Berliner Ensemble's London season, *Punch* (18 August 1965), p. 248.

For the London tour we have to be aware of two things. In the first place, we will be confronting most of the audience with a pantomime, a sort of silent film on the stage, since they don't know German (in Paris we had a festival audience, an international public—and we played only a few days). Secondly, there is an old fear in England that German art (literature, painting, music) is terribly heavy, slow, ponderous, and "pedestrian."

Hence our playing must be quick, light, and powerful. It's not a matter of rushing, but of deliberate speed; and not only of quick playing, but of quick thinking. We must keep up the tempo of a run-through, but in addition engender a sense of quiet power and our own fun. The exchanges of dialogue must not be offered hesitatingly, as if we were offering someone our own last pair of shoes, but must be thrown like balls. It must be perceived that here many artists are at work as a collective (ensemble) to offer the public stories, ideas, and tricks.

Work well![20]

And the speed, lightness, and strength in acting that he demanded to project the thought of a drama to an audience which did not understand its language were no more than an extension of the same polished acting technique that he had demanded of his own actors throughout his entire career, for he never relented, even in the production of his most austerely didactic *Lehrstücke*, in his quest for polish and lucidity in performance. The sort of performance he demands in this letter is the same, essentially, as that which he had demanded of the players of the Augsburg *Stadttheater* in his youth, a style of acting in which word and *Gestus* were so harmonious as to produce a concrete unity as meaningful to the eye as to the ear, a unity which grew organically out of the action of the play. It is this aspect of Brecht's work in the theater which underlies all of his theoretical innovations and which continues to produce superlative performances in the Berliner Ensemble more than ten years after his death. American and English directors of his works, who have no

[20] Brecht, *Schriften zum Theater 6*, p. 389.

direct experience of the sort of theater which Brecht practiced, are often so fascinated with his more *outré* theories that they act as if these theories gave them license to slight the details of production, but such is not the case. The measure of the thoroughness and patient attention to detail that marked all of Brecht's productions is partly revealed by the fact that, in its preparation of the production of *The Resistible Rise of Arturo Ui* for its 1965 London tour, the Ensemble devoted a full three weeks of rehearsal to polish a work which had been in their repertory since 1959.

In this respect no real comparison may be drawn between Brecht and Ionesco, for Ionesco has never had such close ties with the practical side of the theater, and as a consequence his critical writings mention only twice in passing the quality of performance of an individual piece. He tends, even in criticizing the works of another author, to deal with the philosophical, the intellectual, and the more generally aesthetic problems raised by each piece, rather than with the actual production of that piece, thus demonstrating his inclination to the metaphysical rather than the practical side of the theater. Just such intellectual considerations have occupied Ionesco in all of his copious criticism of Brecht, very little of which, as we have already observed, is based on direct experience of Brecht's plays. Generally the aspect of Brecht's theater seized upon is the *Verfremdungseffekt* (alienation or V-effect), as it is cleverly lampooned here in an "interview" between the ego of Ionesco, in his role as a Transcendent Satrap of the Collège du 'Pataphysique, and his alter ego:

ALTER EGO: Well, then, you write didactic, anti-bourgeois theater?
EGO: That's it exactly. Bourgeois theater is magical theater, enthralling, a theater that asks its audience to identify with the hero of the drama, a theater of participation. The anti-bourgeois theater is a theater of non-participation. The bourgeois audience is spellbound by the production. The non-bourgeois audience, the people's audience, has a different mentality: it establishes a distance between itself on the one hand and the hero and the play that it sees. It separates itself from the theatrical portrayal in order to look at it clearly and judge it.

ALTER EGO: Give me some examples.

EGO: Oh—at the Ambigu just now they're playing *Madame sans gêne* to packed houses. It's a bourgeois intellectual audience, one that "participates."

ALTER EGO: How so?

EGO: The spectators identify with the hero of the play. In the orchestra you hear, "Go at him, baby!," "Serves you right!," "You've had it!," and the like. A people's audience is clear-minded; it could never be so naive. Besides, up to our time, all theater has been by the bourgeois for the bourgeois, who have systematically excluded the clear-thinking people's audience.[21]

A little further along in the same "interview," Ionesco goes into more specific detail in explaining how his play *Rhinoceros* supposedly establishes such "non-participation":

EGO: I feel I must tell you how I have succeeded masterfully in avoiding theater of participation. The heroes of my play, except for one, are transformed before the eyes of the audience (for it is a realistic play) into beasts, into rhinoceroses. I hope to evoke disgust in my audience. There is nothing that alienates so well as disgust. Thus I shall have succeeded in estranging the audience from the performance. Disgust is clear-headedness.

ALTER EGO: You say that in your play one of the characters is not transformed?

EGO: Yes, he resists rhinoceritis.

ALTER EGO: Does this mean that the audience is not supposed to identify with the hero who remains human?

EGO: On the contrary, they absolutely have to identify with him.

ALTER EGO: Then you are falling back into the sin of identification.

EGO: That's true. But since there is also the virtue of non-participation or alienation, we can claim that this play achieves a synthesis of a theater that is both bourgeois and anti-bourgeois, thanks to my own instinctive skill.

---

[21] Ionesco, *Notes et contre-notes*, p. 180.

ALTER EGO: You're talking nonsense, old boy!
EGO: I know! But I'm not the only one![22]

While this is a delightful parody of Brechtian "dialectic" as Ionesco understands it, it is also certainly an oversimplification of Brecht's theories. In this respect it is by no means unique, for there is a distinct tendency in Brechtian criticism in general to concentrate on his theories concerning the "epic" theater in a relatively early phase of their development, as postulated in the notes to the opera *Rise and Fall of the City of Mahagonny*.[23]

Few concepts have been so widely misunderstood as have Brecht's epic theater and his *Verfremdungseffekt*. In the first place, neither concept is unique to Brecht's critical thinking. The dramas of the baroque age of German literature, particularly those of Andreas Gryphius and Daniel Caspar von Lohenstein, had been more nearly epic (i.e., narrative) than dramatic in character, and Tieck's dramas, notably *Der gestiefelte Kater*, had made abundant use of *Verfremdung*, intentional destruction of the illusion of reality or of dramatic continuity, though of course for strictly ironic effect. And as early as 1888 August Strindberg, in his foreword to *Miss Julie*, had anticipated Brecht's concern regarding the spectator's loss of capacity for socio-critical thought because of his emotional involvement in the drama, protesting the fact that his heroine aroused a pity and fear in the audience that kept them from seeking a solution to the problem afflicting her.[24] This may seem to be Brechtian on the surface, particularly as Brecht is interpreted by Ionesco and other critics, but there are significant differences between Strindberg's views of life and drama and those of Brecht. In the first place, Strindberg did not believe in the flexibility of the human condition and thus neither foresaw the likelihood of change nor accepted the concept of absolute evil, while Brecht, even in his earliest works, condemned

[22] *Ibid.*, pp. 181–182.
[23] Cf. Brecht, *Stücke 3*, pp. 259–276.
[24] August Strindberg, *Six Plays*, Elisabeth Sprigge, trans. (Garden City, N. Y.: Doubleday Anchor Books, 1955), pp. 61–62.

the exploitation and dehumanization of man as evil and believed profoundly in man's capacity to change this condition. But even more important, Brecht never wanted to exclude emotions and feelings from his dramas; he simply wanted to focus the emotions and feelings of the public upon that which he saw as evil. Hence Brecht's only real theoretical innovation is rooted in his hope to change the world through the medium of the theater, and even in this respect he echoes Schiller in considering the theater an institution for moral education.

It must be remembered, too, that the elements of Brecht's later theories, those formulated after his commitment to Marxism, find their roots in his earliest works. It is difficult to imagine a scene more destructive of the illusion of theatrical reality or of the spectator's emotional absorption in the drama than the closing scene of Brecht's first play to reach the stage, *Drums in the Night*, in which Kragler destroys the flimsy scenery, shouting at the audience, "Don't gape so romantically!" Even more revealing as to the nature of Brecht's view of the theater is the probable source of the idea for this scene, the works of Karl Valentin, the Munich cabaret comedian with whom Brecht had collaborated between 1918 and 1919. In his collected works, Valentin describes a comic sketch that bears striking resemblance to the final scene of *Drums in the Night*. The old stage of the Frankfurter Hof had been scheduled for destruction and replacement. The original plan had been to start the destruction after the last performance of the evening, but suddenly a better idea struck Valentin: why not begin the demolition before the eyes of the audience? The final skit of the evening concerned a peasant who, coming home late one night, is apprehended and scolded by his wife and gets into a squabble with her. As formerly played, the peasant had only shouted and pounded the table, but now a new idea evolved: taking only the actor-peasant into his confidence, Valentin planned to raze the old stage. At the end of the wife's sermon, the peasant seized not just the verbal initiative, but an axe, and he and Valentin began the systematic demolition of set and stage, to the open-mouthed astonishment of all: the peasant's wife, the orchestra, the owner, and the audience, which left the hall marveling at the realism of the scene which had just destroyed the stage and enhanced the illusion.[25] Indeed, the further one reads into the works of Valentin, the more one becomes convinced that the association must have been a very fruitful one for Brecht, for one encounters on every page not only examples of *Verfremdung*, but also the same sort of perversion of logic, destruction of familiar relationships, and distortion of traditional patterns of language that mark even the mature works of Brecht, as well as many works of the theater of the absurd. Brecht has acknowledged his indebtedness to Valentin, writing in *Der Messingkauf* concerning himself as a playwright that he had learned most of all from this clown who appeared in a beer hall, portraying in short skits recalcitrant employees, such as musicians and photographers, who hated their bosses and made them appear ridiculous. While staging the battle scene for *Drums in the Night*, Brecht asked Valentin how soldiers were before a battle, and the famous clown replied, without a moment's hesitation, "They're afraid, they're white."[26] And Brecht did indeed have the soldiers in the first performance of *Drums in the Night* made up with their faces powdered dead white to convey their fear.

When Brecht finally turned to the study of Marxism in the late twenties, he was able to formulate didactic principles for the theater which incorporated and justified the practices he had already instituted on the stage as a playwright and *Dramaturg*. The diary of Brecht's collaborator, Elisabeth Hauptmann, serves to pinpoint the beginnings of his formalized theoretical statements about the middle of 1926, during preparatory work on the proposed play *Joe Fleischhacker*. He had begun to find the traditional "grand" style of theater inadequate for the portrayal of such modern processes as the distribution of wheat and the building of railroads, and eventually he came to the conclusion that if such aspects of the real world had no

[25] Karl Valentin, *Gesammelte Werke* (Munich: Piper Verlag, 1961), pp. 52–53.
[26] Brecht, *Schriften zum Theater 5*, p. 141.

place in conventional drama, then such drama had no place in the real world. His research for *Joe Fleischhacker* led him to the reading of Marx, as we have seen, and Miss Hauptmann reports that during this research he also began to formulate the concept of "epic" theater.[27] His first detailed treatment of this concept was published in 1930 in the notes to the opera *Rise and Fall of the City of Mahagonny*. In actuality an essay attacking the old "culinary" form of grand opera and suggesting a break with operatic tradition, this highly polemic (in an aesthetic sense) piece devotes a scant paragraph to epic theater, which Brecht wanted to use as a basis for an epic form of opera. The heart of this paragraph is the chart which has virtually become his trademark in the western dramatic world, a chart contrasting the modern epic theater with the outmoded dramatic theater:

Dramatic Form of Theater:	*Epic Form of Theater:*
Dramatic	Narrative
Involves spectator in the action on the stage, and	Makes the spectator into an observer, but
Consumes his capacity to act	Awakens his capacity to act
Makes feelings possible for him	Forces decisions from him
Experience	View of the world
The spectator is placed in the middle of the action	The spectator is held at a distance from the action
Suggestion	Argument
Sensations kept at the level of sensations	Sensations carried to the point of cognition
Spectator stands in the middle of the action, participates	Spectator stands opposite the action, studies
Man taken as a known object	Man taken as object of investigation
Man is unchangeable	Man is changeable and changing
Tension concerning outcome	Tension concerning process
Each scene leads to next	Each scene independent in itself
Organic growth	Arbitrary assembly
Linear sequences	Curvelinear sequences
Development the fixed result of evolution	Development in leaps

[27] Elisabeth Hauptmann, "Notizen über Brechts Arbeit 1926" in Peter Huchel, ed., *Sinn und Form: Zweites Sonderheft Bertolt Brecht* (Berlin: Rütten und Loening, 1957), p. 243.

Man as fixed point	Man as process
Thinking determines being	Social being determines thinking
Feeling	Reason[28]

It would seem that no book or article on Brecht is complete without at least a portion of this chart, which is attractive to the general reader simply because it makes clear-cut, black-white distinctions. But it is misleading, especially when taken out of its context as a part of a polemic essay against traditional grand opera, more especially when translated, and most especially when translated ineptly.[29] The most important aspect of Brecht's thought, the avoidance of absolutes, the eternal dialectic process, gets lost when this chart is simply quoted, for that he recognized the contrasts established here as tending toward absolutism is confirmed by the footnote which he appended to it: "This scheme doesn't show absolute opposites, but rather possible shifts of accent. Thus within the process of a single performance either the sensitively suggestive or the purely and rationally argumentative may be preferred."[30] This notation, which appears to have been systematically ignored by many of his interpreters, is the key to an understanding of Brecht's dramatic theories, for here he declares himself free to use whatever mode of theater he feels will work in a given situation.

The foregoing is not intended to suggest that Brecht did not want to effect changes in theater, but rather to point out that his innovations were neither so radical nor so dominant in his work as the chart cited above may seem to imply. For Brecht did want to change the theater as he found it in the early twenties in Germany, and, while the innovations he instituted in many cases predate his commitment to Marxism, it was this commitment that conditioned the articulation of his dramatic theories out of the body of his dramas. To put it

[28] Brecht, *Stücke 3*, pp. 266–267.
[29] Cf. John Willett, *Brecht on Theatre* (New York: Hill and Wang, 1957), p. 37. Willett translates "der veränderliche und verändernde Mensch" as "he is alterable and able to alter," which is meaningless.
[30] Brecht, *Stücke 3*, p. 266.

simply, he saw the capitalistic world as evil, and he felt that the theater public could be made aware of this evil and of the need for change. In short, the theater was to become an instrument of Marxist dialectic. But it could not function thus, so Brecht thought, if it simply aroused the spectator to emotional involvement in the plot and identification with the hero, thence to lead him to an emotional catharsis. What Brecht felt was necessary, as Walter Benjamin so admirably put it, was an *entspanntes Publikum*:

> As a novelist of the last century put it, "There is nothing nicer than lying on a sofa reading a novel." This indicates the degree of relaxation achieved in the enjoyment of a narrative work. The idea generally entertained of the spectator of drama is the opposite: one thinks of a man who, with every fiber tensed, attentively follows an occurrence. The concept of the epic theater . . . seeks a relaxed audience which follows the plot without tension. This audience will certainly always occur as a collective, and that differentiates it from the reader of a novel, alone with his text. Yet this audience, precisely because it is a collective, will feel itself forced to take sides. But as Brecht sees it such taking of sides ought to be reflective and relaxed; in short, that of an interested bystander.[31]

In other words, the spectator ought to be held in a cool, detached, and critical state; indeed, so essential did Brecht find this sense of critical detachment that he repeatedly suggested that spectators be allowed to smoke in the theater: "I even insist that a single man smoking a cigar in the stalls at a Shakespeare performance could lead to the fall of occidental art. He might just as well light a bomb as a cigar. I would like to see the public permitted to smoke at our performances. And I would like it mainly for the actors. In my opinion it is totally impossible for an actor to play unnatural, cramped, old-fashioned drama to a man smoking in the stalls."[32] This hope

[31] Walter Benjamin, *Schriften*, 2 vols. (Frankfurt am Main: Suhrkamp Verlag, 1955), 2: 259.
[32] Brecht, *Schriften zum Theater 1*, pp. 165–166.

may certainly be debunked as naive, but it nevertheless serves to illustrate the frame of mind in which Brecht wanted to keep his audience: for him as an eternally critical cigar-smoker, the man who smoked was defined as a critical man.

The question was how to keep the audience thus detached, non-involved, and critical, particularly since the public was habituated to a theater which provided emotional involvement and catharsis. To prevent such catharsis, which Brecht saw as consuming the capacity of the spectator to think and act critically (hence the rubric *nichtaristotelisch*, non-Aristotelian, used by Brecht to designate his new dramatic forms), there had first to be a different, an epic or narrative, approach to the *Fabel* (plot or story-line) at hand. Peter Szondi has succinctly described this approach by pointing out that the occurrence depicted on the stage no longer represents the entire thematic content of the play, but has rather become the narrative topic of the play. Hence the totality of the spectator's impression comprises not just the occurrence, but rather both the occurrence and the approach taken to it by the production. The attention is focused not simply on the outcome, but on the process of portrayal itself, which fact, so both Brecht and Szondi feel, substitutes an "epic" (i.e., novelistic) freedom to tarry and contemplate for the former goal-directedness of the conventional theater.[33]

To maintain this "epic freedom to tarry and contemplate," the traditional spell cast by the theater had to be broken. The spectator had to be made aware periodically that this was not real life that was taking place on the stage, but rather a theatrical production representing some mutable aspect of the human condition. Hence Brecht turned to use of various forms of *Verfremdungseffekt* (alienation effect, not thus called until 1936), all of which were originally intended to remind the audience that they were experiencing theater, not life. A poem from *Der Messingkauf* expresses this intention eloquently:

[33] Peter Szondi, *Theorie des modernen Dramas* (Frankfurt am Main: Suhrkamp Verlag, 1956), pp. 117–118.

Show that you are showing! Above all the different attitudes
That you show when you show how men comport themselves,
You should not forget the attitude of showing.
The attitude of showing should be basic to all other attitudes.
Here is the exercise: Before you show how somebody
Commits treachery or is seized by jealousy,
Or how he makes a deal, look
At the spectator as if you were saying,
"Look out, now, now this man commits treachery, and this is how he
    does it.
This is the way he is when seized by jealousy; this is the way he made deals
When he made deals." Thereby
Your showing will maintain the attitude of showing.
. . . . And behind your figures
You yourselves will remain visible as the ones
Who are presenting them.[34]

"Show that you are showing" was probably one of Brecht's favorite
expressions as a director ("Zeigt das Zeigen!" is still a cry frequently
heard during the *Probenarbeit* of the Berliner Ensemble), and it is
the basic purpose which underlies his use of the *Verfremdungseffekt*,
especially in his earlier works.

Such unmasking of the process of dramatic showing can be carried off in many ways. It can be accomplished, for example, by
manipulation of and innovation with the basic machinery of the
modern stage: the half-curtain which only partially hides the process
of changing scenery, the brilliant flat white lighting which reveals
the stagy falseness of the set, the operation of the stage turntable to
skew the spectators' view of the action during a scene, the elimina-
tion of spotlights and footlights, and even the exposure of flood-
lighting fixtures are all familiar devices used by Brecht to remind the
audience that they are witnessing a stage production. *Verfremdung*
can also be accomplished in the structure of the play, by a prologue
which anticipates the action to be depicted, by an epilogue which

[34] Brecht, *Schriften zum Theater 5*, p. 275.

sums it up and extracts a moral, or by interruptions of the action during the scene in order to comment upon it; and it is also frequently carried out by the display or projection of titles and legends which anticipate, sum up, or comment upon the development of the action on the stage, much as in the mode of writing of the novelist.

But even more important for Brecht was the *Verfremdung* produced by the actor in his approach to the playing of his role. Probably the simplest and most vivid illustration of this approach was given by Brecht in the following passage from *Der Messingkauf*, appropriately entitled "street scene":

> It is comparatively simple to establish a basic model for epic theater. In practical experiments I generally selected as an example of the most simple, so to speak "natural," epic theater an event which can occur on any street corner: the eyewitness of a traffic accident demonstrates to a crowd how the accident came to pass. The bystanders have either not seen the event or are just not of the same opinion or see it differently—the important thing is that the demonstrator portrays the attitude of the driver or the victim in such a way that the bystanders can form their own opinion about the cause of the accident.
>
> This example of epic theater of the most primitive sort seems easy to understand. Yet it poses astonishing difficulties as an experience for the spectator as soon as it is demanded of him that he bear the burden of reaching a conclusion, that he accept such a demonstration on a street corner as a basic form of great theater, of theater for the scientific age. I feel that this epic theater can prove to be richer, more complex, more highly developed in every detail, but that it basically needs no other elements than those in the demonstration on the street corner in order to be great theater. Yet, on the other hand, it could not be called epic theater if one of the chief elements of the demonstration on the street corner were lacking.[35]

Indeed, in order to achieve the effect of demonstration, of "showing," in acting technique, in order to prevent the actor from disap-

[35] *Ibid.*, pp. 70–71.

pearing without a trace left of himself into the character portrayed, Brecht recommended three procedures to be used during the phase of *Probenarbeit* as an exercise to achieve a distance between the actor and the role he was portraying: recasting all speeches into the third person and into the past tense, and recitation of stage directions and comments along with the speeches. He felt that such practices would cause two nuances of tone to clash, and in the process the second of the two, the text itself, would be "estranged." Yet he saw such exercises as realistic, for they simply emphasize a fact of theater practice: as far as the actor is concerned, everything concerning the play should be seen in a sort of "past tense," for he knows the outcome of the play and can thus judge each speech from the perspective of the consequences it entails. And reciting stage directions ("He stood up angrily, for he had not eaten, and said . . . ," or "He smiled and said all too carelessly . . .") emphasizes the attitude of the character toward the words he is about to speak and thus determines his basic *Gestus*.[36] In short, the technique is designed to interpose a distance between the actor and his role during the *Probenarbeit* which could not later be bridged completely in actual performance. To use Walter Benjamin's words, this technique further enables the actor to "quote" a certain *Gestus* in actual performance, rather than simply to immerse himself totally in the playing of the role.[37] Indeed, Brecht even went so far as to incorporate such "quoted roles" directly into the acting versions of some of his more epic works of the late twenties and early thirties; in a late version of *Three Penny Opera*, for instance, Polly Peachum "quotes" a song originally attributed to Pirate Jenny, and the entire function of the four comrades of *The Measures Taken* is to "quote" the actions and *Gestus* of the young comrade, much as a witness might reenact a traffic accident to show how the accident happened.[38] And it is clear that Brecht intended the technique to serve as much an aesthetic as a didactic purpose in his

---

[36] Brecht, *Schriften zum Theater 3*, pp. 159–160.
[37] Benjamin, *Schriften*, 2: 261.
[38] v. Brecht, *Stücke 4*, p. 258.

theater, for he saw such exercises as a sure check on the sort of over-playing to the galleries that he found so objectionable in the conventional theater of the period.

There is, moreover, a twofold didactic purpose served by such estrangement of roles: the actor is prevented from empathizing with the character he is portraying, and the spectator is thus prevented from empathizing with the portrayal, or so Brecht thought during this phase of his experience of the theater: "The contact between audience and stage is usually established, as is well known, on the basis of empathy. The exertions of the conventional actor are so completely concentrated on the improvisation of this psychic act that we can say he sees the object of his art as that alone. Our introductory remarks have already shown that the technique emphasized by the V-effect is diametrically opposed to the technique that causes empathy. The actor is thereby constrained from improvisation of the empathetic act."[39] And the reason for such avoidance of empathy between actor and role was that Brecht felt that this empathy, particularly when carried to the point of emotional catharsis by the spectator, dulled the latter's critical faculty and consumed his capacity to act, to change the corrupt existing social and economic order. He illustrated the difference between the spectator of the traditional, dramatic, empathetic theater and the spectator of the new, epic, nonempathetic theater thus:

> In no respect was the spectator any longer permitted to give himself up without criticism (and, in practice, without consequences) to identification with dramatic characters through empathy. The performance posited the material and occurrences as a process of estrangement, which was necessary to promote understanding. With all the things taken for granted in traditional theater, real understanding is abandoned. What had been taken for granted had to achieve the impact of surprise. Only thus could the laws of cause and effect be revealed. The actions of men had to be thus, yet at the same time it had to be possible for them to be otherwise. These were great differences.

[39] Brecht, *Schriften zum Theater 3*, pp. 156–157.

The spectator of the dramatic theater says: Yes, I've often felt that way, too.—That's the way I am.—That is quite natural.—That's the way it always is.—The suffering of this person disturbs me because there's no way out for him.—This is great art: everything here is just as it should be.—I cry with those who cry and laugh with those who laugh.

The spectator of epic theater says: I never would have thought that. —That's not the way it ought to be.—That's very surprising, almost incredible.—That's got to stop.—The suffering of this person disturbs me because there really is a way out for him.—This is great art: nothing here is as it should be.—I laugh at those who cry, and I cry at those who laugh.[40]

And it is important that this possible escape from the plight of mankind be shown as socially determined, that nothing be taken for granted or posited as *selbstverständlich* or predetermined by some fate, for the condition of man could indeed be changed by the concerted action of men:

What is gained thereby? The spectator no longer sees the figures on the stage portrayed as unchangeable, beyond influence, helplessly delivered to their fate. He sees: This man is the way he is because the conditions are the way they are. And the conditions are the way they are because man is the way he is. But he is conceivable as well not only as he is, but otherwise, as he could be; and even the conditions could conceivably be different. Thus the spectator in the theater assumes a new attitude, the same attitude with respect to the world of man as portrayed on the stage that he has with respect to nature as a man of this century. He is accepted into the theater, too, as a great changer who is capable of interfering in the processes of nature, who doesn't simply accept the world as it comes, but masters it. The theater no longer attempts to intoxicate him, to provide him with illusions, to make him forget the world, to get him to accept his fate. The theater now presents the world for him to attack.[41]

[40] *Ibid.*, pp. 54–55.
[41] *Ibid.*, p. 102.

This was, in effect, the aesthetic and polemic viewpoint which produced the austerely didactic *Lehrstücke* of Brecht's middle period, such as *The Measures Taken*. But it was a viewpoint from which he soon began to retreat, for these *Lehrstücke* were not generally well received, and the following pieces, such as *The Rifles of Señora Carrar* (a transposition of J. M. Synge's *Riders to the Sea* to a setting in the Spanish Civil War), were characterized by a much richer texture of dramatic variety. This shift in emphasis was accompanied by a concomitant change of stress in Brecht's theoretical writings from purely didactic epic theater to a more permissive view of the theater as an institution for entertainment. The shift is already perceptible as early as 1936, in the essay "Vergnügungstheater oder Lehrtheater?":

> The theater became an institution for philosophers, for the kind of philosophers, to be sure, who wanted not only to explain the world but also to change it. Hence there was philosophizing; there was teaching. And what happened to entertainment? Were we being sent back to school, dealt with as illiterates? Were we supposed to take exams and compete for grades?
>
> According to consensus, there is a great difference between learning and entertainment. The former may be useful, but only the latter is pleasurable. Thus we have to defend the epic theater against the suspicion that it must be an extremely unpleasant, joyless, and even enervating institution.[42]

And by 1948, when Brecht formulated most clearly and succinctly the principles of his theater, his *Little Organon for the Theater*, he formally recognized entertainment as the essential business of the theater:

> It has always been the business of the theater, like all other art forms, to entertain the public. This business vests art with its special dignity; it needs no other excuse than enjoyment, which is certainly unconditional. By no means would theater be raised to a higher level

[42] *Ibid.*, p. 56.

if it were, for example, turned into a marketplace for morality; we should rather have to make sure that it wasn't really lowered, which would immediately occur if it didn't make morality pleasurable— pleasurable to the senses—in which case morality would only stand to gain. We should certainly not be able to suspect it of being didactic, at least in any other respect than to teach us how we can enjoy physical or intellectual pleasure. The theater must, you see, be permitted to remain something thoroughly superfluous, which is to imply that we live for such superfluities. Less than anything else do pleasures need defending.[43]

Of course Brecht still considered genuine learning to be one of the highest forms of entertainment, especially in the scientific age, but the moderation of his approach here from his initial didacticism is obvious.

Brecht had long been concerned with the role of the theater in the scientific age, as witness his use of the term as early as 1931, and he actually considered substituting this term for the rubric "epic theater." In the "Addenda to the *Little Organon*," dating from 1954 and 1955, it becomes obvious to what extent he has moderated his assertions concerning the epic theater:

Even if the term "epic theater" is now to be given up, the stride toward conscious experience which it makes possible now just as it used to is not to be. Rather it is the term itself which is too narrow and vague for the intended kind of theater; it needs more precise definition and must be more productive. Besides, it was too immovably opposed to the concept of dramatic theater and frequently took the latter all too naively for granted, for instance in this sense: certainly we are concerned with occurrences which are presented directly with all the earmarks of spontaneity! (In the same dangerous way we have always, in all of our innovations, taken for granted that it is still theater—and does not, for example, become scientific demonstration.)

[43] Brecht, *Schriften zum Theater 7*, pp. 10–11.

Even the term "theater of the scientific age" doesn't go far enough. In the *Little Organon for the Theater* what can really be called the scientific age is perhaps fully enough explained, but the term itself, in the sense in which it is generally used, is just too pejorative.[44]

The thinly veiled disillusionment with both the epic theater and the scientific age, for which Brecht had earlier held such great hope, is too strong to be missed, but it does not betoken a similar disillusionment with the theater, which remained his one sustained commitment.

In his later years Brecht tended more and more to think of his approach to the theater as a form of dialectic, an exposition of thesis and antithesis, with the spectator being led to form his own synthesis. This mode of thought, which was characteristic of Brecht throughout his career, he also suggested as a satisfactory rubric for his drama in the "Addenda to the *Little Organon*," suggesting that only by dialectic treatment could the "theater of the scientific age" be made pleasurable and viable.[45] He had long since recognized the strongly dialectic elements inherent in his *Verfremdungseffekt*, as indicated by a very sketchy treatment of the dialectics of estrangement in notes dating from 1938.[46] And even Reinhold Grimm, who in his remarkably succinct and perceptive work, *Bertolt Brecht: Die Struktur seines Werkes*, seeks to interpret every aspect of Brecht's work in terms of *Verfremdung*, eventually recognizes that *Verfremdung* inevitably serves the purpose of dialectics:

In order to understand correctly the relationship of Brecht's works to the view of the world they propagate, one must know their structure. As we have ascertained, in the dramas this structure is based above all upon estrangement, hence upon the demonstration of contradictions, which leads to independent analysis and engagement. It is the intention of such drama to awaken productive doubt, the most certain of all certain things, as the young Brecht recognized; such drama re-

---

[44] *Ibid.*, pp. 58–59.
[45] *Ibid.*, p. 59.
[46] Brecht, *Schriften zum Theater 3*, pp. 180–182.

quires "the free orientation of vital questions for the purpose of solving them." This implies that in content Brecht's theater can be thoroughly dogmatic, but never in form. For the latter always functions dialectically. But the irony of dialectics is that, precisely for the reason that Brecht became a writer in the service of a totalitarian regime, he is not useful as a totalitarian writer. Hence it can scarcely surprise us that Russian stages present "culinary" theater and avoid the revolutionary theater of estrangement. Brecht was upsetting to the realized ideology, and he knew it and relished it. The structure of his works is such that they are directed against their own content.[47]

It was indeed precisely this dialectic effect of the form of his works which made Brecht all but intolerable to the Communists, as will be demonstrated with reference to both *The Measures Taken* and *The Life of Galileo*.

In his last published and highly fragmentary theoretical writings, entitled "Die Dialektik auf dem Theater" and dating from 1955 and 1956, Brecht appeared at last ready to abandon the concept of epic theater in favor of the more functionally descriptive and broader concept of dialectic theater, as his preface indicates: "The following work, which was devoted to Section 45 of the *Little Organon*, comes close to suspecting that the term 'epic theater' is too formal for the form of theater intended (and in part for the form practiced). For this consideration, epic theater is a point of departure, but it alone cannot convey the productivity and changeability of society from which sources we must draw our chief pleasure. The term must therefore be considered insufficient, without offering a new one to replace it."[48] And although he balked at providing a new catchword to describe his new concept of the theater, it is certain that this concept was dialectic in nature. That Brecht was in earnest about this development in his dramatic theory, indeed, that his death probably cut short an entirely new line of theoretical thought, if not of creative

[47] Reinhold Grimm, *Bertolt Brecht: Die Struktur seines Werkes* (Nuremberg: Verlag Hans Carl, 1962), pp. 75–76.
[48] Brecht, *Schriften zum Theater 7*, p. 223.

productivity, is evident from Manfred Wekwerth's account of a discussion with Brecht of the *Probenarbeit* for *The Days of the Commune* that took place at Brecht's country home in Buckow just nine days before his death. Wekwerth relates how Brecht turned the discussion to the concept of dialectics in the theater, of which he had spoken frequently in the preceding weeks. He asserted that dialectics offered a way of making events come to life on the stage, and when he noticed that Wekwerth was jotting down a note, he pounced on him: " 'Underline *life* heavily! There are fools who continually mistake the dead for the living.' And in the typical theater this folly had actually been developed to a form of art, to 'clear the table' of the plot of all 'unevenness'—which is to say of all contradictions. But a cleared table was still an empty table. Therefore the challenge of bringing events to life on the stage, as simple as that sounds, could scarcely be overstated."[49] As Wekwerth emphasizes, Brecht had long felt that familiarity had a way of killing off everything live in the events we experience, either in life or in the theater, and that only a dialectical approach could bring such events to life on the stage. Hence to understand his concept of dialectics as dry Marxist didacticism, purely as a means to a political end, is to misunderstand the experience of theater that Brecht sought to provide, for his concept of dialectics had always been more Hegelian than Marxist, and to him the means was often more interesting than the end.

His concern for the theater as a means not only of instructing, but also of entertaining, is reflected in a further development of a new theoretical category which issued from the discussion cited above. Wekwerth recounts that Brecht held his associates back to complain bemusedly that so many, even friends and collaborators, had so frequently misunderstood his theories for the theater, especially when he had attempted to clarify and simplify them. Suddenly it occurred to him that he had omitted from the presentation of his theories something which he had taken for granted as an utterly es-

[49] Manfred Wekwerth, "Auffinden einer ästhetischen Kategorie" in Huchel, ed., *Sinn und Form: Zweites Sonderheft Bertolt Brecht*, p. 265.

sential element of any theatrical experience: the role of the naive. Wekwerth describes Brecht's surprise at this discovery:

> Brecht said that quite naively, without the slightest irony. It was for him a real discovery. He was deeply surprised that his theater had been taken unnaively for years and years. He was shocked: "Most of the people occupied in the theater—and not only the theoreticians— simply don't have this word in their vocabulary. How do they propose to create worthy, sensible theater?" Brecht had long been an implacable foe of the modern experiments of Marxist aesthetics, but now he was on the point of detecting its ignorance of the naive. "They really, earnestly believe there are great beauties in art without naiveté. The naive *is* an aesthetic category, the most concrete of all!" We knew the word *naive* from Brecht's rehearsals, when he often shouted it at the actors on the stage, but we were hearing it now for the first time in such a generalized context.[50]

Just how general Brecht's regard for the naive was is indicated by Wekwerth in his own assertion that the very acting style of the Berliner Ensemble was essentially predicated on the restoration of naiveté, of credulity.[51] Unfortunately, however, Brecht's death followed so soon that he was unable to incorporate such observations into his own theoretical writings. Nevertheless, it should be obvious that to conceive of Brecht as a narrow, didactic, and dogmatic formulater of dramatic principles is to neglect the richness and variety of his practice of the theater. He never accepted as generally valid any one set of aesthetic principles, for his theories abound in contradictions in the true spirit of dialectic thought, as even a superficial glance at his most comprehensive attempt to formulate an aesthetic system for the theater, *Der Messingkauf*, must substantiate. Somewhat bemused at the contradictory complexity of the viewpoints expressed by the philosopher, the actor, the actress, the director, the playwright, and the lighting technician, I finally sought to resolve my

[50] *Ibid.*, pp. 266–267.
[51] *Ibid.*, p. 268.

confusion by asking several members of the Ensemble which of these viewpoints represented the true Brecht. In each case the reply was simple but eloquent: *all*. Hence Brecht's theories clearly do reflect his Marxist commitment, particularly in the sense that they convey of the need to change the world, to remake society along the lines laid down by Marx, Lenin, and Engels. But such theories represent only a part of the creative energy that went into his works, and the most important phase of that creation, the step that took his works from page to stage, was generally characterized more by an uncanny theater sense than by philosophical or political cant.

Indeed, it is precisely this aspect of Brecht's work, his preparation of a play for the stage, upon which much of his reputation as a dramatist rests. It is difficult at best for a reader, even one who can handle Brecht's German, to begin to assess the theatrical power of his dramas. But it is just as difficult for one who has seen these dramas played in the West, even in West Germany, Switzerland, or Austria, to sense what more can be made of his works and what more is consistently made of them by the Berliner Ensemble. Certainly the phenomenal support by the Ulbricht regime that is enjoyed by the Ensemble as a showcase institution contributes no little to its remarkable success, for no purely commercial theater can afford to lavish the months and even years of patient effort regularly expended by the Berliner Ensemble in the preparation of even minor productions. But the aesthetic success of this troupe is due as well to a characteristically Brechtian flair in direction that is its trademark, a flair that is difficult to pin down because of its complexity, but which results in an unmistakably Brechtian lightness, stylization, concreteness, and lucidity.

For some time it has been fashionable in this country to attempt to create "Brechtian" productions, to adopt Brecht's *Verfremdungseffekt* freely, if not indiscriminately, in order to achieve stylization. Unfortunately, however, the result has frequently been little more than illusion-destroying "alienation" for its own sake, which in turn serves as little more than an alibi for inadequate preparation of a work, for acting techniques that are immature, undisciplined, and irrelevant to the exigency or scenic unity of the work. To pretend that such an approach is Brechtian is to do a disservice to both the man and the theater in general, for ultimately much more was involved in Brecht's staging than simply the *Verfremdungseffekt*.

In the first place, it must be emphasized that the text was no more than a point of departure for Brecht. This observation is not meant to deprecate his efforts in the initial writing of a work, for even such a minor text as his adaptation of Shakespeare's *Coriolanus* occupied him and the dramaturgical staff of the Ensemble for more than a year and a half. But it is meant to underscore the fact that the text of a work was never considered more than tentative until the actual work of production was well along, for during this phase scene after scene was polished, trimmed, recast, and occasionally even entirely dropped from the work. Probably the best known product of such a revisory process is his *Mother Courage*: originally written in 1939 during his Danish exile and first performed at the Zürich Schauspielhaus in 1941, it was revived by Brecht in Zürich in 1948 in considerably revised form. Still dissatisfied with the clarity of the production, he reworked it completely for its January, 1949, premiere as his maiden effort in East Berlin, and only then did the definitive text of the work emerge, based upon and collated to the pictorial record of an actual dress rehearsal in his *Modellbuch*.

Actually, it is such *Modellbücher* as have been published that constitute the best evidence available in the West of Brecht's directorial touch. Much more than mere records of blocking, set design, or use of properties, such works as the *Couragemodell 1949*, the *Antigonemodell 1948*, the *Aufbau einer Rolle* (detailing Laughton's 1947 and Ernst Busch's 1959 reading of the role of Galileo), or the monumental *Theaterarbeit* (covering the Berliner Ensemble's productions of *Mr. Puntilla and His Man Matti, The Mother, Mother Courage*, Lenz's *The Tutor*, Gorki's *Wassa Schelesnova*, and Hauptmann's *The Beaver Coat*) can provide fascinating insight into the scope of Brecht's theatrical practice. Literally no detail of production is too slight to escape his scrutiny, for painstaking record is made of every aspect of the total picture presented on the stage. And the astonishing thing about these records is the way in which the Brechtian touch, the lucid, concrete *Gestus*, emerges from the still photographs. Helene Weigel's muted cry of anguish as Mother Courage's son is executed, Charles Laughton's studied off-handedness as Galileo tantalizes a young monk with a forbidden manuscript, Ernst Busch's bitter self-reproach as Galileo condemns his own cowardice—all of these are exemplary moments of realized theater, and they are by no means isolated instances in the model books, nor in the productions of his works.

Fortunately for those of us who have come to his works too late to encounter the living Brecht, this directorial flair has survived its progenitor, thanks to the staff of young *Dramaturgen* so painstakingly trained by Brecht during the years after his return to Berlin. The methods of production used by the Berliner Ensemble today are essentially those developed by Brecht, and watching the Ensemble at work can provide startling insights into the nature of his success. I, for one, shall never forget a morning spent watching the Ensemble reworking *The Resistible Rise of Arturo Ui* for its 1965 London tour. The point under attack was the opening of Scene 15, the cemetery scene, in which Ui/Hitler is wooing the widow of Dullfeet, whom he has just had exterminated. The scene represents Hitler's take-over of Austria (the widow) after the assination of Chancelor Dollfuß, and something in the blocking of the scene, which had been in the company's repertory for almost six years, had failed to satisfy the director, Manfred Wekwerth. For two hours on end he had Ekkehard Schall and Felicitas Ritsch run through the first few seconds of the scene again and again, and, amazed at the perseverance of the two, I finally jotted a supercilious note to myself that Wekwerth didn't know what he was after. But suddenly, almost imperceptibly at first, something new began to emerge from the scene, particularly as the coffin of Dullfeet was moved slightly closer to the point of entry, and Ui's hubris began to take on a new dimension. Wekwerth pounced upon the detail, asked the actors to exaggerate it, polished it so that it lent an entirely new perspective to the scene, and finally had the actors "fix" the new *Gestus* in the reading of their roles. It was a memorable moment, but only one of many that came out of the three weeks of work devoted to sharpening the production.

It is just this sort of touch in production which makes Brecht's works difficult to assess for the reader of his texts, yet which lies at the root of his success in the theater. For seldom does his theater create the great psychological conflict or the violent confrontation which we have come to regard as the stock-in-trade of the theater. The incongruities of life which he attacks are generally far too subtle to permit of the sort of exaggerated treatment which creates the traditional grand theatrical moment. Yet these subtleties, these deft touches of detail, when grasped and effectively played by the Berliner Ensemble, contribute to the congruity of each work and eventually enhance the entire complex of the work, providing the unmistakably Brechtian touch, which is best described as the realization of theatrical concreteness, not as the realization of the polemic.

As has already been observed, it is considerably more difficult to reconstruct a line of theoretical development for Ionesco than it is for Brecht, for Ionesco's theories reflect his lack of concrete experience in theatrical production in their abstractness. To put it baldly, he is generally less concerned with the effect of his theater upon an audience than he is with its satisfaction of his own aesthetic and emotional needs. In his early reaction to the drama, however, he does appear to bear some resemblance to Brecht in his negative assessment of the mode of theater currently in vogue:

> A theatrical production held no magic for me. Everything seemed a little ridiculous, a little painful. I couldn't understand how one could be an actor, for example. It seemed to me that the actor was doing something unacceptable and reprehensible. He was renouncing his own being, abandoning it, changing his own skin. How could he accept being another person, playing a role? For me that was a kind of coarse trick, blatant and inconceivable.

And yet the actor did not become some other person, but only pretended to be, which I felt to be worse. That seemed painful and in a way dishonest. "How well he acted," said the audience. As far as I'm concerned, he acted badly, and acting is a bad thing.[52]

And what makes acting a bad thing for Ionesco is the appearance of live actors on the stage seeking to play their roles "realistically," for he feels that such portrayal robs him of his own freedom of imaginative illusion, such as is afforded him by the novel or even by the cinema:

> Fiction didn't bother me at all in the novel, and I accepted it in the cinema. Novelistic fiction, like my own dreams, struck me in a natural way as a possible reality. The playing of cinematic actors didn't provoke in me that indefinable malaise, that same embarrassment, as did theatrical acting. Why didn't theatrical reality have an effect on me? Why did its truth seem false to me? And this falseness— why did it seem to assume the guise of truth, to take the place of truth? Was it the fault of the actors? of the text? of myself? I think I understand now what it was that upset me about the theater; it was the presence on the stage of flesh-and-blood people. Their material presence destroyed the fiction. There seemed to be two kinds of reality: concrete, material reality impoverished, emptied, and limited by living, everyday men moving and speaking upon the stage; and the reality of the imagination; face to face, overlapping, irreconcilable to each other; two antagonistic universes incapable of uniting, confounding each other.[53]

Thus Ionesco goes much further than did Brecht in his critical reaction to the theater of his contemporaries, for while Brecht had found some aspects of the Augsburg theater of the twenties praiseworthy, Ionesco finds no redeeming feature at all in the mid-century theater of Paris, but attacks the basic premises of all conventional theater. To him it appears entirely self-contradictory and self-defeating:

[52] Ionesco, *Notes et contre-notes*, pp. 3–4.
[53] *Ibid.*, pp. 4–5.

Yes, certainly, that was it: every gesture, every posture, every cue spoken on the stage destroyed, as I saw it, a universe which that gesture, that posture, that cue were designed to bring to life, destroyed it even before it could be brought to life. For me that was an utter abortion, a kind of mistake, a kind of foolishness. If you cover your ears so that you can't hear the orchestra playing dance music, but keep on watching the dancers, you can see how ridiculous they seem, how senseless their motions appear. Similarly, if you were attending the rites of a religious cult for the first time, the whole ritual would seem meaningless and absurd to you. It was in such an incredulous frame of mind that I attended the theater, and that's why I didn't like it, didn't feel it, and didn't believe it.[54]

But Ionesco had not always attended the theater in such a critically sophisticated frame of mind, as witness his reaction as a child to the puppet shows in the Luxembourg Gardens. He recounts how he stood, transfixed for hours at a time by the spectacle of the puppets speaking, moving, and clubbing each other. But he did not laugh at this spectacle, for far from entertaining him, it gave him an insight into human affairs that he holds even today: "It was the very picture of the world that I knew, weird and unlikely, but more true than truth itself; it revealed itself to me in a form infinitely simplified and caricatured, as if to underscore the grotesque and brutal truth. And even later, up till I was fifteen, every theatrical work would excite me, would make me sense that the world was unfamiliar, strange, a sensation with roots so deep that it has never left me. Every performance awakened in me this sensation of the strangeness of the world, which nowhere appeared to me more clearly than in the theater."[55] The grotesque and brutal view of the world described here, represented by the primitive Punch-and-Judy shows to which he reacted as a child, was later to become a major philosophical concern in Ionesco's dramas; what is at issue here is what caused him to become disillusioned with the theater as an art form. This

[54] *Ibid.*, p. 5.
[55] *Ibid.*, pp. 7–8.

disenchantment grew out of his increasing awareness of and sensitivity to the technical trickery of the theater: "When did I begin to dislike the theater? From the time when, as I became a bit lucid and acquired a critical turn of mind, I became aware of the tricks, of the great contrivances of the theater, that is to say from the time when I lost all my naiveté. Where are the great actors of the theater who could give it back to me? And in the name of what possible magic does the theater claim the power to enthrall us? There is no magic now, nothing sacred is left: no reason, no justification would suffice to resuscitate our lost naiveté."[56] This sense of lost naiveté as a fault of modern theater is just as strong for Ionesco as it is for Brecht, since both see it as the principal shortcoming of contemporary drama. And like Brecht, Ionesco feels that this lack of naiveté is unique to the drama as an art form, for, while he can think of only twenty or at most thirty dramatists in the whole history of the theater who possess the lucid naiveté necessary to move an audience, he insists that the paintings, poems, and novels that still speak to us are numbered in the thousands.[57]

But unlike Brecht, who looked to the narrative form of epic theater to restore naiveté to the drama, Ionesco is unequivocal in his rejection of any hybrid form, feeling that the theater can achieve its renewal only through its own unique idiom, through heightened exaggeration of its own unique effects:

Thus if the value of the theater lies in its exaggeration of effects, it is necessary to exaggerate them even more, to underscore them, to accentuate them to the maximum. To force the theater out of that intermediate zone where it is neither theater nor literature is to restore it to its own frame of reference, to its own natural boundaries. We ought not to hide the trickery, but to make it even more visible, deliberately evident, to go to the extreme in the grotesque, the caricature, beyond the realm of the pale irony of witty drawing-room comedies. No more polite comedies, but rather farce, the outer limit of parody. Humor,

[56] *Ibid.*, p. 8.
[57] *Ibid.*, pp. 10–11.

yes, but with the slapstick methods of burlesque. A tough, broad, excessive form of the comic. No dramatic comedies, not any more. But return to the unendurable. Force everything to the point of paroxysm, where lie the sources of tragedy. Create a theater of violence, violently comic and tragic.[58]

But while he demands a theater of paroxysm, of burlesque, of travesty, of extremes, he does not advocate the extreme simply for its own sake, for he is desperately concerned with conveying a sense of the universality of human experience in his own theater. Indeed, one of the principal points of his criticism of Brecht is directed at what he conceives of as Brecht's purely topical orientation, his lack of universality. In an attack on a favorable review of *Mother Courage* by the critic Bernard Dort, he states his distrust of pacifist plays which depict war as the ruination of mankind because it produces so much suffering and death. That there is more death in wartime he does not deny, but he sees this fact as a purely topical truth, which pales beside the permanent truth that death exists, that all men must die. For example, he cites *Endgame*, by Samuel Beckett, as more true, more universal than any quasi-historical drama about war, saying that it is closer to the lamentations of Job or the tragedies of Sophocles or Shakespeare than to the shoddy theater called *engagé*.[59]

Indeed, it is in the works of Shakespeare that he finds an archetypal example of the non-topical, universal truth which he feels ought to be the domain of drama, for in *Richard II* he finds mirrored the eventual fate of all men:

> To choose a great example in our own field, in theater: when the fallen Richard II is a prisoner in his cell, abandoned, it is not Richard II that I see, but all the fallen kings of the world; and not only all the fallen kings, but also our beliefs, our values, our desecrated, corrupt, outworn truths, the decay of civilizations, destiny itself. When Richard II dies, it is the death of all I hold dear that I witness; it is I who die

[58] *Ibid.*, pp. 12–13.
[59] *Ibid.*, pp. 40–41.

with Richard II. *Richard II* makes me acutely aware of the eternal truth that we forget in the course of history, the truth that we never consider, that is simple, infinitely banal: I die, you die, he dies. Hence, in the last analysis, it is not history that Shakespeare is writing, although he uses history; it is not just some story, but rather *my* story that he tells me, *my* truth beyond time, transcending time beyond all time, recalling a universal and inevitable truth. Indeed, it is of the nature of a dramatic masterpiece that it is supremely exemplary: it reflects my image, it is a mirror, it is drawn from the conscience, history directed beyond history toward the deepest truth.[60]

And it is just this sort of universal truth concerning the human condition that Ionesco feels can best be conveyed through the dramatic idiom, the language of theater, a language which is—or should be—constantly in flux:

All men die in solitude; all values decay into contempt: this is what Shakespeare tells me. "The cell of Richard II is really the cell of all our solitudes." Perhaps Shakespeare wanted simply to tell the story of Richard II; if that were all he had told, this story of someone else, he would not have touched me. But the prison of Richard II is a truth which has not passed away with history: its invisible walls still hold firm while so many philosophies and systems have collapsed. And all this still holds true because the language is that of living proof, not that of discursive and demonstrative thought; the prison of Richard II is there before me, beyond any demonstration; the theater *is* this eternal living presence; it corresponds, without doubt, to the essential structures of tragic truth, to theatrical reality; its proof has nothing to do with the precarious truths of abstract thought, nor with the so-called ideological theater: it is a matter of theatrical archetypes, of the essence of theater, of the language of theater. Of a language lost in our times, when allegory and academic illustration are substituted for the image of living truth, which it is necessary to rediscover. Every language evolves, but in evolving, in renewing its idiom, it does not abandon itself and become something else; it rediscovers itself constantly

60 *Ibid.*, p. 18.

at each historical moment. One evolves in conformity to oneself. The language of theater can never be anything but the language of theater.[61]

Here it must be emphasized that it is the constant evolution and renovation of the theatrical idiom that concerns Ionesco. He does not seek a single set of fixed principles to guide the writing or production of drama; rather he constantly explores the frontiers of possibility for renewal and expansion of the dramatic idiom, for he insists that this language cannot be fixed as a system:

> Indeed, by the very nature of things, as soon as a regime is established, it is already outworn. As soon as a form of expression is known, it is already out of date. A thing once said is already dead, reality is beyond it. It is a petrified thought. A mode of speaking—and thus a mode of being—imposed or even admitted is already inadmissible. The man of the avant-garde is like an enemy at the very center of the city he is intent upon destroying, against which he is rebelling, for like a regime, an established form of expression is also a form of oppression. A man of the avant-garde is the opponent of an existing system. He is a critic of that which exists, a critic of the present, not its apologist. To criticize the past is easy, especially when the regimes in power encourage or tolerate it; it is nothing more than a solidification of the status quo, a sanctification of the sclerosis, a cringing before tyranny and convention.[62]

Hence any approach to the drama which is systematized or which can be characterized in absolutes must be regarded with suspicion, for to Ionesco that which has assumed a systematic form is already dead.

To explain his approach to the theater, his role as a playwright of the avant-garde, Ionesco draws a parallel between modern painting and music and modern drama, saying that while the idioms of painting and music have always been limited by the cultural styles of the

[61] *Ibid.*, p. 19.
[62] *Ibid.*, p. 27.

times, they have never lost their uniquely pictorial or musical character. He insists that what appeared, at certain junctures in time, to be experimental formalism was actually nothing but the attempt of painting to rid itself of non-painterly elements of literature, anecdote, history, or photography. What seemed to be a disintegration of accepted pictorial style was actually a kind of purification, a rediscovery of the basic elements of painting: pure line, form, and color. What he demands of theater is a similar process of disintegration and purification, a rejection of false, parasitic elements in drama, a return to "pure" theater.[63] He also remains characteristically adamant in his insistence that theater be regarded only as theater, as an art form unique in itself and valid for its own sake. Above all it is not a platform from which didactic or polemic themes may be expounded, for he sees the artist as neither a pedagogue nor a demagogue, but rather simply as an artist, one whose creative effort serves only his own spiritual needs and which asserts itself just as a tree asserts its being as a tree. Like a tree, the theater should not try to be a particular kind of theater or try to explain itself or assume a more comprehensible form; it should simply "be itself," pure theater, secure in the knowledge that audiences will recognize it as theater, just as they recognize a tree as a tree.[64]

Thus Ionesco seeks to write a form of drama that is pure, universal, non-systematic, paroxysmal, and experimental. The problem remaining, how to call such a drama into being, is complicated by the fact that he is as non-specific and non-systematic in his positive recommendations regarding the creation of drama as his remarks concerning systematized thought would suggest that he might be. His observations concerning both the writing and the production of drama tend to be scattered and random, and they certainly do not as yet reflect the total development that has occurred in his dramatic works. Generally speaking, his published theoretical writings all tend to propound the same sort of grotesque, exaggerated, guignolesque

[63] *Ibid.*, pp. 19–20.
[64] *Ibid.*, p. 29.

theatrical technique as that suggested in the passage cited on the theater of violence. Above all, he demands freedom to explore the extreme limits of the idiom of the stage, accepting no other restraint than the technical limits of stage machinery[65] (which limits, it must be observed, he has certainly stretched considerably with the demands of such works as *Amédée, The Aerial Pedestrian,* and *Rhinoceros*). And he expects more from drama than merely a form of literature, for it can only be realized in the theater, when it has been brought to life upon the stage. Although he expects the words of his plays to effect a renewal of the dramatic idiom, he feels that this renewal can find its culmination only in the materialization of the theatricality of his words, in the *mise en scène* which provides the uniqueness of the experience of theater:

> If you think that the theater is only a theater of words, it is difficult to conceive that it may have an autonomous language of its own. It can only be subservient to other forms of thought expressed in words, subservient to philosophy or morality. Matters are different if you consider that words are only one of the shock elements of the theater. In the first place, the theater has its own way of using words, as dialogue, words in combat, in conflict. If they amount to no more than discussion in the works of some authors, that's a big mistake on their part. There are other means of making words more theatrical: by carrying them to the point of paroxysm in order to reveal the true dimension of theater, which lies in its capacity for exaggeration. Even the tone of voice ought to be raised to the extreme; the language must almost explode in its futile attempt to convey meanings.
>
> But there is more than just words: the theater presents a story which is brought to life anew in each performance, and it is also a story that can be seen coming to life. The theater is just as visual as it is auditory. It is not a sequence of pictures, like the cinema, but a construction, a moving architectural arrangement of scenic pictures.
>
> Everything is permitted in the theater: to incarnate characters, but also to make concrete our anxieties, our inner presences. It is indeed

[65] *Ibid.*, p. 32.

not only permitted, but even recommended to make the properties play roles, to bring objects to life, to animate scenery and make symbols concrete.

Just as words are extended by gestures, acting, and pantomime, which take over when words become inadequate, the elements of the set may in turn accentuate the words.[66]

And the way in which he suggests that his works be played is quite revealing as to the generally dialectic nature of his own theater:

To uproot us from the everyday, from the customary, from the mental laziness which hides the strangeness of the world from us, we have to be virtually clubbed. Without a new virginity of the mind, without a new, purified awareness of existential reality, there is no theater, there is no art; reality must somehow be dislocated, after which it can be reintegrated.

To this end, a process of playing counter to the text may be adopted. A serious, solemn, ceremonial interpretation may be grafted upon a senseless, absurd, comic text. On the other hand, to avoid the ridiculous sentimentality of easy tears, it is possible to graft a burlesque interpretation on a dramatic text, to underscore by farce the tragic meaning of the play. Light makes shadows darker; shadow accentuates light.[67]

Ionesco recommends this technique of playing against the text repeatedly in his remarks concerning the production of his own plays, and in so doing he demonstrates the limitations of his understanding of Brecht. The technique as he describes it could scarcely be more Brechtian in its attempt to achieve *Verfremdung* through detachment from daily life, through dislocation of reality, and through forcing the spectator to take a fresh look at the world around him. In its effect this technique is as dialectical as that of Brecht's epic theater, which seeks to make the spectator laugh at the characters who cry and to cry over those who laugh.

[66] *Ibid.*, pp. 15–16.
[67] *Ibid.*, pp. 16–17.

On the other hand, Ionesco's approach to the problems of acting technique could scarcely differ more widely from that of Brecht. It is true that he appears superficially to follow Brechtian principles of *Verfremdung* in asking that the actors refrain from appearing too natural (as Brecht would have put it, avoid a total submersion of self in the role): "Avoid psychological acting, or rather give it a metaphysical dimension. Theater lies in the extreme exaggeration of feelings, exaggeration that dislocates flat, everyday reality. Dislocation and disintegration of language, too. If, on the other hand, I was bothered by actors that appeared inadequately natural, perhaps it was because they were or wanted to be too natural: in renouncing their own identity, they perhaps reassumed it in another way. They must not be afraid of being unnatural."[68] But Ionesco's theoretical basis for demanding "unnatural" or non-psychological acting technique is obscure; he appears to want unnaturalness purely for its own sake. Brecht avoids psychological acting partly because he distrusts it, because he recognizes that he cannot know the psyche of another being in any depth. But he can know the conditions in which the other exists, and he can know the archetypal actions that arise out of these conditions (the *Gestus*). And he feels that the *Gestus* and the conditions are the materials out of which theatrical experience can be made. Entirely lacking in Ionesco's theoretical writings is the profound insight held by Brecht into the range and variety of possibilities of the art of acting, to the ways of conveying a sense of reality through well-defined and fixed *Gestus*, and lacking as well is Brecht's respect for the creative power of the actor. A letter to the first director of *The Chairs* serves as an example of Ionesco's approach to the actor and his craft:

> Give yourself up to this play, I beg you. Don't diminish its effects, either the large number of chairs or the frequent ringing of bells which announce the arrival of the invisible guests, or the lamentations of the old woman, who must be like a wailing woman of Corsica or Jerusa-

[68] *Ibid.*, p. 13.

lem; everything must be exaggerated, excessive, caricatured, painful, infantile, without finesse. It would be just as great a mistake to mold the play as it would be to mold the interpretations of the actors. As for them, you just have to push the button to start them moving: tell them all the while not to relent, but to go all out, to the very extreme. For great tragedy there must be great sarcasm. Just this once let yourself be molded by the play.[69]

While Ionesco is certainly within his rights here in begging the director to let himself be molded by the play, he places undue constraint upon the creative imagination of the actor by demanding that he play his role in such an exaggerated and childish manner, quite without finesse. In this respect he is considerably less flexible than Brecht, whom he accuses of inhibiting the viability of the actor's craft by requiring that the player remain outside the role—which is not, as we have seen, a categorical requirement of Brecht's theater. Indeed, in comparison with a fairly straightforward student production, the revival of the original production of *The Chairs* by Jacques Mauclair and Tsilla Chelton at the Théâtre Gramont in 1965, retaining the acting approach suggested above by Ionesco, was severely limited in its success by the woodenness of the portrayals.

On the whole, however, Ionesco's theoretical requirements for the theater do appear to bear striking resemblance to those of Brecht, which fact has prompted Reinhold Grimm, for one, to question Ionesco's unequivocal rejection of Brecht's principles, since he sees *Verfremdung* as the basic concept of both.[70] This similarity is all the more striking when one considers that it is the outgrowth of the diametrically opposed political attitudes of the two. Brecht developed his concepts of the epic or dialectic theater in order to demonstrate the evils of the capitalistic system; he sought to present an estranged and exaggerated picture of these evils in order to provoke his audience to seek a remedy, specifically (at the theoretical level, at least)

[69] *Ibid.*, p. 166.
[70] Reinhold Grimm, "Brecht, Ionesco, und das moderne Theater," *German Life and Letters* 13 (April 1960): 224.

Communism. Ionesco, on the other hand, developed his theories of the dialectical anti-theater in order to portray even more fundamental evils and weaknesses of the human community; he seeks to present an estranged and exaggerated picture of the world in order to provoke thought, not so much concerning a remedy, for he sees none, as concerning the very nature of these evils. Yet this is not to suggest that the two are identical in their theoretical approach to the theater, for nothing could be further from the truth. There are, it is true, striking parallels and similarities, but these are operative only on the philosophical level. Where Brecht differs from Ionesco most clearly is in his practice of theater, for while Ionesco is but little concerned with the reaction of audiences to his plays, Brecht was entirely motivated by such reaction, was always striving to produce an effect. Nor is this effect exclusively polemic, for as Manfred Wekwerth has noted, Brecht always took the basically dramatic as the starting point for his work in the theater. Hence it should come as no surprise that the resultant works do not consistently carry out his theoretical or polemic intentions.

CHAPTER FOUR / *Engaged Drama*

I am for the measures of the Communist Party, which fights
against exploitation and ignorance for a classless society.

BRECHT[1]

I'll defend myself against everyone, against the whole world!
I am the last human, and I'll stay just that until the end!
I won't capitulate!

IONESCO[2]

WHILE IT IS TRUE that both Brecht and Ionesco first devoted themselves to writing works of what may be termed *théâtre gratuit*, dramas
expressing no exclusive political orientation, neither really hit his
stride as a playwright until he had adopted the political attitude
which was to be the dominant philosophical manifestation of his
mature works. Hence, while such works as *Baal, In the Jungle of the
Cities, The Bald Soprano*, and *The Lesson* contain the seeds of both
technical and philosophical developments that were to come later,

[1] Bertolt Brecht, *Stücke 4* (Frankfurt am Main: Suhrkamp Verlag, 1962), p. 259.
[2] Eugène Ionesco, *Théâtre III* (Paris: Gallimard, 1963), p. 117.

98

they present problems of interpretation which do not properly fall within the scope of this investigation. Thus the principal focus of this study will be concentrated on the later works of both men from the outset.

As was remarked at the outset of Chapter Two, it is absurd to suggest that the significance of a work of literature may be exclusively dependent upon the political ideology held by its author; nevertheless, significant works themselves do occasionally spring from purely polemic intentions. Yet what lends such works their significance is not their polemics, but the degree to which they transcend mere ideological statement, the degree to which the intuition of the artist enables him to see beyond the ideological perception of the world which provides his stimulus—in short, the degree to which the polemic is superseded by the poetic. As cases in point in this study, let us take for each playwright the work in which he makes the most clearly articulated statement of his own particular viewpoint: Brecht's *The Measures Taken*, which is a Communist *Lehrstück* intended to teach the necessity of subjecting the self to the discipline of the party, and Ionesco's *Rhinoceros*, which is intended to demonstrate the dehumanizing influence of any ideology. In the end, however, both of these works become more than topical statements or sententious documents, for both deal ultimately with the situation of man in twentieth-century mass society; both provide deep and strikingly similar insights into the antithetical opposition between the need of the individual to retain and assert his identity and the demand of the socio-political establishment that he relinquish it.

Brecht made his purpose in writing *The Measures Taken* quite clear in an introduction to the piece written in 1931:

> The didactic play *The Measures Taken* is no work of theater in the usual sense. It is a presentation by a mass chorus and four actors. In our production today, which is really to be more of an exposition, four actors play these roles. But they can also be staged in a quite simple, primitive way, and that is precisely their chief purpose.
>
> The content of the play runs briefly as follows: Four Communist

agitators stand before a party tribunal, portrayed by the mass chorus. They have spread Communist propaganda in China and in the process have had to shoot their youngest comrade. In order now to prove the necessity of this measure to the tribunal, they demonstrate how the young comrade had conducted himself in different political situations. They demonstrate that the young comrade was a revolutionary as far as his feelings were concerned, but that he possessed too little discipline and failed to follow his intellect, so that he unwillingly became a serious danger to the movement. The purpose of this didactic play is thus to teach about improper political behavior. This performance is supposed to pose for discussion the question whether such a presentation may have any politically instructional value.[3]

In short, his intention was to embody in the figure of the young comrade a sympathetic yet negative example to demonstrate the necessity of obeisance to party discipline. To see how he attempts to accomplish this end and why his attempt falls short of its aim, it is necessary to take a closer look at the plot and dramatic structure of the work.

The Measures Taken, which is a *Lehrstück* derived, with the two school operas, *He Who Says Yes* and *He Who Says No*, from Arthur Waley's English translation of the Japanese *No* play *Taniko*,[4] is set in China during the turbulent revolutionary era of the 1920s. Four Communist agitators have just returned from China to report the success of their mission to a *Kontrollchor* which represents the corporate conscience of the party. But they must also report the death of a young comrade, whom they have shot and thrown into a quick-lime pit, so that no trace remains of his body. Called upon to account for this measure (hence the title of the play), the four proceed to act out the incidents which led to the execution, each in turn playing the role of the young comrade. At the last party outpost before crossing

---

[3] Bertolt Brecht, *Schriften zum Theater 2* (Frankfurt am Main: Suhrkamp Verlag, 1963), pp. 138–139.

[4] Martin Esslin, *Brecht: The Man and His Work* (Garden City, N.Y.: Doubleday Anchor Books, 1960), p. 46.

the Chinese border the four request a guide acquainted with the countryside around Mukden, their objective, and the young comrade volunteers his services. He declares his *Einverständnis* with the principles and practices of the party, and before starting across the frontier all five pledge themselves to work exclusively for the good of the party, effacing their private personalities and individualities by a ritual descent into anonymity which is symbolized by the donning of masks.

Once within China, the young comrade proves to be less than an asset to the mission, for he repeatedly endangers its success through his inability to control his emotions; he has not succeeded in completely subjugating his personality to the mandates of the party. Assigned to exploit the pitiable lot of coolies pulling rice barges along a river, he succumbs to his sympathy, finds a way of ameliorating the conditions under which they work, delays their rebellion, and is consequently recognized as an agitator and pursued. When another man is arrested for passing out propaganda broadsides that the young comrade has distributed, he seeks to avert injustice by attacking a policeman, thus again revealing himself, endangering his mission, and defeating the purpose of the party's propaganda. Sent to negotiate for arms with a rich merchant who might support the revolution in hope of reward from the party, he finds the man's crassness so repulsive that he refuses to eat with him and breaks off the negotiations in a state of outrage. Finally, unable to bear the plight of the starving, oppressed coolies any longer, he gives in to his human sympathy, rips off his mask, thus revealing himself as an agent from Moscow, and seeks to lead the coolies in a premature uprising which can only end in disaster. Their mission now hopelessly compromised, all five agitators are obliged to flee for their lives from the forces of the Kuomintang. The four original agents seek to contrive a way to save the young comrade by spiriting him across the border, but this seems impossible, so they decide that he must disappear completely. When the situation into which he has precipitated the mission is explained, the young comrade admits his guilt, sees that there is no other way out, and asks to be liquidated. His four comrades tell him to lay his head upon their arms and close his eyes; then they shoot him and hurl his body into a quicklime pit, where it is completely consumed. The *Kontrollchor* absolves the four agitators of all guilt in the death of the young comrade, stressing the fact that the ultimate success of the mission—and thus, by extension, of the party—is of far greater importance that the life of one of its members. The end, after all, justifies the means.

But even more illuminating than the plot of *The Measures Taken* is its dramatic structure, for this work serves as the very embodiment of Brecht's most extreme theories of *Verfremdung*. The extremity of the attempt at *Verfremdung* in this play can best be illustrated by a brief comparison with its immediate forbear, *He Who Says Yes*. Also an adaptation of *Taniko*, *He Who Says Yes* is, technically speaking, a relatively straightforward piece. In it the success of a mission seeking to bring relief to an epidemic-stricken village is threatened by the sickness of one of its members, a student who has come along to fetch medicine for his mother. Realizing that his infirmity endangers the expedition and the well-being of his village, the boy consents to his own death, much as the young comrade had expressed *Einverständnis* regarding the necessity of his death to protect his co-workers from his own weakness. But when *He Who Says Yes* was first performed by the students of the Karl-Marx Schule in Berlin/Neukölln, in early 1930, the student actors who played the roles complained that the death of the boy seemed harsh and unnecessary and suggested all manner of adaptations to avoid the execution at the climax of the piece.[5] Brecht provided a temporary palliative in the form of *He Who Says No*, in which the dramatic situation is altered so that it is not social necessity, but rather tradition, that demands the death of the boy; this demand is evaded by calling for a new tradition, "The custom of thinking anew in each new situation,"[6] and the boy is permitted to live.

[5] Cf. Brecht, *Stücke 4*, pp. 248–251.
[6] *Ibid.*, p. 245.

But when Brecht took up the same theme again as the topic of *The Measures Taken*, it seemed obvious that something would have to be done to allay the empathy of both actors and spectators for the hero, to focus the attention on the social necessity for the death of the young comrade, so that the didactic effect of the play would not be dissipated through emotional identification with and sympathy for the genuinely human hero. To accomplish this end, Brecht first adopted a traditionally epic form, that of the *Rahmenerzählung*, or "framed tale," familiar to the German audience as a device popular in the *Novellen* of nineteenth-century poetic realism (though equally familiar to the reader of Shakespeare as the play within a play). From the second speech of the play it is known that the young comrade has already been killed, and thus there can never be any hope in the spectator for his salvation, even when his companions are doing their utmost to find an alternative solution to their dilemma. Since the doom of the hero is a foregone conclusion, the spectator should, theoretically at least, be relaxed, should escape the emotional suspense inherent in conventional illusionistic tragedy and be able to seek the causes of that doom. In short, the audience is asked to judge, with the *Kontrollchor*, whether the execution of the young comrade be justifiable. But here it must be observed that such a dramatic construction is by no means an innovation in the theater; it is strongly reminiscent of Greek tragedy in the best Aristotelian sense, for the fate of the hero of such a tragedy is never at issue, yet the sympathy of the audience for the hero is by no means thereby forestalled.

But Brecht went even further in his attempt to discourage empathy, for he never allows the young comrade to appear "in person." His part is played by each of the four agitators in turn, and it should be noted here that the role of one of the agitators was written for a woman and played in the premiere by Helene Weigel.[7] Hence it

---

[7] Cf. Reinhold Grimm, "Ideologische Tragödie und Tragödie der Ideologie," *Interpretationen 2: Deutsche Dramen von Gryphius bis Brecht* (Frankfurt am Main: Fischer Bücherei, 1965), p. 309.

becomes even more difficult for the spectator to identify himself with the young comrade, for such identification is predicated in part upon a similar identification with the personality of the actor playing the role. Here the role is played by four different persons, and there must of necessity be in such a portrayal an unevenness which would prevent the emergence of a single personal entity, becloud the individuality of the young comrade, and render identification with him unlikely.

The essentially narrative mode of presentation is designed to diminish even further the emotional impact of the play. As the four agitators re-create for the *Kontrollchor* the events that have led to the death of the young comrade, they rarely act out the incidents directly, but rather describe them as they are pantomimed by other members of the cast. Generally the third person and the past tense are used in such description, as exemplified here by the last speech attributed to the young comrade: "He said again: In the interest of Communism/In agreement with the progress of the proletarian masses/Of all nations/Saying yes to the revolutionizing of the world."[8] In such a technique is found the embodiment of the attitude of the actor as the demonstrator rather than the portrayer of the role, as called for by Brecht in his comments on the street scene and on the use of quotation in the third person as a means of achieving distance between actor and role; it should be observed here that the practice in a play antedated the articulation of the theory by at least four years. Only in the recruitment of the young comrade and in his four transgressions against party discipline is any sort of direct conventional dramatic portrayal employed.

Yet even the theatricality of each of these brief scenes is canceled out by that which follows, for at each of these junctures, as, indeed, at every developmental point in the play, dramatic action is suspended in favor of dialectic discussion between the four agitators and the *Kontrollchor* to underscore the didactic point: one must entirely subjugate one's being to the party, for the collective goal

[8] Brecht, *Stücke 4*, p. 306.

must take precedence over the individual conscience. An example of such an interruption is found as the piece approaches its climax, after a dispute in which the young comrade has condemned the impersonality of the party and finally forswears his commitment: "Because I am right I cannot yield./With my two eyes I see/That misery cannot wait."[9] Yet at this juncture the intonation of platitudes by the *Kontrollchor* is for once overshadowed by the outburst of the young comrade, who has entirely capitulated to his own emotionality: "None of that is valid any more. In the face of battle I discard everything that was still valid yesterday, announce that everything is in accord with everything else, and do only that which is human. Here is a rebellion. I take my place at its forefront. My heart beats for the revolution!"[10] The other agitators remonstrate with the young comrade, urging him not to give them away, but he has been transported beyond their influence by his own compassion for the human misery he has seen. He rips off his mask to reveal himself as an agent from Moscow and thus plunges his companions into extreme danger.

In the following two scenes, however, dialectic reason is restored as the principle which guides the party. The four agitators review their situation as they had seen it at the time and arrive again at the conclusion that there was no other way out than to obliterate the young comrade. When the party questions this conclusion, the question is referred to the audience:

THE CONTROL CHORUS:
You found no way out?

THE FOUR AGITATORS:
Because of the pressure of time we found no way out.
As one animal helps another
We wished to help him, who
Had fought with us in our cause.
For five minutes, harried by our pursuers,

[9] *Ibid.*, p. 298.
[10] *Ibid.*

We tried to think
Of a better possibility.
Now you try to think
Of a better possibility.

PAUSE

Thus we decided:
Now to cut off our own foot from our body.
It is frightful to kill.
Yet we would kill not only others, but even ourselves,
    when necessary,
Since this deadly world
Can only be changed by violence,
As every living being knows.
As we said, it is not yet granted
To us, not to kill. Only with our
Unshakeable will to change the world
Did we undertake the measure.[11]

The simple direction *Pause* is the key word in this passage, for here Brecht sought to realize the goal of the epic theater as he had formulated it in the same year in his notes to the opera *Mahagonny*: to awaken the activity of the spectator, to force him to make decisions, and to drive him to cognition of the truth. But the truth to which he thus leads his spectator is a negative one if it is taken only in its immediate context, for the cognition demanded is simply *Einverständnis* on the part of the audience in the necessity for the execution of the young comrade. The broader implications of this cognition will be treated later; at issue here is that Brecht actually sought in this work to apply consistently the epic principles he was in the process of formulating. And the conclusion of the work is consistent, for the shooting of the young comrade and the disposal of his body are not enacted, but simply narrated in a matter-of-fact tone: "Then we shot him and/Threw him down into the quicklime pit./And

[11] *Ibid.*, pp. 304–305.

when the lime had swallowed him up/We returned to our work."[12] All that remains is the absolution of the agitators by the *Kontrollchor*, which admits the necessity of the measure taken.

A further element of *Verfremdung*, one all too frequently overlooked by interpreters who have experienced Brecht only through reading, is introduced by the music, for Brecht collaborated on *The Measures Taken*, which is actually a dramatic cantata with prose passages sung in recitative, with the composer Hanns Eisler. Generally speaking, Eisler, who filled in as the composer after Brecht had openly broken with Paul Hindemith over the treatment of the score,[13] employed two musical idioms in his approach to the text, a quasi-liturgical style and jazz. Indeed, it is the musical necessity imposed upon the text which accounts for what some critics have deprecatingly referred to as its dryness, sterility, and almost naive simplicity.[14] The liturgical style is generally used to accentuate the pronouncements and praises of the *Kontrollchor*, as Brecht points out in his notations to the play.[15] But whereas the music of the party takes on a strongly ritualistic character, the music of corrupt capitalist society is reminiscent of the highly satiric jazz of *Three Penny Opera* and *Mahagonny*:

> The music to Part Five ("What Is a Man, Really?") is an imitation of a type of music which mirrors the basic attitude of the businessman, jazz. The brutality, stupidity, license, and self-contempt of this type could be represented by no other musical form. Nor is there any other music which could have so provocative an effect on the young comrade. (Yet a rejection of jazz not stemming from a rejection of its social function would be a step backward.) You see, one must be able to distinguish between true jazz as technical prowess and the abominable commercial stuff that the entertainment industry makes of it. Bourgeois music was in no condition to develop further the progressive

[12] *Ibid.*, p. 307.
[13] Cf. Brecht, *Stücke 4*, p. 308.
[14] Cf. Ronald Gray, *Brecht* (London: Oliver and Boyd, 1961), p. 51.
[15] Brecht, *Stücke 4*, pp. 311–312.

aspect of jazz, that is, the capacity to improvise, which makes the musician into a technical specialist. Here there was a possibility to achieve a new unity between freedom of the individual and discipline of the collective (improvisation with a fixed goal), to emphasize *das Gestische*, to subordinate the method of the music to its function, and thus to transform styles of playing without transition.[16]

Hence the music was intended to play an important role in the overall *Verfremdung* he considered necessary for his epic theater, and it continued to play an important though less dominant part in many of his later works.

Thus Brecht sought in *The Measures Taken*, his most thoroughly engaged work, to employ every possible means to destroy the "culinary" theater and establish a new form of epic and didactic theater serving the Communist cause. The extent to which he failed in this respect can best be determined by analysis of reviews and criticisms of the work in the party press. Generally speaking, Marxist critics tend to acclaim Brecht the poet for his songs of praise to the party, the Soviet Union, and the Communist movement in general. But they castigate Brecht the polemicist for having written an intellectualized piece lacking concreteness and representing a typically petit-bourgeois view of the party. Karl Thieme, for example, reporting the discussion of *The Measures Taken* which took place a week after its premiere, describes the party's embarrassment over the execution of the young comrade:

> The discussion concentrated chiefly on the killing of the young comrade, and above all the Communists didn't want to admit that this is a Communist practice. The Communist way, they said, was exclusion from the party, not the killing of a comrade. The chairman thought he could substantiate this by asserting that physical death would not be so tragic for the comrade (or better, for any political man) as would exclusion. The position of the Communists was clearly expressed thus: wherever revolutionary theory was taught, the work expressed it with

[16] *Ibid.*, p. 312.

classic clarity, for instance in the passage about the eyes of the individual and the eyes of the party. But where revolutionary practice was at issue, Brecht didn't measure up, because he didn't know party practices. In general it was noticed that the Marxists present were in great conflict with their natural feelings.[17]

And Alfred Kurella, who correctly recognized the theme of *The Measures Taken* to be the conflict between emotion and reason, chided Brecht for conceiving of this conflict in a purely idealistic way, so that the confrontation between emotion and reason is portrayed metaphysically rather than dialectically. He felt that such a portrayal resulted from a lack of practical experience of Marxism, that real understanding of the party would have forced a less harsh resolution of the conflict:

The authors [Brecht and Eisler] would have made a great contribution if they had worked out a genuinely Marxist solution to this problem by correctly exposing the real roots of the confrontation between feeling and intellect. They would not have been forced to create an artificial *ad hoc* milieu, but would have taken a fragment of reality from the history of the struggles of the proletarian masses; they would then have portrayed the falseness of the absolute intellectual opposition between feeling and intellect by opposing on the one hand an action that was objectively fallacious—i.e., harmful to the revolution—resulting from a predominance of feeling, with, on the other hand, a similar error, resulting from a predominance of intellect. They would have progressed further and would at least, by hinting at the concrete problems of revolutionary struggle in their Chinese city, have portrayed the class roots of the erroneous action in either case, and would have formulated their "instruction" accordingly.[18]

The charge that he had no gut-level feeling for Marxist practice must

---

[17] Karl Thieme, "Des Teufels Gebetbuch," *Hochland* 29, no. 5 (February 1932): 412.

[18] Alfred Kurella, "Ein Versuch mit nicht ganz tauglichen Mitteln," *Literatur der Weltrevolution* 4 (1931): 103.

have stung Brecht, but the criticism that wounded him most deeply, as a life-long opponent of the bourgeoisie, was that which Kurella directed at the petit-bourgeois nature of the work: "The conflict between feeling and intellect is thus a basic experience of the bourgeois intellectual who is in the act of aligning himself with the revolutionary proletariat. And it is not only a basic experience of the bourgeois intellectual! It is repeated in the case of many a worker who has kept his distance from the revolutionary movement and has fallen under the influence of bourgeois ideas. This problem is thus not irrelevant, but Brecht's solution has not been reached by materialist dialectic. In its idealized posing of this question it is certainly an intellectualized petit-bourgeois work."[19] And even *Die Linkskurve*, the organ of the proletarian revolutionary writers in Germany, approved Brecht's songs of praise to the party, only to cast doubt upon the authenticity of his portrayal of Marxist practice: "One feels that he does not draw his knowledge from experience, but rather deduces from a theoretical viewpoint. The work's false synthesis of its political and artistic consequences is a result of fallacious analysis of Brecht's assumptions. In all this there is reflected an abstract attitude toward the complicated and manifold struggle and experience of the party."[20] Ultimately, it must be observed, Brecht's insight into the logical consequences of the totalitarian nature of the party was borne out by the Moscow purge trials of the mid-thirties and similar travesties on justice that occurred in the satellite countries after the war, for the spectacle of an official who had fallen into disfavor with the regime expressing his *Einverständnis* in his own guilt and in the justice of his own sentence became a recurrent feature of these trials.

Yet later critics, who should find it considerably more difficult to confute Brecht's intuitive grasp of the consequences of party discipline, continue to be embarrassed by *The Measures Taken*, and for the same reasons. Ernst Schumacher, for instance, takes Brecht to

[19] *Ibid.*
[20] Unsigned review in *Die Linkskurve* (24 January 1931), p. 12.

task for exposing the party's dirty laundry and disregarding its higher goals:

> Had Brecht used the actual practice of the party as his point of departure, he would have forgone a proletarian revolutionary presentation in an absolute sense of his highly personal theme of *Einverständnis*. With this presentation he only offered the reactionary bourgeois press an opportunity to fulminate about a "bolshevist assassination" and to slander the Communist Party. The demonstration of the most extreme situation of underground struggle was ill-suited to the task of preparing the way for understanding of the goals of the Communist Party of Germany, which were directed at national and social liberation, and to the task of furthering acquiescence in its practice among the non-Communist workers and other strata of society.[21]

And Werner Mittenzwei carries the same critical viewpoint a step further to point out what he feels are the aesthetic weaknesses of the piece, its abstractness and overgeneralization:

> The aesthetic weakness of *The Measures Taken* lies in the fact that its characters show no independence with respect to the general idea, the ethical principle; they are really no more than personifications of categories. Yet this weakness can only be appreciated if the political and aesthetic position occupied by Brecht, like other writers of the Thirties, is kept clearly in view. The writing of these authors was directed against bourgeois individualism and bourgeois psychology. They thereby attacked the bourgeois way of "creating men" by psychology. However justified and necessary was the rejection of bourgeois psychology, which smothers all social problems in superficial soul analysis, it was still wrong to extinguish the independence of the individual. The dialectic unity of the individual and the social, however, had already been shattered in Brecht's works because his intellectual formulation of the problem was undialectic, since he emphasized an abstract necessity.[22]

[21] Ernst Schumacher, *Die dramatischen Versuche Bertolt Brechts, 1918–1933* (Berlin: Rütten und Loening, 1955), pp. 367–368.

[22] Werner Mittenzwei, *Bertolt Brecht von der "Maßnahme" zu "Leben des Galilei"* (Berlin: Aufbau Verlag, 1962), p. 68.

In short, Communist critics, both those who wrote at the time of the work's premiere and those who look at it in retrospect, find *The Measures Taken* to be damaging to the party, for it propagates a view of the party which is too candid regarding what they hold to be a minor problem, considering the long-range goals of Marxism. In other words, they had not been sufficiently "estranged" by Brecht's dramatic construction to react objectively to it, for they universally identify themselves with the party as represented by the *Kontrollchor* and the agitators and seek to correct the image of the party that the play projects. Out of deference to such criticism on the part of those whom he had sought to serve, Brecht—or so we are given to believe —withheld *The Measures Taken* and his other *Lehrstücke* from production, as is indicated by the following notation from *Stücke 5*: "To avoid misunderstanding, the minor works *The Baden Didactic Play on Acquiescence, The Exception and the Rule, He Who Says Yes* and *He Who Says No, The Measures Taken*, and *The Horatians and the Curatians* are designated as *Lehrstücke*. This term is applied only to works instructive solely to the players; they thus require no audience.

"The playwright has repeatedly rejected performances of *The Measures Taken*, since only the young comrade can learn from it, and he can learn only if he has also played one of the four agitators and sung in the *Kontrollchor*."[23] But if this notation really be Brecht's own, then he was certainly indulging in a Schweikism, for the assertion is patently misleading in two respects. First, it represents a deliberate confusion of the *Lehrstücke* in general, which Brecht had clearly intended for the edification of the public (see above, pp. 99–100), with the two school dramas, *He Who Says Yes* and *He Who Says No*, which he had intended to edify only the participants. But even more misleading is his statement about *The Measures Taken*, for the stage directions quite specifically assert that the role of the young comrade (who, the notation tells us, is the only one who can learn from the experience, and then only if he has played the role

[23] Brecht, *Stücke 5*, p. 276.

of one of the agitators) is to be played by each of the four agitators in turn. Hence Brecht's apparent recantation of his early aberration is not a recantation at all, but a joke at the expense of his Communist critics.

While those whom Brecht had attempted to aid by writing *The Measures Taken* had reacted so unfavorably to the work, the author himself would have been alienated by the reaction of current western critics, most of whom seize upon it as a great tragedy which, as Martin Esslin puts it, demonstrates "the tragic dilemma facing adherents of a creed that demands the subordination of all human feeling to a dry and abstract ideal."[24] Indeed, interpretation of *The Measures Taken* as a work prophetic of the evils of Marxism is one of the principal levers by which western critics have sought to pry the poet Brecht loose from his willful commitment to the East. Jürgen Rühle provides a typical example of such an attempt to "save Brecht for the West" in his highly polemic book, *Gefesseltes Theater*: "The *Lehrstück*, *The Measures Taken*, which no theater in either West or East has dared to stage, aside from *Agitprop* presentations, is a documentary of gruesome, statuesque greatness, almost comparable with a Greek tragedy in its force and consistency—except that the thunderbolts of nemesis which mercilessly slaughter men are no longer hurled down by the Olympian council of the gods, but by the Politburo of the bolshevist party."[25] Indeed, Herbert Lüthy goes so far as to call *The Measures Taken* "the only bolshevist drama."[26] And even Reinhold Grimm, who has written what is otherwise the most thorough and sensitive analysis of the piece, is so carried away by its failure as a Communist didactic play that he terms it a tragedy in the classic sense of the word:

What really happens in Brecht's *Lehrstück* on the practice of the

[24] Esslin, *Brecht*, p. 233.

[25] Jürgen Rühle, *Gefesseltes Theater* (Munich: Deutscher Taschenbuch Verlag, 1963), p. 220.

[26] Herbert Lüthy, "Vom armen Bert Brecht," *Der Monat*, no. 44 (May 1952), p. 128.

Communist Party, which seems to set itself at such a distance from all traditional drama? Really nothing more than that a man becomes inextricably entangled in a complex of freedom and necessity, in a contradiction of two absolute values. Both values confront him as inevitable ethical challenges: he can never fulfill the one without violating the other. Thus he must incur guilt, however he may decide. And hence death becomes the only solution for the irresoluble conflict.

That is tragic; tragic in the strict sense of the word as it developed in German classicism. Goethe offers the most succinct and pregnant formulation thereof: "The tragic," he wrote on June 6, 1824, to Chancellor Müller, "is based upon irresoluble antitheses." Elsewhere he similarly remarked that tragedy depended simply and basically upon a conflict permitting no solution, which might arise "out of any contradiction of circumstances at random."[27]

What Grimm finds so fascinating in this tragic aspect of the work is that it is precisely the aspect to which the Communist critics object as irrational. He goes on to defend the irrationality out of which the tragedy arises:

The tragic element, as it appears in *The Measures Taken,* is such an irrational element that it can at no cost be tolerated where the general and unlimited rational permeability and perfectibility of the world is postulated. Brecht agreed that, while he meant to write a purely Marxist drama, he had fallen victim to the dialectics of his own creativity: as a Communist *Lehrstück, The Measures Taken* should have demonstrated the absolute feasibility of the right attitude, yet instead of that it proved, as a tragedy of conflicting duties, the impossibility of doing that which was absolutely right. Since by the nature of its formal structure it will always function to instruct, it provides the spectator either foreground details without meaning, or on the other hand perceptions which must seem highly suspect from the viewpoint of the teaching propounded.[28]

[27] Grimm, "Ideologische Tragödie," p. 316.
[28] *Ibid.,* p. 318.

Thus, to put it baldly, while Communists attack the work for depicting the party in a bad light, if not falsely, most western critics praise it as a great ideological tragedy because it exposes the true dilemma of the party member. Unfortunately, there has been no attempt to view the work objectively enough to determine what it represents in Brecht's development as a playwright. Even Robert Brustein, who very persuasively suggests that Brecht wrote such works less for the enlightenment of other ideologues than as a self-disciplinary measure,[29] does not pursue the observation further. And yet it needs to be pursued further, for *The Measures Taken* represents a pivotal point around which the rest of Brecht's works turn.

In the first place, with the other *Lehrstücke* and *Schuldramen*, it represents a decisive turning point in the formal aspect of Brecht's works. In the place of the ebullient language and the profusion of poetic forms which had marked such early pieces as *Baal, In the Jungle of the Cities, Drums in the Night,* and even *A Man's a Man,* and in place of the richness of dramatic and poetic texture which distinguished the pieces tending toward engagement, *Three Penny Opera* and *Mahagonny, The Measures Taken* manifests a cold, detached, and impersonal approach to problems of poetic and dramatic form that lends it a stark austerity so extreme as to border on poetic asceticism. It is matched in its rigorous imposition of discipline upon the creative spirit only by the other *Lehrstücke*. That Brecht ultimately recognized this approach as barren is evidenced by the fact that *The Measures Taken* represents a pinnacle of austerity in his works that he never reached, or indeed even tried to reach, in his subsequent plays. Much has been made of the way in which Brecht abandoned the form of the *Lehrstück* after the rejection of such works by the party on philosophical grounds. Disappointed though he may have been by the didactic failure of these works, he actually had far better reason to forsake the primitivistic didactic theater on purely aesthetic grounds, for he recognized it as a blind alley, as his *Little Organon for the Theater* clearly indicates.

29 Robert Brustein, *The Theatre of Revolt* (Boston: Little, Brown, 1962), p. 251.

But philosophically speaking, *The Measures Taken* represents an even more important turning point for Brecht, one which did not, as might have been expected from the negative reaction of the party, alienate him from Marxism, but rather drew him even closer to it in spirit. The most significant passage in the play with regard to this development is intoned by the *Kontrollchor* at the moment when the agitators and the young comrade submit to the extinction of their identities by donning masks: "He who fights for Communism/ Must be able to fight and not to fight/Tell the truth and not tell the truth/Render services and deny services/Keep promises and not keep promises/Expose himself to danger and avoid danger/Be known and be anonymous./He who fights for Communism/Has only one of all virtues:/That he fights for Communism."[30] But the young comrade is by his very nature unable to meet these demands of the party, for he is naive in Schiller's sense of the word; he does not reflect, but rather reacts directly to the situations into which he is thrust. Like Baal, Shlink, Garga, Kragler, Macheath, Paul Acker-mann, and even Galy Gay, his response is unpremeditated; it is a discharge of the force which lies at the root of his being, and even though an intellectualized positive creed has been imposed upon that being which the central figures of earlier dramas had lacked, the inner force is still too powerful to be suppressed. Apprised of the truth, he had to utter that truth as he saw it without equivocating. Seeing a duty to the suffering coolies, he had to carry out that duty. Having made a promise to himself, he had to keep that promise. And seeing the need to fight, he could not but fight, though the conditions of battle must surely render his struggle a futile sacrifice. Like all of Brecht's earlier heroes, he falls victim to his own passion, and he does so because he lacks *List*, the cunning which Brecht was to designate four years later as the most important quality needed by the writer who sought to utter the truth.

It is significant that the young comrade is the last of Brecht's

[30] Brecht, *Stücke 4*, pp. 265–266.

heroes to be so completely defenseless against himself, so totally lacking in *List*. But it is even more significant that it is the last work in which Brecht himself operates without *List*; in no subsequent play did he say the truth as he saw it so directly and unequivocally as in *The Measures Taken*. From this point on his characters become increasingly *listig*, ranging from the innate folk cunning of Pelagea Wlassowa in *The Mother*, Gruscha in *The Caucasian Chalk Circle*, and Shen-Te in *The Good Woman of Setzuan* to the highly developed, self-seeking wiliness of Azdak in *The Caucasian Chalk Circle*, Galileo in *The Life of Galileo*, and Menenius in *Coriolan*, to name but a few. It must be remarked that nowhere is this *List* seen as a negative quality; it always lends appeal to the character in whom it is embodied, even in characters like Galileo and Menenius, whom Brecht saw as impeding the rise of the proletariat. And nowhere is the effect of this quality of *List* more deeply felt than in Brecht's approach to his own works. In *The Measures Taken*, as in the rest of his preceding works, he had been without the quality, expressing the truth directly as he felt it. There can be no doubt that in 1930, as a neophyte Communist, Brecht genuinely felt that there was an inherent contradiction between the needs of the individual and the demands of the party, and this contradiction found unequivocal expression in his play. Having been duly censured by the party for his transgression in so forthrightly expressing his feelings, he found ways of circumventing and placating the dictates of socialist realism and still expressing what he felt to be the truth; he learned, as it were, to play the game by the ground rules imposed upon him by the party and still to win.

In brief, then, it would be difficult to find a more spectacular instance of the failure of polemic intentions than *The Measures Taken*. Intended to serve the Communist cause by exemplifying the necessity of discipline, of submergence of self for the collective good, it succeeded only in alienating the Communists and providing philosophical ammunition for their enemies. It is by no means a tragic masterpiece, as some would have it; it is far too barrenly austere, harshly stylized, and lacking in humanity for that. It is at best an interesting minor work, when compared with the powerful dramas Brecht had already written previously and was to write later. But it is also an extremely significant and pivotal work in which may be found the key to Brecht's approach to commitment in his subsequent plays. Above all, it demonstrates clearly the limitations of the didactic intention, for, although his intention had been transparent in its simplicity, Brecht's intuitive and artistic grasp of the nature of the party enabled him to see far beyond the ideology which had provided his stimulus.

Although he has been outspokenly antididactic in his theoretical writings, Ionesco readily admits that in certain of his dramas, notably *Rhinoceros*, he has been tempted to write a form of "committed drama." When asked by an interviewer for *Les cahiers libres de la jeunesse* whether the resistance of Bérenger at the end of *Rhinoceros* signified the surrender of Ionesco to polemic drama, he replied,

All right, let's admit that you have caught me out in a flagrant contradiction and that I was tempted to write "engaged drama," to plead and accuse. But we always more or less contradict ourselves in life. The most important philosophers contradict themselves even within their own systems. But a poet who writes first one sort of work, and then another? I don't believe it is necessary to surmount, to resolve contradictions. That would be to impoverish them. It is necessary to let contradictions blossom in complete freedom; perhaps our contradictions will resolve each other by opposing themselves in dynamic equilibrium. Let's see what that will lead to.

I may on one occasion write free, gratuitous theater, and then *The Killer* or *Rhinoceros*, but even then I am not judging, but telling a story which happened to Bérenger. And I solicit interpretations, which I may well reject. I don't judge? Well, maybe I do, at that. To plead is also to have judged: and in this case I believe that Bérenger, my hero in *Rhinoceros*, is exactly (as Sartre said so well in an interview he accorded you) one of those men who "in an oppressive society, in its political form a dictatorship to which all appear to consent, bears witness to the stand of those who do not consent: for it is then that the worst is averted." That certainly seems to me to fit Bérenger.[31]

Ionesco goes even further than claiming ironically that Sartre's definition of the dissenter against totalitarianism fits his Bérenger: he also describes an experience related to him by the writer Denis de Rougemont, who had been present at a Nazi demonstration in Nürnberg in 1938. He goes into considerable detail in his description of de Rougemont's emotional state as Hitler's party neared his vantage point and the hysteria around him mounted into a crescendo which almost swept him up in the frenzy of the mob. But suddenly something welled up from within him which enabled him to withstand the collective delirium: "At that moment it was not his mind that resisted, not arguments issuing from his intellect, but his entire being, his entire 'personality,' that balked. That is perhaps the point of departure of *Rhinoceros*; it is doubtless impossible, when one is assailed by arguments, doctrines, intellectual slogans, by propaganda of all sorts, to give an on-the-spot explanation of one's refusal. Of course, later on discursive thought will substantiate this refusal, this natural inner resistance, this response from the soul."[32] Of course, in conceding that the cancerous growth of Nazism in Germany during the thirties served as the specific stimulus for *Rhinoceros*, Ionesco by no means restricts the thematic content of his play to condemnation of Nazism alone. Rather he takes this movement as a model, as an archetype of ideologies in general, and he uses it to demonstrate the essentially dehumanizing effect of all ideological movements. Hence the piece is not so restrictive in its polemic intention as was Brecht's *The Measures Taken*, for while Ionesco selects the Nazi movement to serve simply as a model of ideologies in general, Brecht, motivated by his belief in the necessary course of history, was much more concrete in his didactic intention.

[31] Ionesco, *Notes et contre-notes*, p. 97.
[32] *Ibid.*, pp. 176–177.

The Measures Taken may thus be seen, speaking solely from the viewpoint of Brecht's intention, as a positivistic, didactic work in the interest of Communism, while Ionesco is quick to point out that his artistic purpose in *Rhinoceros* is considerably broader than mere "didacticism": "*Rhinoceros* is, to be sure, an anti-Nazi work, but it is above all also a work directed against all collective hysteria and the epidemics which assume the guise of reason, but which are nevertheless serious maladies for which ideologies are no more than alibis. If you perceive that history has lost its sense of reason, that the lies of propagandists are there to mask the contradictions between the facts and the ideologies that propagate them, if you take a clear look at reality, that will be enough to deter you from succumbing to irrational 'reasons' and to escape the delirium."[33] Indeed Ionesco himself still delights in recounting how, before the London premiere of the work, an eminent English critic told him that the piece had little chance of success in London, despite the fact that he had a distinguished production team (Orson Welles directed Sir Laurence Olivier and Joan Plowright), and notwithstanding the success of *Rhinoceros* in Germany, France, Spain, and Argentina, ". . . because Germany and France experienced Hitler, Spain had Franco, and in Argentina there was Peron. But there had never been a dictator in England. Nevertheless, *Rhinoceros* was a hit even in London. That shows, I think, that the work is more than merely topical."[34]

And yet, in his criticism of Joseph Anthony's New York production of the work, Ionesco reiterates his polemic intention quite clearly:

> Properly speaking, my piece is not a satire: it is a fairly objective description of a process of growing fanaticism, of the birth of a totalitarianism that grows, spreads, conquers, transforms a world, and transforms it totally for the simple reason that it is totalitarian. The production must follow and point out the different phases of this

[33] *Ibid.*, p. 177.
[34] Ionesco recounted this anecdote during my interview with him on 11 September 1965.

phenomenon. I tried hard to tell the American director that; I clearly indicated, in the few interviews I was able to get, what the play was about. It was to denounce, to expose, to demonstrate how an ideology is transformed into idolatry, how it pervades everything, how it brings the masses to hysteria; how a thought, reasonable enough for discussion at the outset, could become monstrous when leaders, then totalitarian dictators, regents of islands, acres, or continents made of it a powerful stimulant, a potent dose of which exerts a monstrous malignant power on the "people," who become a crazed, hysterical mass. I made it clear that I was not just attacking conformism, for there is a kind of non-conformity which is conformist to the extent that the conformism it attacks is simply something vague. A non-conformist play can be entertaining; an anti-totalitarian play, for example, cannot. It can only be painful and serious.[35]

But however Ionesco chooses to interpret it, it is clear that *Rhinoceros* is, with *The Killer*, the most clearly articulated statement of his political views.

As such, remarkably enough, it is his most nearly conventional piece from the viewpoint of dramatic structure and technique. Unlike his earlier anti-plays, *The Bald Soprano*, *The Lesson*, and *The Chairs*, it weaves a genuine and linear plot in which generally well-developed characters (as opposed to purely typological figures) react in a dramatic situation constructed so as to provide exposition, rising action, and a climax. Indeed, there are only three technical elements or characteristic dramatic idioms which seem to relate this work to his earlier ones: metamorphosis (here of human beings into rhinoceroses), proliferation (of rhinoceroses), and what can only be described as a form of contrapuntally developed dialogue in which two conversations are juxtaposed so that the patent absurdity of one illustrates and emphasizes the less obvious absurdity of the other. Gone is the childish, guignolesque manner of acting which Ionesco had recommended for his earlier pieces, particularly *The Chairs*; he criticizes Anthony's Broadway production for employing just the

---

[35] Ionesco, *Notes et contre-notes*, p. 186.

sort of slapstick burlesque treatment of the roles that he had previously so admired:

> I also saw on the stage boxing matches which don't exist in the text, which the director interpolated—I wonder why? I have often been in conflict with my directors: either they weren't daring enough, and diminished the content of the text in not carrying out the stage directions to the limit, or else they "enriched" them by weighing them down with false jewels, with cheap gimcracks without value because they were useless. I don't write literature. I write something quite different; I write theater. I want to make it clear that my text is not just dialogue, but also stage directions. These directions are to be respected just as the text is respected; they are necessary, and they are also sufficient in themselves. If I didn't indicate that Bérenger and Jean were supposed to fight and to tweak each other's noses onstage, it's because I didn't intend them to.[36]

What Ionesco thus appears to demand is a fairly straightforward, psychological acting approach to the main roles. This "new" approach is not restricted to his later works, for when it was pointed out to him that the revival of the Tsilla Chelton-Jacques Mauclair production of *The Chairs*, with its grossly burlesque acting technique, was both less ludicrous and ultimately less horrifying in its implications than a straightforward and psychological American student production, Ionesco agreed that the essence of both comedy and tragedy lay more in the structure of the piece than in a guignolesque acting technique.[37] In short, in *Rhinoceros* he takes himself more seriously as a dramatist, and he has retreated from his earlier demand to let the limits of the theater be determined only by the limitations of stage machinery, as well as from his express desire to create a new dramatic idiom, for in this work he returns to an almost traditional mode of theater.

To appreciate how conventional the work is, it is first necessary

[36] *Ibid.*, p. 185.
[37] A finding of the interview cited above.

to take a closer look at the plot and the structure of *Rhinoceros*. The first act takes place in a typically French setting: a sidewalk cafe in an unnamed provincial town, on a pleasant Sunday morning. Bérenger, the hero, arrives late for an appointment with his complacent bourgeois friend Jean, who proceeds to upbraid him for his slovenliness, lassitude, and alcoholism. As he does so, the bourgeois tranquility of the scene is shattered by the appearance of a rhinoceros, which thunders by close offstage, much to the discomfiture of all save Bérenger, who is so hung over that he scarcely notices the occurrence. But the disturbance is transitory—at that, it elicits only expressions of mild surprise ("ça alors!," roughly, "how about that!") and, when the dust has settled, the smug Jean continues to remonstrate with his dissipated friend until he finally extracts a promise to reform. This development is accompanied by what has become a highly stylized and distinctive *Gestus* in Ionesco's works: a discussion between a pedantic logician and an old man which quickly becomes ludicrous in its distortion of logic, since the logician is capable of proving syllogistically that any being is a cat: "Another syllogism: all cats are mortal. Socrates is mortal. Therefore Socrates is a cat."[38] This conversation serves contrapuntally to demonstrate the lack of genuine communication between Jean and Bérenger, for their earnest discussion, on the surface so important to Bérenger's "conversion" to a bourgeois mode of life, soon breaks down to such an extent that they simultaneously use phrases identical with those used in the disjunctive discourse between the patently insane logician and his gullible pupil, as the mechanism of logic triumphs over logic itself:

JEAN: . . . Bring yourself up to date.
BÉRENGER: How can I bring myself up to date?
LOGICIAN: I subtract two paws from these cats. How many will each one have left?
OLD MAN: It's complicated.
BÉRENGER: It's complicated.

[38] Ionesco, *Théâter III*, p. 25.

LOGICIAN: On the contrary it's simple.

OLD MAN: Maybe it's easy for you, but not for me.

BÉRENGER: Maybe it's easy for you, but not for me.

LOGICIAN: Exert your mind, and we'll see.

JEAN: Exert your will, and we'll see.

OLD MAN: I don't see.

BÉRENGER: I really don't see.

LOGICIAN: I have to tell you everything.

JEAN: I have to tell you everything.

LOGICIAN: Take a sheet of paper and figure it out. You subtract six paws from two cats, and how many does each cat have left?

JEAN: Here's what you've got to do: dress properly, shave every day, and put on a clean shirt.[39]

As the inability of the two friends to communicate approaches a point of outright rupture, the scene is suddenly upset by the passage of a second (or perhaps the repassage of the first) rhinoceros, which tramples to death the cat that had served as a stimulus to the demented set of syllogisms posed by the logician. Again the response does not fit the occasion: clichés of mild surprise and of sympathy for the cat's owner are uttered, but quickly attenuated as the action degenerates into a pointless debate as to whether the rhinoceros in question had one horn or two horns, whether it was Asian or African. Taken in context with the depraved reasoning of the logician, this development is ominous in portent and pointed in its criticism of bourgeois reaction to the menace of totalitarianism, for if any being may be proven to be a cat (Jew, Negro, heretic, bourgeois, or capitalist), and a rhinoceros (Nazi, racist, religious fanatic, or bolshevist) can kill a cat with impunity because no member of society recognizes the danger or cares sufficiently to act, then that society is doomed. Bérenger is the only one who retains his sense of proportion in this scene, for he perceives that the question of "unicornity vs. bicornity" is quite academic in view of the danger manifested in the beast itself. But in the end he is more concerned with his own private

[39] *Ibid.*, pp. 26–27.

problem, the alienation of his friend, than with the menace of the rhinoceros, and the problem remains unsolved.

The second act opens the next day in the law office where Bérenger is employed. At curtain a lively discussion concerning the events of the previous day is in progress, yet again it does not focus upon the important issue, the danger represented by a rhino on the loose, but degenerates into a pointless quarrel concerning the veracity of newspaper reports of the incident. Mlle. Daisy, having observed the second passage of the beast, vouches earnestly for its existence, and she is supported by M. Dudard, a young man on the way up, who is trying to win her favor. But nothing they say can convince old M. Botard, a self-appointed savant, to accept the possibility that a dangerous monster is on the loose. The director of the office, M. Papillon, remains unconcerned, except to urge his employees to return to their work, which they do momentarily until Bérenger arrives, late as usual. After a few moments, however, the dispute breaks out anew and grows quickly to its former intensity, only to be interrupted by the breathless arrival of Mme. Boeuf, seeking her husband, an absent employee. She reveals that she has been chased into the office by a rhinoceros, which at this moment is heard thundering up the stairs. But the staircase collapses under its bulk, and it contents itself with trumpeting piteously from the ground floor until Mme. Boeuf suddenly recognizes the beast as her missing husband. The rhino answers her cries with a "violent but tender" trumpeting, and she leaps down the demolished stairwell, lands astride its back, and is carried off. Of this act of immolation the cynical M. Botard observes that it was her duty. The scene ends as the others are rescued from their precarious haven by the fire brigade.

In the second scene of Act Two, Bérenger drops by the flat of his friend Jean in order to patch up the quarrel between them. Jean is feeling out of sorts from the outset and becomes increasingly so as the scene progresses, although he will not admit that anything is wrong with him. It soon becomes obvious that a metamorphosis is taking place: his skin turning green and tough, his voice growing hoarse and less comprehensible, and a bump developing in the middle of his forehead, the smug Jean, the pillar of bourgeois society, is actually turning into a rhinoceros himself. But the process does not shake his complacency, for he steadfastly asserts that the symptoms of "rhinoceritis" are characteristics of the strong, and he finally embraces his transformed being, renouncing moral standards and proclaiming the primeval integrity of the laws of nature. The transformation complete, Bérenger cries out for help, only to discover that the concierge has turned into a rhinoceros, as has his wife, and that the streets are teeming with the beasts. He departs the scene in terror, shouting "Rhinoceros!" at the top of his voice.

The third act is set in Bérenger's flat, where M. Dudard has come to succour the indisposed anti-hero. Bérenger has by now developed such a paranoid fear of rhinoceritis that he constantly seeks assurance that his voice is normal, that his skin is not turning green, and that there is no incipient bump in the middle of his forehead. He rushes alternately to the mirror to reassure himself and to the window to shout "Salauds!" ("Bastards!") at the herds of rhinos thundering by offstage. In attempting to allay Bérenger's fears, Dudard inadvertently reveals that both M. Papillon and M. Botard have fallen victim to the epidemic. Gradually he begins to rationalize the right of the beasts to exist, and finally he wonders whether one ought not to give it a try. When invited to stay for lunch after Daisy arrives, he replies, with ominous portent, that he'd rather eat on the grass, and he takes his leave in haste and with obvious relish. It soon appears to Bérenger and Daisy that they are the only humans left on earth, and the diffident anti-hero finally summons enough courage to profess his love for her and suggest that they attempt to regenerate the human race, serving as a new Adam and Eve. But this is too much for Daisy, who has already begun to manifest the symptoms of incipient rhinoceritis: a rationalization of the brute animality of the beasts as "natural" accompanied by a sharp and localized headache, the sure sign of a budding horn. Soon she fancies that the trumpeting and stampeding rhinos are singing and dancing, indeed, that they are god-like, and she deserts Bérenger to join them.

The anti-hero, left alone to face a rhinocerized world, first re-affirms his humanity and vows to defend it to the end. But much as the Bérenger of *The Killer* had wilted when face to face with the killer, he becomes conscious of the desperate weight of his loneli-ness, weakens, and begins to conceive of himself as an ugly outcast in a world of beautiful rhinos, and he tries to make the metamorpho-sis himself. But like Denis de Rougemont, he finds something at the core of his being which resists the change; his essential humanity is too deeply ingrained to be cast off by a willful act. Hence his final cry, "I'm the last human, and I'll stay just that till the end! I won't capitulate!"[40] is not a courageous reaffirmation of the principle of humanity, but rather a cry of desperation, of resignation to a fate as a pariah. Thus Bérenger does not live up to Sartre's description of the dissenter as quoted by Ionesco, for he does not actively support those who do not consent, but only passively submits to the dictates of his own private nature. The final curtain falls neither on a heroic nor on a tragic figure, but rather on a pathetic one.

The central symbol of the play, the metamorphosis of human beings into rhinoceroses, clearly engenders a genuine sort of *Verf-remdung*. It does not do so in the sense that it suspends belief, for Jean's metamorphosis onstage can be made frighteningly concrete and credible. Nor does it do so in the sense that it discourages iden-tification with the central figure, for Bérenger is the only sympathet-ically portrayed figure in the play, the only one who seems cut of the whole human cloth. But it distinctly engenders *Verfremdung* in that it attempts to force the spectator to experience the phenomenon of the growth of a totalitarian movement in an entirely new light, to sense it emotionally as an increasingly oppressed yet essentially naive being. Here the importance of naïveté for an appreciation of Ionesco's work must be emphasized, for it is the concern upon which his choice of symbol is predicated. What is aimed at in this play is

[40] *Ibid.*, p. 117.

not the intellectualized cognition of totalitarianism as a Bad Thing, for such a realization amounts to just the sort of a cliché to which Ionesco so stridently objects and which he so effectively satirizes. No, what is sought in this play is rather an instinctive, highly emotional, and direct experience of the onslaught of a Movement, and the symbol chosen to represent that Movement, the rhinoceros, is quite fitting, at least theoretically speaking. To convey the stark terror of a society gradually falling into the grips of such a movement, no political party, no religious faction, no temporal human convention, real or imagined, would do, for the connection between abstract party and historical Party is too easily made and intellectualized. This is why it is difficult to read or see plays such as Sartre's *Dirty Hands,* Giraudoux's *Tiger at the Gates,* Frisch's *Andorra,* Hochhuth's *The Deputy,* or even Brecht's *The Resistible Rise of Arturo Ui* without experiencing a faint sense of embarrassment; the identification of the evil is too invitingly easy, and such plays all too readily resuscitate old and familiar horrors from their very first scenes, thereby preventing the spectator from gaining a new and personal experience of totalitarianism in action. The moment the spectator recognizes the totalitarian nature of the movement portrayed as specifically Nazi or Communist, he responds in cliché-ridden patterns of thought which issue from what he has read or heard of such movements, and he is all but incapable of experiencing the horror in a state of naïveté, from the viewpoint of those who experienced it in its original form. In short, to write a play specifically critical of Nazism in the 1960s is tantamount to beating a dead horse.

Thus what Ionesco attempts to do by using a non-human "institution" in this play is to suspend intellectual cognition of the evil in order to convey emotionally the growth of such horror from its apparently harmless and even quite ludicrous beginnings. His choice of symbol, the rhinoceros, fits the situation quite admirably, as the French critic, Claude Sarraute, has perceived: "I don't know if you've noticed, but when people no longer share your opinion, when they can no longer understand you, you have the impression of addressing yourself to monsters. To rhinoceroses? For example. They have a mixture of candor and ferocity. They would kill you in good conscience if you didn't think as they do. And history has clearly proved in the course of this quarter-century that people thus transformed don't simply resemble rhinoceroses, but really become rhinoceroses."[41] In other words, the reputation of the rhinoceros as a short-tempered, myopic, and stupid beast of immense physical strength suits him well for the role of a member of a totalitarian party. Of course, the very valid question remains whether, even if Ionesco's choice of metaphor is accepted, such a choice as the rhinoceros can sustain a three-act play, or whether it must inevitably wear thin before it has served its purpose. One thing, however, is certain: the choice of the rhinoceros as the symbol was predicated upon a desire to force the audience to see the menace of totalitarianism in general in a new light.

Unfortunately, *Rhinoceros* has apparently never been performed in such a way as to carry out Ionesco's intention. Originally staged at the Düsseldorf Schauspielhaus as *Die Nashörner* (German translation by Gustav Sellner) by Karl-Heinz Stroux on November 6, 1959, with Karl-Maria Schley as "Behringer" and Max Mairich as "Hans," the play was received enthusiastically by public and critics alike, but an unsigned review in *Der Spiegel* provides some insight into one of the reasons for such a reception: "The generally good stage orchestra plays a few bars of 'S. A. marschiert' and lands a solid blow in the German solar plexus with this stroke of irrepressible memory."[42] The tune referred to is "Horst Wessel Lied," the marching song of the *Sonderabteilung*, Hitler's brown-shirted elite guard, and it is quite understandable that such an accompaniment to the thundering hoofbeats of stampeding rhinos would evoke a deeply emotional response from a German audience. But even Jean-Louis Barrault's produc-

[41] Claude Sarraute, "Propos de *Rhinocéros*," *Le Monde* (19 January 1960).
[42] Unsigned review, "Nashorn marschiert," *Der Spiegel* (11 November 1959), p. 58.

tion, which opened at the Odéon Théâtre (Théâtre de France) in Paris on January 26, 1960, was not free of such "help" to the spectator. Pierre Marcabru, writing in *Arts*, criticized Barrault for forcing an overly restrictive interpretation of the play by having the victims of rhinoceritis trumpet "Lili Marlene" as they goose-stepped by.[43] Marcabru is correct in this assessment, but he could have gone further, for such gratuitous assistance does more than simply force a too narrow interpretation: it actually defeats the author's purpose by focusing the attention of the audience on the wrong aspect of the play. In essence, what Ionesco is saying here is not simply that totalitarianism is evil because it engenders blind, thoughtless, and inhuman behavior, but rather that what he conceives of as the bourgeois mode of thinking is evil because *it* is blind, thoughtless, and inhuman and because *it* engenders totalitarianism. The villains of the piece are thus not the rhinoceroses, but the logicians, the storekeepers, the Botards, the Dudards, the Jeans, the Daisys, and even the Bérengers, for it is they who virtually call rhinoceritis into being by their callous complacency and by their fear of being different. Anything which distracts the attention of the spectator from their behavior dilutes the essence of the play: rhinoceritis is simply a failing of the bourgeois personality, as Jean's metamorphosis makes clear, since it is only a physical metamorphosis. Hence to identify the rhinocerized restrictively as Nazis is to make them appear somehow different, somehow more evil and dangerous than the beings from which they evolved, the smug bourgeois, whom Ionesco regards as the most dangerous of the human species.

The English and American productions of *Rhinoceros* failed as well to convey the effect Ionesco had intended (here it should be noted that for once Ionesco *is* concerned with the effect of his play upon the audience, as his frustration over the production makes clear), but for a different reason. Concerned with commercial success, Welles and Anthony apparently tried to turn the work into a

---

[43] Pierre Marcabru, "Un rhinocéros à qui Barrault a coupé les cornes," *Arts* (27 January 1960), p. 6.

piece of boulevard comedy. Harold Clurman of *The Nation*, who saw both the London and the New York productions, recognized Ionesco's reputed debt to Kafka and to the Marx Brothers in his attempt to convey his apprehensions regarding humanity through dark humor. But Clurman felt that in both productions only the Marx Brothers came through, for only the gags were effective. He found the first act hilarious, ". . . but there is a faint touch of college theatricals throughout, and no sense of the relationship of the fun and games to the very unfunny central theme. . . . There is a Disney style at the outset, childlike and childish, which intimates that the piece is a one-joke affair. . . . The final act and its last speech are not kept in view; the production proceeds moment by moment and conveys no sense of unity of theme. . . . Hence the final scene degenerates to the level of flat realism."[44] Henry Hewes of *Saturday Review* took a similar view, for while the Paris reviews had praised the remarkable brutality conveyed by William Sabatier as Jean,[45] Hewes found Zero Mostel's reading of the role terribly funny, ". . . yet [he] doesn't suggest the self-deluded man Ionesco intended, but rather a man with a superb ability to see through the foibles he is satirizing. The other actors are too consciously working at showing themselves up, too little concerned with the emergency of the drama; indeed, they seem to avoid it. . . . The self-conscious and farcical inventiveness are not tied to the play's needs, and instead of being moved by the final act, one feels that it has taken too long to relate the outcome. One feels a judicious yearning for another sort of performance."[46] Richard Schechner, the editor of *Tulane Drama Review*, goes considerably deeper into the matter in his comparison of the U.S. productions of *Rhinoceros* and Friedrich Dürrenmatt's *The Visit*, for he uses these two examples as grounds for condemnation of the commercialism of what he terms "our commodity theatre":

[44] Harold Clurman, "*Rhinoceros*," *The Nation* (28 January 1961), p. 85.

[45] Dussane [pseud.], "*Rhinocéros*," *Mercure de France* 338, no. 1159 (March 1960): 449.

[46] Henry Hewes, "Rhinoceros on the Loose," *Saturday Review* (26 January 1961), p. 51.

In the production of *Rhinoceros*, as in that of *The Visit*, our commodity theatre was unwilling to confront us in their pure form with plays which said that we are responsible for our communal fate. In both cases the scope of the play was reduced to an individual matter, and individual matters can always be "the other fellow's fault." Dürrenmatt and Ionesco intended us to feel as if we were Gülleners or townsfolk susceptible to rhinoceritis. We were asked to accept history as *our own* fact, brutal and uncomfortable as that fact may be. But our theatre "saved" us from the indictment of these plays by making us feel that we were Bérenger and Ill, the oppressed and not the oppressors. Leaving the theatre "we" were innocent, "they" were guilty.[47]

If Hewes and Schechner yearn for another sort of performance, it should be expected that Ionesco would share this yearning. As it happened, he was present at a partial rehearsal of the New York production, and he recorded his dissatisfaction with the interpretation on his return to Paris:

The public success of *Rhinoceros* in New York cheers me, surprises me, and saddens me a little, all at the same time. I attended only one rehearsal, almost complete, before the dress rehearsal of my play. I must say that I was totally baffled. I believe I understood that they had turned a hard, ferocious, agonizing character into a comic one, a feeble rhinoceros: Bérenger's friend Jean. It also seemed to me that the director had transformed an indecisive character, a hero in spite of himself, allergic to rhinoceritis, Bérenger, into a sort of hardened, clear-headed intellectual, a sort of unruly revolutionary who knew what he was doing.[48]

In his negative reaction against the reviews of this production, which were unanimous in praising the drollness of the work, Ionesco clarifies his own intention and shows what a variety of serious interpretations may be drawn from the work:

[47] Richard Schechner, "*TDR* Comment," *Tulane Drama Review* 7, no. 4 (Summer 1963): 13.
[48] Ionesco, *Notes et contre-notes*, p. 185.

In effect, we witness the mental transformation of an entire community; the former values are lost, are knocked askew, while others are born and imposed. A man stands impotently by and watches the transformation of his world, against which he can do nothing, he no longer knows if he's right, he debates without hope, he is the last of his species. He is lost. That is found to be funny. All the New York critics agree. On the other hand, Barrault made of it a tragic farce—a farce, to be sure, but an oppressive one. Moretti, the Italian actor who has just died, one of the greatest actors of the world, turned it into a sad and touching drama. Stroux, the Düsseldorf director, and his lead, Karl-Maria Schley, treated it as a stark tragedy without any concession, tinged with mortal irony. The Poles made it into a heavy drama. But Mr. Anthony, advised by I don't know whom, in any event not by the author, turned it into a funny and non-conformist thing.[49]

Although Ionesco appears here to consider the Barrault production the best interpretation of *Rhinoceros* that had been staged, at least one critic saw greater possibilities to the piece than Barrault was able to realize. In his review of the original production, Pierre Marcabru of *Arts* praised the work as a whole, but faulted Barrault for overplaying the farcical elements of the first two acts to the great detriment of the third.[50] But a year later, when Michel Bouquet took over the role of Bérenger, Marcabru felt that he supplied the necessary tragic vision which Barrault had lacked:

A while back I reviewed *Rhinoceros*, a play which I didn't particularly like at its creation. There was a profound hesitation in the face of the intentions, a hesitation which found its alibi in the pirouettes and parades of boulevard humor. It was clever, prudent, and witty, and closer to Labiche than to Ionesco. Barrault kept his distance and held to a farcical first act, the worst one, to the disadvantage of the other two. The tragedy was abandoned or conjured away. He had to avoid upsetting the souls of the Parisians, so susceptible when it comes to their tranquility.

49 *Ibid.*, p. 186.
50 Marcabru, "Un rhinocéros," p. 6.

With Michel Bouquet, it's another matter. From the first exchanges you know that Bérenger is not responsible for the social universe, that he simply puts up with absurdity, that Bérenger is a loner even before the rhinoceroses have turned up. The adventure of the individual is recognized: there is Bérenger, and there are the others. And the malaise of being in the milieu of others and of not finding oneself there illuminates the whole first act.[51]

In other words, Marcabru felt the same sort of dissatisfaction felt by Schechner vis-à-vis the Broadway production. As Schechner would have hoped, a production based upon a more tragic view of the piece had, as Marcabru reports it, a different effect, but it was not the effect that either had hoped for:

As one sees, the play takes on a different character. It remains profoundly reactionary. But it is instinctively so. It is not at all reactionary with respect to this or that political mystique. It is so totally, as a whole. And at precisely this point, it becomes anarchist. Neither the interest of ideas nor that of classes counts at all. Nothing is assumed. The human adventure consists thus in this ignorance of the others, in this essentially tragic blindness that is involuntary, that is submitted to as fate is. Bouquet makes this fate sensually palpable to us; it touches us, it wounds us; general ideas are blurred, and life goes on.[52]

But in recognizing that Barrault's interpretation had not prepared the way for the complexities of the third act, and in praising Bouquet's reading for its portrayal of Bérenger as a man who opposes the rest of the world from the outset as an outsider, Marcabru has unconsciously put his finger on the inherent polemic weakness of the play, that which keeps it from being in its total effect an indictment of the bourgeois habits of the audience. Such earlier pieces as *The Bald Soprano* and *The Chairs* had lacked any sort of genuine central figure, and they had consequently been reasonably successful gen-

[51] Pierre Marcabru, "Un rhinocéros chasse l'autre: Bouquet remplace Barrault: Une pièce rénait," *Arts* (11 January 1961), p. 5.
[52] *Ibid.*

eralized attacks on bourgeois society as a whole. In them, every institution that had been exposed had come under direct and merciless
attack, and bourgeois audiences had found nothing within the play
to help rationalize any sort of defense against the criticism leveled
at them. But *Rhinoceros*, in providing Bérenger as a central figure
who is obviously victimized by the institutions being attacked, bourgeois complacency and conformity, thereby provides a means of
escape. Negative and passive though it may be, the character of
Bérenger as Ionesco conceived it is human, and the spectator is virtually invited to identify with the oppressed hero. Hence it is not
solely "our commodity theater," as Schechner puts it, that attenuates
the social criticism he seeks in *Rhinoceros*, but rather the central role
of the play itself, for there is no conceivable way in which Bérenger
can be played so as to alienate the spectator, to close the escape hatch
of identification with victimized humanity. Doubtless Ionesco sought
to accomplish such alienation by having Bérenger attempt to change
into a rhinoceros himself, but the gesture is too feeble, and Bérenger's
humanity is too convincing to discourage identification. An analogous situation occurs in Franz Kafka's novella *The Metamorphosis*,
but Kafka manages to keep the reader at a distance from his protagonist, Gregor Samsa, by allowing only him to be transformed into
a gigantic insect. Clearly Samsa evokes some sympathy, since he is
obviously victimized by the members of his family and other bourgeois figures. But identification with him is effectively forestalled by
the fact that he alone has taken on non-human form; it is, after all,
difficult to generate much empathy for a bug, even for a victimized
one. Thus Kafka achieves his purpose, keeping the reader at a critical
distance from the protagonist, and as a consequence the reader is
made concretely aware that the metamorphosis which has occurred
is simply a physical one that does no more than bring Samsa's phys-
iognomy into congruity with his inner being. And yet while the meta-
morphoses brought off in *Rhinoceros* are of the same nature, as the
cases of Jean and Botard make quite clear, Ionesco has unwittingly
provided an escape hatch from the reality he is attempting to convey

in the person of Bérenger, his immutably human anti-hero. The trap is all too inviting, for so engrossed are we in the fate of this man alone against the brutalized herd that we are all but incapable of perceiving his complicity in that fate. And once such empathy is gained, once the identification is made, Schechner is right: "we" are indeed innocent, "they" are guilty, and the play's critical edge is blunted. In short, what started out as an anti-bourgeois polemic has, by the quite conventional mystique of theater, been transformed into the universal allegory of a solitary man confronted by an implacable fate.

While it is considerably more profound and thought-provoking in its analysis and evaluation of the work than most commentaries, Marcabru's review is typical of the general nature of French criticism of the play, for in France *Rhinoceros* has received little attention as a literary document. Criticism has generally taken the form of a review of a specific performance, most commonly of the Barrault first production. Predictably, such reviews have been mixed and contradictory, for Ionesco remains a controversial playwright, even with the acceptance of his works at the Théâtre de France (*Rhinoceros* and *The Hiatus*) and the Comédie Française (*Hunger and Thirst*). But the remarkable thing about the reviews of *Rhinoceros* is that some of Ionesco's most consistent defenders appear to have turned upon him. It is only to be expected that such deeply entrenched theatrical conservatives as Robert Kemp of *Le Monde* and Jean-Jacques Gauthier of *Le Figaro* (who likened himself to Bérenger as the only "normal" human among the applauding rhinoceroses of the audience[53]) would react negatively to an Ionesco premiere. But even Jacques Lemarchand of *Le Figaro Littéraire*, one of Ionesco's earliest critical defenders and closest friends, faulted the Barrault production for its narrow, too specifically anti-Nazi interpretation of the work and criticized the play itself as being too clearly a *pièce à thèse*, lacking the sense of human mystery he had come to expect in

[53] Jean-Jacques Gauthier, "À l'Odéon: *Rhinocéros* d'Eugène Ionesco," *Le Figaro* (26 January 1960).

Ionesco's works.[54] Bertrand Poirot-Delpech similarly criticized the work for its theatrical conformity, saying he missed the originality and depth of such earlier pieces as *The Bald Soprano* and *The Lesson*.[55] In other words, in turning to a more conventional mode of theater in a play with strongly polemic undercurrents and overtones, Ionesco seems to have alienated the avant-gardist critics, yet he has won no friends among the conservatives.

On the other hand, Anglo-American criticism of the work, with the exception of the reviews already cited, tends to take a more theoretical and purely literary approach to *Rhinoceros,* possibly because the West End and Broadway productions were too deeply flawed to permit any real critical judgment. But again there is considerable discord regarding the significance of the work. Martin Esslin stands at one extreme by lumping *Rhinoceros* together with Ionesco's early works as absurd theater, since he finds the absurdity of Bérenger's defiance, predicated as it is upon the same instinctive feelings that he condemns in the metamorphosed rhinoceroses, is as great as the absurdity of the conformity of the bourgeoisie, and he makes a very lucid comparison of the absurdity of Bérenger's situation with that of Gregor Samsa in Kafka's *Metamorphosis*.[56] But in trying to make a case for his rubric, "Theater of the Absurd," Esslin reduces the term to a catch-all, for *Rhinoceros* bears only superficial resemblance to the earlier works which prompted the coining of the term, and it has much wider implications than, for instance, *The Bald Soprano*, which is clearly absurdist in both content and form.

George Wellwarth represents the opposite view in his assertion that *Rhinoceros*, unlike *The Killer*, has no moral, but is simply a horror story which parallels the rise of Nazi hooliganism. He does see

54 Jacques Lemarchand, "*Rhinocéros* d'Ionesco à l'Odéon," *Le Figaro Littéraire* (27 January 1960), p. 14.

55 Bertrand Poirot-Delpech, "*Rhinocéros* d'Eugène Ionesco au Théatre de France," *Le Monde* (24 January 1960).

56 Martin Esslin, *The Theatre of the Absurd* (Garden City, N. Y.: Doubleday Anchor Books, 1961), pp. 126–127.

a ray of hope in Bérenger's symbolic act of rebellion, which he interprets as an act of faith in human independence which undermines the tyranny that reigns at the end.[57] But in understanding this act as one of selfless heroism, Wellwarth fails to see that Bérenger is, as his preoccupation with his own affairs at the end of Act One makes clear, simply a bourgeois in whom the submersion of humanity is imperfect, for had his "symbolic act of rebellion" occurred before it could be no more than symbolic, the catastrophe might have been averted. Bérenger in fact passively shares the guilt of the Dudards, the Botards, and the Jeans, in spite of his unalterable humanity.

Leonard Pronko comes considerably closer to a clear perception and statement of the literary stature of the play in his defense of *Rhinoceros* against the *New York Times*'s allegation that it had a "purely political theme."[58]

> There are political implications in the play, but there is nothing *purely* political about it. It so happens that the political implications strike us more forcefully today, whereas in another era the savage and thoughtless animals might stand for something else. Indeed, preceding plays for Ionesco suggest that this preponderance of unthinking, if not dead, matter is but another materialization of that oppressive universe which is constantly crushing in upon us and preventing us from realizing the spiritual possibilities which lie inherent in human nature.
>
> The terror implicit in the situations is alleviated, as is usually the case in Ionesco's theater, by the grotesque symbol that has been chosen. The idea of a man becoming a rhinoceros is, of course, fantastic. Yet within the framework of the play the characters accept it so naturally that they become laughable. It is only when we realize how naturally we accept the monsters we encounter in our own lives that the laughter freezes on our lips.[59]

[57] George Wellwarth, *The Theater of Protest and Paradox* (New York: New York University Press, 1964), pp. 66–67.

[58] Unsigned news story, "Ionesco's *Rhinoceros*," *New York Times* (3 November 1959), p. 36.

[59] Leonard Pronko, *Avant-Garde: The Experimental Theater in France* (Berkeley and Los Angeles: University of California Press, 1962), pp. 106–107.

Pronko displays equal sympathy toward Ionesco in his grasp of the play's portent as a lamentation over the absence of independence and individuality within contemporary society which inevitably produces totalitarianism of one sort or another.

The most penetrating and knowledgeable analysis of the play's import is made by a critic who does not seek to exemplify any personal literary theory by reference to *Rhinoceros*, Richard Coe, in his remarkably perceptive and incisive book on Ionesco:

> The fell disease of rhinoceritis is the condemnation, not of *any* ideology to which man may feel the need to conform, but specifically of the *Nazi* ideology. Not that the allusion is in any way historical; Fascism is far from belonging exclusively to the past, and indeed, the urgency of the play, the menacing tempo of its dramatic rhythm, makes it very much a warning to be heeded here and now. The average audience is all too eager to find any excuse not to apply a dramatic moral to itself, and it was probably in an attempt to avoid the pitfall of "history" that Ionesco deliberately omitted all references which might associate the drama with a specific place and epoch. Having avoided the particular, however, he found himself caught out on the general; for all too many of the critics, their safe refuge in history being denied to them, have retaliated by turning the play into an *abstraction*—a "universal parable" on the subject of "conformism." Universal it may be; but when "universality" is used as an excuse for making oneself deaf to a call to action, then it is time to restate the particular.[60]

In brief, then, *Rhinoceros* is a highly problematic play which, like Brecht's *The Measures Taken*, certainly had as its stimulus a single politically didactic concept. As Coe has pointed out, Ionesco, unlike Brecht, attempted to generalize the dramatic moral by avoiding the "pitfall of history," that is, by using a non-human symbol not readily identifiable with any particular creed or political movement. Unfortunately, productions of the work have generally either negated

[60] Richard Coe, *Eugene Ionesco* (Edinburgh: Evergreen Pilot Books, 1961), pp. 90–91.

the effect of Ionesco's attempt at generalization by identifying the symbol too obviously, or they have disregarded its portent entirely and played it strictly for laughs. But what is important for this investigation is not so much the failure of productions to carry out the author's intention, but rather the nature of that intention *per se*, for, as Coe again points out, "*Rhinoceros* is as explicit and committed a statement as one could wish: a warning of the most peremptory order against the ever-present menace of the Fascist appeal to the instinct."[61]

It seems ironic that, in their most clearly committed works, Brecht and Ionesco stand not only at extremes of dramatic technique, but also at technical extremes with respect to their own earlier and subsequent works. Brecht's *The Measures Taken* stands at the epic extreme of theater, the playwright having spared no effort to destroy what he considered an outworn, outmoded convention of theater. But in *The Measures Taken* Brecht himself stands at the epic extreme of his career; his subsequent works may be regarded as a retreat from the austerity of epic form that was to culminate in *The Days of the Commune*, which is, as one English reviewer has put it, a perfectly conventional though Marxist melodrama. Ionesco's *Rhinoceros*, on the other hand, represents an extreme of dramatic technique, the conventional, realistic, and illusionistic theater, yet it also represents an extreme in his career, for Ionesco has sought, in his later works, to develop a new mode of what might be called mythological or metaphysical theater.

It is even more ironic that, in their most engaged works, two writers as far apart philosophically as Brecht and Ionesco appear to share a common view of political engagement; stated baldly, the dominant theme of both works may be summed up in two words, totalitarianism dehumanizes. It is certain that the four agitators and the *Kontrollchor* of *The Measures Taken* are every bit as blind, thoughtless, and inhuman as Jean, the logician, Botard, and eventually the pachyderms of *Rhinoceros,* who will obliterate the human-

---

[61] *Ibid.*, p. 96.

ity represented by Bérenger standing in their path just as surely as the agitators liquidated the young comrade. However, there are both distinctions and similarities of a philosophical nature existing between the two works which need further clarification. To deal first with one of the salient distinctions, although both works make a statement with regard to the relationship between the individual and society (the Communist Party in *The Measures Taken* and the bourgeoisie in *Rhinoceros*), it must be observed that the two playwrights hold diametrically opposed viewpoints. While both are critical of the condition of society (indeed, for both the point of departure is contempt for and distrust of the bourgeoisie), Brecht looks at the individual as an element of the societal mechanism, while Ionesco regards the individual only as an individual. Nowhere is Brecht's viewpoint more in evidence than in his own play concerning the rise of the Nazi movement, *The Resistible Rise of Arturo Ui*. In this piece, a parable play that equates Hitler's rise to power with that of a Chicago gang czar, Brecht analyzes the social, economic, and political factors contributing to the accession to power of Hitler/Ui, and he works from a similar viewpoint not only in *The Measures Taken*, but also in all of his other plays since his conversion to Marxism. He sees man as socially conditioned in his behavior, and the social structure is the focal point of his view as a playwright. In *The Measures Taken* the societal mechanism takes three forms: that of the party, as represented by the *Kontrollchor* and the agitators, that of the bourgeois, and that of the proletariat, here represented by the exploited coolies. The young comrade is an outsider who does not fit into any of these categories, and it is clear that Brecht has little sympathy with him. Indeed, the young comrade embodies just the sort of weakness which Brecht had attacked as early as *Drums in the Night* with placards reading "Don't gape so romantically!" Of course, as Robert Brustein has suggested, there is always a vein of the romantic in Brecht which, despite his most persistent efforts, he has never been able to exorcise or subdue completely, and this romantic element is a complicating factor in *The Measures*

Taken, as in the rest of his works. On the whole, however, his concern is basically for the role played by the individual within the societal mechanism, and his view of humanity is principally social.

Of all the aspects of Brecht's works, it is this socially mechanistic orientation which upsets Ionesco the most, and he has expressed himself quite unequivocally concerning his own view of humanity:

> It is evident that the theater cannot remove itself from the social universe. But for Brecht there is only one social problem: that of class conflict. In reality, that is only one aspect of society. Even my relationships with my neighbor are societal relationships. The relationships between a married couple or two lovers are societal, as well. Since man is not alone, everything is necessarily social. One can speak of marital sociology, of neighborly sociology, of industrial sociology, alas, of the sociology of concentration camps or religious communities, of scholastic or military sociology, or of the sociology of labor, all of which means that social problems and conflicts are not exclusively problems of class. To reduce the social dimension to that is to diminish both society and humanity.[62]

This statement represents a lack of understanding of some of Brecht's later works, particularly of *The Life of Galileo*, as will be shown in the next chapter, but it does emphasize Ionesco's rejection of society as the basic consideration of mankind. Thus, while his first three plays may be taken exclusively as social criticism of the bourgeois, every work from *Victims of Duty* on has been written from the viewpoint of the individual, and *Rhinoceros* is no exception. In his later works Ionesco does not ask how society works to determine individual behavior; he poses what is essentially a far more basic question: what is it in the makeup of the individual human that (in *Rhinoceros*) permits one man to accept totalitarian rule but forces his neighbor to resist such rule with all the strength of his being? That he generally finds no clear-cut answer is indicative of the stress that he puts on the essential mystery of the individual human spirit.

[62] Ionesco, *Notes et contre-notes*, p. 114.

A closer look at the individuals portrayed in the two dramas at hand reveals a striking similarity, for both the young comrade and Bérenger are passive, victimized anti-heroes. Each falls victim to his own weaknesses, and these weaknesses are also similar: Both are the products of a bourgeois background, yet both are ultimately brought to their fates by their unalterable humanity. The young comrade, as party critics recognized and Brecht later agreed, exemplifies the attitude of the bourgeois intellectual who recognizes the necessity for class struggle and who tends to identify with the proletariat in that struggle, but who had not exorcised his bourgeois sense of individuality enough to work within the discipline of the party. Bérenger, on the other hand, is completely unaware of class struggle; he is so constrained by bourgeois habits of lethargy, complacency, and self-concern that he is unable to act when the occasion demands action. The young comrade makes his own death necessary in the eyes of his party because he cannot control his human compassion for the suffering coolies, and Bérenger renders his own salvation impossible because he is too human even to assume the guise of a dehumanized party member to protect himself from the rest of the herd.

But here the similarity ends, for while both Brecht and Ionesco condemn the bourgeois elements manifest in their respective heroes, they are at odds regarding the problem of the humanity of the individual. As we have seen, the young comrade is the last of Brecht's heroes to be entirely without *List*, the quality of cunning, and it is the combination of his humanity and his artlessness that impairs his effectiveness as a party member and ultimately brings about his death. Bérenger, however, is an archetypal Ionesco hero, for all the central figures of his works are essentially weak, helpless, and artless; they cannot defend themselves, either against the machinations of bourgeois society (in *Rhinoceros, Victims of Duty, The Lesson, Jacques, The New Tenant,* and *The Killer*), or against the demands of their spouses (in *Amédée* and *Exit the King*), or least of all against their own natures (in all his works, but most urgently in

The Aerial Pedestrian and *Hunger and Thirst*). Philippe Sénart, in describing Bérenger's weakness and passivity, has actually provided a generalized description of all the heroes of Ionesco, who are simply not made for this world:

> He doesn't know how to sustain himself. He was not made for this world. Neither shaved nor combed, he wears a rumpled suit, he yawns, he slumps his entire frame on an iron chair in a sidewalk café. He doesn't give the impression of a thinker, but of a rake. He who is saluted in the press reviews as the champion of humanism, the defender of irreplaceable values, opposing and resisting fascism, doesn't he seem to be out of a work by Courteline? Once more he hasn't gone to the office all day. But if he drinks, it's still for philosophical reasons: disgust, discouragement, lassitude. He can do no more. He is "tired of living." He doesn't "apply himself to life." He is "unadaptable." He supposes it is "abnormal to live." Hence, coming from a work by Courteline, he can be enlisted by Sartre, seen by August Comte. Doesn't he proclaim, in his own way, that society consists of more dead people than living? Yet he is still not prepared for great battles. One event is the talk of the town where he lives: a cat has been trampled by a rhinoceros. The moment has not yet come when M. Ionesco would tell us that we are all cats. Even Bérenger shrugs his shoulders. "Don't get involved. It doesn't affect us." The death of a kitten can't trouble the universal conscience. Even less the siesta of Bérenger.[63]

In short, Brecht asserts that the individual is helpless unless he is cunning enough to defend himself in the conflict between the demands of society and the demands of his own spirit; but Ionesco asserts that he is helpless, period.

In essence, then, the two dramas discussed here are both direct outgrowths of the didactic or polemic intentions of their authors. Brecht's *The Measures Taken* was a dismal failure as a didactic work, for it was considered subversive by those whom it was intended to serve and hailed as a profound indictment of Communist

---

[63] Philippe Sénart, *Ionesco* (Paris: Éditions Universitaires, 1964), p. 39.

inhumanity by those whose institutions it was intended to subvert. But in its failure as a *Lehrstück* it achieved its slight measure of artistic success, for it thereby transcended its purely topical statement and acquired considerably broader implications—this despite its application of Brecht's most extreme theories concerning the renovation of the drama. On the other hand, Ionesco's *Rhinoceros* is generally counted as less than an artistic success, largely because it was so narrowly interpreted in production that it became too clearly didactic—this despite its adherence to generally accepted conventions of theater. In short, neither lived up to its author's hopes, and the disillusionments thus experienced doubtless played a large role in conditioning the change in viewpoints regarding form and content which both Brecht and Ionesco were to undergo and which in turn conditioned their later more confessional works.

CHAPTER FIVE / *Concerns beyond Engagement: Confessional Drama*

The old days are past, and it is a new age. Soon mankind will
know about its home, the heavenly body on which it lives.
What is in the old books can't suffice any longer.

BRECHT[1]

MARIE: Another wisdom will replace the former one, greater folly,
greater ignorance, quite different, quite the same. Let that console
you, let that cheer you up.

THE KING: I'm afraid. I'm dying.

IONESCO[2]

IT IS PROBABLY FORTUNATE that the polemic dramas of Brecht and
Ionesco met with so little success, for both playwrights turned away
from didactic theater to seek a more generally acceptable and more
genuinely theatrical dramatic idiom. This is not to suggest that

---

[1] Bertolt Brecht, *Stücke 8* (Frankfurt am Main: Suhrkamp Verlag, 1962), pp.
10–11.

[2] Eugène Ionesco, *Théâtre IV* (Paris: Gallimard, 1966), pp. 55–56.

either relented in his political (or, for Ionesco, apolitical) views, for the contrary is true, since their works continue to be demonstrably conditioned by their politics. But exclusively political considerations no longer provided the chief creative stimulus, for each turned for his subjects and themes to more fundamental concerns, concerns which indeed preceded his overt commitment and which are more universally germane to the problems of human existence in the twentieth century, and these concerns are again both similar and disparate. Not only the philosophical aspects of their works are affected by the relaxation of didactic emphasis; as might be expected, there are further developments in dramatic technique which are commensurate with the expanded philosophical view. In the works which will serve as a point of departure for this chapter, Brecht's *The Life of Galileo* and Ionesco's *Exit the King*, Brecht had long since abandoned the more *outré* elements of his epic theater and reverted to a relatively conventional dramatic structure, while Ionesco had turned away from the fairly traditional mode of theater he had adopted for *Rhinoceros* and undergone at least a partial reversion to a form of drama approaching his early works of anti-theater. In short, in turning to his more fundamental concerns, each became free from the restrictive influences inherent in his own form of didacticism. The political inclination of each is still in evidence, but it no longer dominates the creative imagination to such an extent as it had in the didactic pieces.

Walter Weideli has termed Brecht's *The Life of Galileo* his most epic work,[3] but this designation cannot be applied in the restrictive sense in which Brecht used the term in the late twenties. Indeed, *The Life of Galileo* is epic only in that it is novelistic in construction, for it spans twenty-eight years, encompassing the entire development of the mature Galileo, rather than concentrating on a single dramatic high point. But this is certainly not a distinguishing feature of the work, for in this respect it had ample precedent, as witness Goethe's *Faust*, Schiller's *Wallenstein* trilogy, and Shaw's *Saint Joan*,

---

[3] Walter Weideli, *Bertolt Brecht* (Paris: Éditions Universitaires, 1961), p. 134.

to name but a few similarly epic works. What does distinguish *The Life of Galileo* from Brecht's earlier, more "epic" (in his sense of the word) works is its lack of the sort of stage trickery or obtrusive *Verfremdung* so characteristic of *Mother Courage* and *The Caucasian Chalk Circle* or earlier works such as *Three Penny Opera* or *The Measures Taken*. Gone is any attempt in the structure of the play to objectify or "estrange" the characters, for all major figures of the play remain essentially in character throughout the course of the action. Yet this is not to suggest that Brecht here at last abjured the sort of *Verfremdung* he had practiced in other works, for Galileo's approach to life is fundamentally "estranging": he stands the accepted facts of the universe on their heads to expose them as empty shibboleths. What distinguishes this work from *Mother Courage*, for example, is that its *Verfremdung* functions organically; it is systematically worked out in the figure of Galileo as an essential aspect of his character, not grafted onto the work as something strikingly external or dissonant. Helene Weigel had to step out of her role as Anna Fierling in *Mother Courage* to sing a song about the course of the war and its effect on her family; such songs interrupt the sense of dramatic continuity, keeping the spectator off balance, remote, and critical. In *The Life of Galileo*, the *Verfremdung* is still present, but because it is not so obvious to the spectator as it is in *Mother Courage*, its ultimate effect is even more dialectical, since both the sensual and the intellectual aspects of humanity are here fused in a single character seen from a single consistent viewpoint. In this work there is only one element which seems to attempt to produce what Walter Benjamin termed the *entspanntes Publikum*, for virtually the only remnants of Brecht's early style are the captions projected upon the curtain to reveal the content, the *Grundgestus*, of the scene to come. But taken in context with the rest of the drama, these captions and the brief choruses which accompany them seem little more than a characteristic Brechtian gesture, a signature, so to speak, which does not attenuate the tensions created by the scenes themselves. It is true that Brecht praised both Charles

Laughton and Ernst Busch for not allowing themselves to become entirely absorbed in the role, for maintaining the attitude of "showing" how Galileo behaved rather than "becoming" Galileo,[4] but the same may be said, for instance, of Laughton's reading of *King Lear* at Stratford-on-Avon in 1959, which interpretation actually produced heightened tensions.

But the decisive respect in which Brecht has drifted away from his earlier practices lies in the nature of the tensions that are created in *The Life of Galileo.* Whereas in his earlier works, both dramatic and theoretical, he had sought to discourage tension regarding the outcome (*Spannung auf den Ausgang*) in favor of a more epic interest in the progress (*Interesse für den Fortgang*) of the work, this piece is consciously pointed toward a specific outcome, as Rolf Geißler takes pains to point out:

> *Galileo,* like no other work of Brecht, poses a problem that is inextricably bound up in the life and development of its central figure. Hence *Galileo* evokes the impression of a drama constructed on Aristotelian principles. Contrary to Brecht's opinion, this drama may thus easily be approached by the traditional means of dramatic interpretation without missing Brecht's intention entirely. It is characteristic of this mode of construction that the decisive role is played by the conclusion. Thus even the problem posed by science, as portrayed in *Galileo,* becomes meaningful and accessible to interpretation only from the viewpoint of the conclusion, the last scene in which Galileo appears.[5]

But while Geißler is certainly correct in his assertion that it is the conclusion that played the decisive role in Brecht's formative thinking concerning *The Life of Galileo,* it is the drama as a whole that works upon the spectator, and such is the power of the character that

---

[4] Bertolt Brecht, *Aufbau einer Rolle: Laughtons Galilei* (Berlin: Henschel Verlag, 1962), p. 11.

[5] Rolf Geißler, *Zur Interpretation des modernen Dramas: Brecht, Dürrenmatt, Frisch* (Frankfurt am Main: Verlag Moritz Diesterweg, 1962), p. 49.

Brecht created that his intention regarding the conclusion is almost inevitably defeated when the work is played. For this is, more than any other of Brecht's works, the drama of a single character, and there is certainly more of Brecht in the figure of Galileo than there is in any other role he created. Indeed, so many are the parallels between the life of Galileo and that of Brecht, including some anticipatory parallels which may reveal a great deal about Brecht's return to East Berlin, that the work may best be understood as confessional. As such, it is one of his most complex works, and its complexity is compounded by the existence of three different versions of the final scene, the latter two of which represent a major shift in his own viewpoint regarding the use of *List*. (For the purposes of this study, Scene 14 of the Suhrkamp edition will be considered the final scene, since Scene 15 is generally omitted in production of the work.[6]) But the complexities posed by this final scene can only be appreciated when they are seen in the perspective of the work as a whole.

The first scene sets the tone for the general complexity of the work, for it has a number of closely related expository functions concerning the nature of the hero, a highly ambivalent yet profoundly human figure. Brecht's own notes concerning the production he staged in collaboration with Charles Laughton in Beverly Hills in 1947 are quite revealing in regard to this exposition, for he wanted to demystify the learned man and breathe genuine life into the role: "Laughton's work began with discarding from the role all the pale, intellectualized textbook clichés regarding stargazers. Above all it was necessary to turn the scholar into a man. Just the word 'scholar' connotes ridicule when used by common folk; it smacks somewhat of 'overtraining,' of passivity. The scholar was an impotent, bloodless, eccentric figure, conceited and ill-suited to life. In his approach to Galileo, Laughton kept in mind the engineer

---

[6] Cf. Käthe Rülicke, "*Leben des Galilei:* Bemerkungen zur Schlußszene" in Peter Huchel, ed., *Sinn und Form: Zweites Sonderheft Bertolt Brecht* (Berlin: Rütten and Loening, 1957), p. 269.

of the Great Arsenal of Venice. He had eyes for seeing, not for glowing; hands for working, not for gesticulating."[7] To portray the man under the scientist's robes, Brecht appropriately enough divested him of those robes, for the first scene, set in Padua in 1609, opens with the morning toilette of the 45-year-old Galileo. It was Brecht's desire that the actor bring to this mundane act a sense of *Beginnerfreude*, the joy of starting anew,[8] and this sense is easily conveyed in production, for Galileo's robust and earthy vigor in scrubbing his body portrays his sensual pleasure in that body. When he is interrupted by his young assistant, Andrea, who brings him a breakfast of milk and bread, he turns with equal gusto to devouring his breakfast and instructing his favorite pupil. Both actions are seen simply as emanations of the life force within him, for he cannot live without eating, and he cannot live without teaching what he knows to be the truth. In this instance, the truth at issue happens to be astronomy, for Galileo has examined the hypotheses of Copernicus and has determined that the Ptolemaic system of astronomy, which held that the earth was the center of the universe, must be debunked. As Andrea investigates and describes a model of the Ptolemaic universe, Galileo embarks upon a long and ruminative monologue in which he reveals his boundless enthusiasm for the future. No longer is man to sit on a ball at the center of the universe, shut in by the crystal spheres of the Ptolemaic system, living in unquestioning servitude to an absolute authority residing at the very midpoint of creation, for it is the dawn of a new age. He has already seen this new age manifested in the actions of simple workmen, who after a discussion of a few minutes abandoned an age-old system for moving granite blocks to adopt a new and better one. He senses that he is participating not simply in the birth of the new sciences of physics and astronomy, but rather in a rebirth of the human intellect, for the spirit of this new age will call all old values and absolutes into question, and man, borne by a new courage and con-

[7] Brecht, *Aufbau einer Rolle*, p. 15.
[8] *Ibid.*, p. 14.

fidence in his own intellect and perception, will be freed to find a new way in a new world. Yet, lest this all sound like head-in-the-clouds intellectual idealism, Brecht shows in the next line of development that we are still dealing with a pragmatic, earthy man whose feet are solidly planted on the ground and who believes only what his senses tell him, for he demonstrates the Copernican theories to Andrea in such concrete, non-technical terms that even the boy can perceive their patent logic.

The two are interrupted in this informal lesson by the intrusion of one Ludovico Marsili, a wealthy young dilettante whose patrician family have decided to have him tutored in science by the renowned Galileo. Thereby another aspect of Galileo's character is revealed, for, while he obviously lives to teach, he resents being dependent for his existence, in which he takes all too much pleasure, on the whims of such dabblers, and he resents even more the time he must steal from his own studies and research to earn his keep. As luck would have it, though, he does learn from this particular dabbler of the recent invention in Holland of the telescope. His curiosity aroused, he agrees to take on the new pupil, dismisses him, and sends Andrea out to buy a pair of lenses of the sort Ludovico has described. At this juncture the curator of the university arrives to announce that he has rejected Galileo's request that his salary be doubled to a thousand scudi a year. In reply to Galileo's rancor over the niggardly means on which he must subsist and the time he must sacrifice by taking on students to expand these means, the curator points out the one advantage of teaching at Padua: Venice is the only republic in Italy where the Holy Inquisition has no say, where academic freedom reigns. In another city, Florence, for example, a scientist might be paid more and have more free time for his own research, but such research would be pointless, for any ignorant monk of the Inquisition could simply forbid publication of the truths arrived at. Shrugging off Galileo's pointed remarks concerning the chief exception to this rule, the case of Giordano Bruno, who had been delivered into the hands of the Inquisition and burnt at the stake for teaching the Copernican theories, the curator reminds Galileo that scudi are worth what scudi will buy, for instance, the proportional compass which he had invented and which had enriched the coffers of Venice. Galileo dismisses this instrument as a toy, but suddenly he remembers the telescope described to him by Ludovico, becomes thoughtful, and remarks casually that he may have something of that nature in development. Urging Galileo to carry on with such profitable work, the curator leaves, and at this moment Andrea returns with the lenses ordered. Made wary by the curator's remarks concerning Bruno, Galileo cautions the boy not to discuss his teachings in public, as they are only unproven hypotheses, and then he proceeds, with only mild interest, to fabricate a crude telescope, which does indeed magnify distant objects. The scene ends with Galileo's confident assertion that this toy will bring him five hundred scudi.

The second scene is set in the Great Arsenal of Venice, as Galileo is presenting his "new invention" to the republic. After his highly servile and self-effacing speech, he turns to his colleague Sagredo to reveal that he has turned the new instrument upon the moon and made some startling observations. The brief exchange of dialogue that ensues bears striking resemblance to the technique of absurd contrapuntal development so characteristic of Ionesco's works, for at one side of the stage Galileo and his friends are earnestly discussing the research made possible by the telescope, while at the other side the gentlemen of the court are uttering expressions of banal delight over the trivia magnified by the instrument:

GALILEO (*softly*): I can't promise that I can endure this carnival. These people think they're getting a profitable toy, but it's much more. Last night I had a look at the moon with it.

SAGREDO: What did you see?

GALILEO: It doesn't generate its own light.

SAGREDO: What?

COUNCILMAN: I can see the fortifications of Santa Rosita, Signor Galileo. On the boat over there they're eating lunch. Baked fish. I'm hungry.

GALILEO: I tell you, astronomy has been stuck for a thousand years be-
cause we didn't have a telescope.
COUNCILMAN: Signor Galileo!
SAGREDO: They're talking to you.
COUNCILMAN: With this thing you can see too well. I'll have to tell my
women not to bathe on the roof any more.
GALILEO: Do you know what the Milky Way is made of?
SAGREDO: No.
GALILEO: I do.
COUNCILMAN: For a thing like this a fellow can ask ten scudi, Signor
Galileo.[9]

This passage serves as a foreshadowing of the later reaction of
others to Galileo's scientific discoveries, but he pays no attention
to such mundane remarks, so absorbed is he in thought concerning
the scientific significance of the instrument. When Ludovico somewhat sarcastically congratulates him on his "invention," he replies
unabashedly that he has improved it, and he is so distracted at the
prospects of the use of the telescope that he registers no pleasure
when the curator and the Doge inform him that his extra five hundred scudi are secure.

This scene serves to demonstrate Galileo's innate capacity for
List and his feeling that the end justifies the means, for he has no
scruples concerning his use of the discoveries of others and is quite
willing to practice deceit and cunning to gain his own ends, to exploit the selfish interests of others in order to serve his own interests.
In this respect there is certainly a striking parallel between Brecht
and the figure of Galileo he has drawn, for Brecht's lack of respect
for the literary property of others has been all too well publicized.
The charge brought against him by the critic Alfred Kerr of plagiarism of the K. L. Ammer translation of François Villon's ballads
for use in *Three Penny Opera* created a minor scandal, but Brecht
characteristically dismissed the whole incident as trivial, since he
had used the lines for quite another literary purpose and had sim-

[9] Brecht, *Stücke 8*, pp. 33–34.

ply neglected to acknowledge the use of the translation.[10] Especially since there is no historical evidence that Galileo pirated a Dutch discovery and took credit for it to fatten his own purse (indeed, in his journal he explicitly describes how he came by the information, gives due credit to the Dutch inventor, and describes his painstaking work to improve the instrument),[11] it is apparent that such an interpretation by Brecht is autobiographical. Yet it serves in no way to discredit Galileo as a man, for those whom he has bilked are portrayed, particularly in the following scene, as such crass and banal bourgeois creatures that one tends to admire Galileo for outsmarting them and using their own means, in spite of their own blindness to the real significance of the telescope, for the benefit of science. A further parallel exists in the fact that Brecht was relatively safe and free in his exile, as was Galileo in Padua, but he still felt attracted to Germany, dangerous as it was before, during, and after the war, for only there could he find the means (in his case, linguistic means) to continue his experiments in drama. The parallel becomes even more striking through analysis of the next scenes; in the meanwhile, Brecht sat out the war in Santa Monica, grubbing out an existence by serving as a technical adviser or collaborating on an occasional film script, such as *Hangmen Also Die*, the while creating the plays which were to win him popular and critical acclaim after the war, yet which had no immediate prospects for production so long as he remained in exile.

Scene Three is set in Galileo's study in Padua on January 10, 1610. At curtain, Sagredo is seated at the telescope, describing the phenomena he observes on the moon, which phenomena can only be interpreted as evidence that there are mountains and valleys on the lunar surface. When Galileo asks him how he would interpret what he sees, Sagredo expresses his incredulity, for what he has seen

---

[10] Cf. Martin Esslin, *Brecht: The Man and His Work* (Garden City, N.Y.: Doubleday Anchor Books, 1960), p. 38.

[11] George Schwartz and Philip W. Bishop, *Moments of Discovery: The Origins of Science*, 2 vols. (New York: Basic Books, 1958), 1: 244.

contradicts two thousand years of astronomical theory. When it is further pointed out to him that the dark areas of the moon are faintly illuminated by light reflected from the earth, that the earth is in fact the same sort of a heavenly body as the moon, his incredulity turns to fear, and he warns Galileo that ten years earlier Bruno had been burnt at the stake for a similar assertion. Galileo's retort emphasizes his faith in man's powers of observation and reason:

SAGREDO: Not ten years ago a man was burnt at the stake in Rome. His name was Giordano Bruno, and he had said the same thing.
GALILEO: Of course. And we are *seeing* it, Sagredo. What you *see* is that there is no difference between heaven and earth. Today is January 10, 1610. Let mankind enter in its journal: heaven dispensed with.[12]

At this point the two are interrupted by the precipitate arrival of the curator, who has just learned the truth about Galileo's supposed invention: it is a worthless copy of a device already manufactured in Holland and even now being unloaded in the harbor of Venice from a Dutch ship in gross lots. Shocked at the appellation "worthless," Sagredo urges the curator to have a look through the telescope, so he can appreciate the research made possible. But the curator's response again foreshadows a later development: having lost faith in Galileo's integrity, he refuses to indulge his own curiosity, and he has even lost interest in the practical application of the discoveries Galileo has made for the science of navigation. At his affronted departure, Galileo invites the now apprehensive Sagredo to share some of the other discoveries he has made. In the process of checking the positions of the satellites of Jupiter, they make a startling discovery: these smaller bodies rotate around the planet, and the belief that lay at the foundation of the Ptolemaic system, that the stars are fixed to crystal spheres rotating around the earth, is irretrievably destroyed. Sagredo, aghast at the portent of this discovery, asks Galileo if he knows what it means to humanity to say that the

12 Brecht, *Stücke 8*, p. 39.

earth is merely a single astral body among millions, and not the center of the universe. Galileo's response again emphasizes his—and Brecht's—unshakeable faith in the power of human reason:

GALILEO: Yes, and that the immense universe with all its stars doesn't revolve around our tiny earth, as any fool might think.

SAGREDO: That there are only stars out there!—Then where is God?

GALILEO: What do you mean?

SAGREDO: God! Where is God?

GALILEO: Not there! Just as he couldn't be found here if there were beings out there looking for him here.

SAGREDO: But where *is* God?

GALILEO: Am I a theologian? I am a mathematician.

SAGREDO: First of all you are a man. And I ask you, where is God in your system?

GALILEO: In us or nowhere!

SAGREDO: (*shouting*) Just as Bruno said!

GALILEO: Yes, just as Bruno said.

SAGREDO: But that's why he was burned! Not ten years ago!

GALILEO: Because he could prove nothing! Because he only *said* it![13]

Sagredo, who has much deeper insight into the nature of men, remonstrates with Galileo to abjure his absurd belief in the human faculty of reason, but Galileo persists and even announces his decision to apply for a position in the court of the Medici in Florence. To this end he has named some newly discovered stars after the Grand Duke Cosmo, a boy of nine, and has composed a letter of application. To Sagredo's criticism that the letter is too servile, he retorts that a man who wants to rewrite the truth has to crawl on his belly to be accepted, and besides, he despises those whose brains are incapable of filling their bellies, again emphasizing the twofold nature of his being. He simply will not relent in his faith in man's belief in what he sees; if worst comes to worst, he will simply take disbelievers by the scruff of their necks, thrust their heads to

[13] *Ibid.*, pp. 46–47.

his telescope, and defy them to deny what their eyes tell them. He withstands all of Sagredo's warnings and remonstrations concerning the natural enmities of popes and princes toward discoveries which may upset the order they have imposed on the world; Galileo is unshakeable in his intention to abandon the security of Padua for the leisure and affluence of Florence.

At the beginning of the fourth scene Galileo has indeed moved to Florence. All versions of the scene in print open with a brief interlude in which the childishness of the young Grand Duke is emphasized by a confrontation with Andrea which ends in puerile fisticuffs, but this sequence was cut during the *Probenarbeit* in 1955 as nonessential, and even distracting, and it is seldom performed.[14] The real action of the scene begins when Galileo confronts the scholars of the court with his discoveries and invites them and the young Grand Duke to observe the satellites of Jupiter through his telescope. But these scholars are by no means disposed to do so; rather, they have come to debate, preferably in Latin, whether such satellites *need* to exist, whether the Aristotelian system, with the beauty, harmony, and symmetry of its crystal spheres, ought to be questioned. Galileo, flabbergasted at such fatuous reasoning by men of science, simply repeats his invitation that they take a look through his telescope and decide for themselves whether the "unnecessary" satellites exist or not. Again the court scholars demur, this time casting doubt on the reliability of the instrument and thereby sending Galileo into a fit of anger which he barely succeeds in controlling. But his anger is as pointless as are his arguments and entreaties that scientists must learn to believe their senses if they are to discover the truth. Finally enraged, Galileo threatens to go among the common people, the workers, with his discoveries, but even this threat goes for naught, as the Grand Duke's entourage departs for a court ball, leaving Galileo groveling in their wake, still begging somebody, anybody to observe the phenomena through his telescope. The scene ends as the chamberlain returns momen-

[14] Brecht, *Aufbau einer Rolle*, p. 27.

tarily to announce ominously that Galileo's claims are to be investigated by Christopher Clavius, astronomer to the Papal College in Rome.

Scene Five was originally two scenes, but in 1947 it was condensed into two brief subscenes, and during the *Probenarbeit* of 1955 it was finally dropped as contributing nothing to the development of the piece.[15] Its one contribution is indeed slight, but it is revealing, particularly with respect to Brecht's intention in cutting it. It depicts Galileo's actions during the Florentine plague of 1612: Unperturbed at the prospect of death by disease, he remains in the city in order to gather further proofs to present to the Papal College. While this detail of his life is borne out by biographical data,[16] it is plain that in Brecht's eyes it bordered too closely on physical heroism to be consonant with the character he sought to portray, especially as his concept of Galileo's sociological role in history began to change, as will be discussed later in consideration of the three versions of the final scene.

The action picks up again in Scene Six, which is set in an antechamber of the Collegium Romanum, the Vatican's research institute, which is investigating Galileo's discoveries. Galileo is seated patiently at one side awaiting the decision, while a group of monks and prelates entertain themselves at his expense, play-acting as if the world were actually spinning and they are at pains to keep from falling off. Their raillery is cut short by the emergence of two astronomers of the Collegium, who are outraged that the great Clavius bothers to investigate the heretical nonsense of this upstart. At their exit, a thin monk expresses his fear of the new theories, which shake the foundation on which his faith rests. And an even more violent exception is expressed by a very old Cardinal who enters and demands to see the creature who would propagate such vile teachings. Confronting Galileo, he upbraids him unmercifully, but thereby also reveals the egocentric basis of the faith he professes to hold:

[15] Rülicke, "Bemerkungen," p. 317.
[16] Schwartz and Bishop, *Moments of Discovery*, 1: 246.

You want to demean the earth, though you live on it and get everything from it. You foul your own nest! But I, for one, won't put up with that. I am not just some being on some tiny star circling somewhere for a little while. I walk securely on solid earth, the midpoint of the universe; I am at the midpoint and the eye of my creator rests on me, on me alone. Around me, fixed on eight crystal spheres, turn the planets and the mighty sun, created to illuminate my surroundings. And me, so God can see me. Thus obviously and indisputably everything turns about me, man, the result of God's exertion, the creature at the focus, the image of God, eternal and . . . (he collapses).[17]

This tirade is intended to demonstrate the error of the thin monk's reasonably expressed doubts by magnifying them to a point of absurdity, which is emphasized by the entrance of Clavius, who strides dramatically across the set, pauses before his exit, and quietly utters three words which are to shake the earth: "He is right." At this point all exit in consternation, except for a young monk, a member of the papal commission, who is later to become a disciple of Galileo. He turns to the vindicated scientist and acknowledges that he has won out, but Galileo insists that it is reason that has triumphed. Yet even this triumph is short-lived, for its hollowness is foreshadowed by the ominous appearance of the Cardinal Inquisitor, who enters to inspect the instrument of heresy, the telescope, at curtain.

Scene Seven can only be understood as the dialectic consequence of the foregoing, for in it the victory of reason is undone. As Galileo, his daughter Virginia, and Ludovico arrive at a ball at Cardinal Bellarmine's house in Rome, it becomes evident that the two young people are in love, and Galileo is expansively contented. His mood is darkened, however, by the arrival of the Cardinals Bellarmine and Barberini, who intimate that the Church is less than happy with his findings, although it is willing to accept and use the astronomical navigation charts which are the practical result of these findings. It is obvious that the two prelates respect Galileo, for they treat him

---

[17] Brecht, *Stücke 8*, pp. 91–92.

with the utmost deference and dignity, but they recognize that his discoveries will, if made public, undermine the authority of the Church. A long and witty dialogue ensues in which Galileo matches scriptural quotations with the Cardinals, but it is all to no avail, for Bellarmine finally informs him that the Holy See has decided to suppress the Copernican teachings as foolish, absurd, and heretical, and he cautions Galileo against appearing to question the infallibility of the Church. As Barberini and Bellarmine lead Galileo out in silence, stunned and unmanned by the flagrant defiance of reason and perception, the Cardinal Inquisitor enters to collect the transcript of the discussion which two monks have been surreptitiously taking. About to leave, he encounters Galileo's daughter, engages her in conversation, and ascertains the name of her Father Confessor, making it obvious that the Inquisition now considers Galileo a marked man.

The eighth scene brings yet another dialectical complication: the previous scene has portrayed the rejection of Galileo's discoveries by the Church, and this one depicts the reluctance of the people, as personified by the young monk who had conceded the victory of science in Scene Six, to accept his findings. In his description of Laughton's reading of the role, Brecht stresses the depth of Galileo's frustration:

> If Galileo perceives the *No* of the Church in the seventh scene, then in the eighth he experiences the *No* of the people. It comes from the mouth of the monk, a physicist himself. Galileo, at first surprised, sees the relationship: the peasant is not defended by the Church, but rather the contrary, where science is concerned. It was Laughton's theatrical innovation to make Galileo so deeply touched that he put all attempts at refutation in a defensive tone, almost of instinctive defensive anger, and he made the throwing down of the manuscript a gesture of helplessness. He put all the blame on his irresistible thirst for knowledge, just as a sex criminal might put the blame on his glands.[18]

---

[18] Brecht, *Aufbau einer Rolle*, p. 30.

But this is not to suggest that Galileo, or, for that matter, Brecht, is insensitive to the young monk's reasons for abandoning astronomy; it is because they understand and sympathize with the oppressed peasantry that they insist on dissemination of the truth, which the peasants may fear, but which will ultimately free them. The monk makes a pathetic plea for the right of his parents, exploited peasants of the Campagna, to believe in the sanctity of the earth as the center of their universe, saying that they draw the strength to struggle on in their miserable lives from the cycle of the seasons, the annual liturgical cycle, and the assurance that the eye of God is on them. He wonders what would happen to them if they were told they lived not at the midpoint of creation, but on one insignificant clump of stone among many; he fears that old, illiterate, and worn out as they are, they will feel cheated and betrayed and will lose the faith that has sustained them.[19] But Galileo rejects this line of reasoning out of hand, insisting that the existence of poverty is an injustice which can be combatted only by knowledge of the truth and that the misery of the peasants does not necessarily produce virtue, which can flourish as well in prosperity and happiness. When the monk asks him if the truth will not triumph even without their help, Galileo can no longer restrain himself, but bursts out: "No, no, no! Only as much truth gets through as we push through. The victory of reason can only be the victory of rational men. You describe your Campagna peasants as if they were the moss on their own huts. How could anyone think their needs could be endangered by the sum of the angles in a triangle? But if they don't get moving and learn to think, even the finest irrigation systems won't do them any good. God damn it, I see the godly patience of your people, but where is their godly anger?"[20] This outburst acquires considerably greater significance later, in the light of Galileo's recantation, and even more in the light of Brecht's revision of the final scene, but for the moment

[19] Brecht, *Stücke 8*, pp. 111–112.
[20] *Ibid.*, p. 116.

it portrays Galileo as a forthright and intransigent champion of the truth. In the next instant he tosses a bundle of manuscripts carelessly at the monk, tells him that they concern the forces controlling the tides, and challenges him to withstand the temptation to read such heretical matter. The young monk has no will to control his curiosity, for he hurls himself upon the new material like a starving man upon food, and he is totally engrossed in his reading almost before Galileo's words are out of his mouth.

But at the start of the next scene there has been a dialectical transformation quite akin to that which occurs in *Mother Courage*, when Courage curses the war for having killed her child at the end of Scene Six, only to proclaim in her next words at the start of Scene Seven that she won't have her war spoiled for her. Here Galileo has acceded to the demands of the Inquisition that he abjure his astronomical studies and has turned to a considerably safer field of investigation, the study of floating bodies. And, though even in this field he continues to attack the teachings of Aristotle (as Brecht continued to do in the field of dramatic theory), he has mellowed a great deal in the eight years that have passed since the last scene, for he simply ignores the questions and entreaties of his assistants, the young monk now among them, regarding the investigation of sunspots. Even a plea to his vanity as a famous scholar falls on deaf ears:

ANDREA: . . . Why don't we investigate the sunspots, Signor Galileo?

GALILEO: Because we're working with floating bodies.

ANDREA: Mother has washbaskets full of letters. All of Europe is asking for your opinion. Your reputation has grown so much that you can't keep still any longer.

GALILEO: Rome has let my reputation grow because I've kept silent.

FEDERZONI: But now you can't afford your silence any longer.

GALILEO: Nor can I afford to be roasted over a wood fire like a ham.

ANDREA: Well, do you think the sunspots have anything to do with this matter?

(*Galileo doesn't answer.*)

ANDREA: All right, let's get back to the pieces of ice. At least they can't hurt you.[21]

In short, in the eight years that have passed, Galileo has developed a concern for his own life and comfort. But at this juncture Ludovico arrives to visit Virginia, and in the course of his conversation he casually reveals that the Pope is dying and that Cardinal Barberini, a scientist and a friend of Galileo, has been mentioned as his successor. A stir of excitement runs through the assemblage at this news, but Galileo maintains a facade of disinterested calm as he enjoys a glass of wine, savoring both its flavor and the idea that now his research in astronomy may find a sympathetic ear in the Holy See. The only thing holding him back is his concern for his daughter's future, for he knows that she loves the young nobleman, and he and his family are conservative aristocrats whose daughter-in-law must be able to assume a dignified posture in the family pew in church. But when Ludovico reveals that he is concerned lest news of further scientific discoveries which contradict official scriptural interpretation cause unrest among his peasants, whom he has taken pains to suppress, he delivers unwittingly the final nudge which provokes Galileo to continue his studies; he will not have the earth stand still simply to keep the castles of the rich from tumbling down. He orders preparation of the equipment to observe the sunspots, even considering publishing his findings in Italian, rather than the traditional Latin, so that the common people whom Ludovico wants to keep ignorant will have access to them. Ludovico breaks off his engagement with Virginia and leaves in anger, making a thinly veiled threat that neither the aristocracy nor the Church which they support will stand idly by while their world is being undermined. Undismayed, Galileo turns his full attention to the preparation of his instruments, yet his directions to his colleagues reveal that he is not proceeding without due caution, caution which bears considerable resemblance to Brecht's own methods of conduct *vis-à-vis* a hostile authority:

[21] *Ibid.*, pp. 124–125.

Yes, we'll question everything again, everything! And we won't go forward in seven league boots, but at a snail's pace. What we find today we'll erase tomorrow and not write again until we've found it again. And as to what we want to find, we'll view it with special distrust once it is found. Thus we turn to observation of the sun resolved to prove that the earth stands still. And only when we have foundered, are completely beaten, sitting and licking our wounds in desperation, only then will we begin to think we might have been right after all, that the earth indeed turns. (*With a wink.*) If every other supposition but this has turned to dust in our fingers, then no more mercy for those who have done no research and still talk. Take the cover from the telescope and point it at the sun![22]

This scene offers a further parallel between Galileo's career and that of Brecht. Like Galileo, Brecht had endured a period of enforced silence during his exile in this country. Like Galileo, he had been unable to find any audience sympathetic to his interpretation of the nature of the world. His testimony before the House Committee on Un-American Activities in 1947 provides a case in point, for Brecht begged to be permitted to read a prepared statement in which he compared the Communist witch-hunt he saw developing here after the war with the techniques and modes of thought of the Nazis. The chairman read the statement in private, but he declined to have it made a part of the record of the proceedings, calling it "a very interesting story of German life," but saying that it was not germane to the hearings. The sense of frustration apparent in Brecht's reaction finds strong echoes in *Leben des Galilei*, particularly in the scene in which Galileo is unable to get the scholars of the court of the Medici to observe the phenomena which have led him to his theories. And Galileo's reaction to the prospect of a new ruling authority, a pope of scientific bent, sheds considerable light on Brecht's return to East Berlin; the appeal of this return rested as much on the hope that the regime would be sympathetic to his research (for so he regarded his plays, as witness the fact that they

[22] *Ibid.*, pp. 138–139.

originally appeared in a series of pamphlets called *Versuche*: attempts or experiments) as it did on his desire to have the time, the means, and above all the opportunity to put his works into production. Similarly, Galileo exudes confidence and satisfaction in returning openly to research (it is revealed that his weakened eyesight has been caused by his secret observations of the sun), reveling in the thought that now his findings may find an audience, as his decision to publish them in Italian indicates.

The following scene attempts to depict the effect that the propagation of Galileo's findings had on the people of Italy, and in so doing, it comes closer than any other scene in the work to the "old" Brecht, the "epic" Brecht of *A Man's a Man, The Baden Didactic Play on Acquiescence, Three Penny Opera*, and *Mahagonny*. Set against the background of the pre-lenten carnival of 1632, it employs a favorite device of Brecht's, later used again in *The Resistible Rise of Arturo Ui*, a carnival barker or street singer who cynically describes the actions of the people in a crude ballad as the carnival crowds frolic and cavort about him, displaying their insolence toward the authority of the Church and their masters. According to this ballad singer, where before there had reigned a sort of order established by the Church and supported by the aristocracy, now all is in chaos: the altar boy deserts the mass, the apprentice lies abed, the mason builds his own home with his master's stone, and the peasant attacks his landlord, while his wife "wastes" her tithe on milk for her children. And all this because Galileo has announced that the earth revolves about the sun. At the end of the ballad, the crowd on stage presents a chaotic procession in which one institution after another is ridiculed and flouted, and finally a gigantic and grotesque puppet labeled "Galileo Galilei" is brought on stage, accompanied by a child bearing a Bible whose pages have been crossed out. When well staged, this is a scene of enormous evocative power, portraying in the most concrete terms the unrest of the times.

The following scene restores relative order to the stage, but it also displays the fundamental disorder and unrest of the state. Galileo, whose vision has failed badly, has come to the palace of the Medici to present the Grand Duke his latest book, but he is apparently being intentionally ignored. Even the rector of the University of Florence, who had in Scene Nine been positively obsequious in his deference to Galileo, now pretends not to see him. The only person at court who still honors him is the iron founder Vanni (a unique figure in Brecht's works, since he is an industrialist, yet a positive figure), who chafes at the way economic progress is being impeded by the reactionary attitude of the Church. Yet he warns Galileo that Florence is no longer safe for him and offers to escort him to a safe refuge. Galileo at first scoffs at the idea that he might fall into the hands of the Inquisition, for he is still certain of the support of the Grand Duke and the personal sympathy of the Pope. But when the Grand Duke finally appears and refuses to accept the book proffered, asking instead about the condition of Galileo's eyes and warning him not to spend too long at his telescope, even he finally becomes wary. He instructs Virginia to go to a nearby inn where he has been keeping a wagon laden with empty wine casks as insurance against the eventuality of persecution. But before they can make good their escape, they are accosted by a high official of the court, who informs Galileo that the Grand Duke is no longer in a position to refuse the request of the Holy Inquisition that he be subjected to a hearing in Rome, and he escorts both Galileo and his daughter to the coach of the Inquisition, which awaits them before the palace.

Scene Twelve, set in the chamber of Pope Urban VIII (formerly Cardinal Barberini), is certainly one of the most successful scenes of modern dramatic literature in the way in which it renders a symbol concrete. At the beginning of the scene the Pope, who is about to be clad by his bodyservants in the vestments of his office, has admitted the Cardinal Inquisitor for an audience. From the outset he resists the urging of the Inquisitor that Galileo's teachings be banned and he be forced to recant. Standing in a simple shift, he is a man, the same Barberini we have encountered before, a gentle, rational man of scientific bent who recognizes the benefits of Galileo's astronomical charts and insists that neither they nor their author be touched. As the Inquisitor's argument develops—and it is essentially the same line of thought as that expounded earlier by the young monk and portrayed by the carnival scene, that there is too much unrest in the world as it is—Barberini is being dressed, and as he accepts, blesses, and dons each successive item of raiment, he becomes progressively less the man Barberini and more the Pope, Urban, the ultimate embodiment of the institution that is the Church. As such, respect Galileo though he may as a man, he cannot indulge in human weakness if that weakness may threaten the institution of which he is head. He continues to resist the arguments, but his resistance weakens with the addition of each vestment:

THE POPE: Finally, the man is the greatest physicist of this age, the light of Italy, and not just some madman. He has friends. There's Versailles. And there's the Viennese court. They'll call the Holy Mother Church a morass of decadent prejudice. Hands off him!

THE INQUISITOR: Practically speaking, we wouldn't have to go far with him. He's a man of the flesh. He'd give in immediately.

THE POPE: He has more pleasures than any man I know. He thinks out of pure sensuality. He can't say no to an old wine or a new idea.—And I don't want any condemnation of physical facts, no battle cries like "Long live the Church!" or "Down with reason!" I allowed him his book on the condition that it express the closing thought that the Church, not science, had the last word. He kept the bargain.[23]

Barberini's transition to Urban, the weakening of his defense of man and reason, becomes clear in the second speech of the Pope above, and finally, when he is in full raiment, he gives in, with the reservation that Galileo be treated humanely:

(*Pause. The Pope is now in full raiment.*)

THE POPE: The utmost I'll permit is that you show him the instruments.

THE INQUISITOR: That will do, Your Holiness. Signor Galileo understands instruments.[24]

[23] *Ibid.*, pp. 159–160.
[24] *Ibid.*, p. 160.

Thus Galileo's recantation is prepared for, and it is based upon his twofold nature as a man of science and a man of the flesh.

Yet the success of this scene ultimately depends upon the subtlety of its staging, for there is a danger that it can be too successful, too specifically directed against the Church. Indeed, it is just such an anticlerical interpretation that East German critics frequently fell back upon in their attempt to rationalize the propaganda value of the work and minimize its embarrassment of the oppressive Ulbricht regime. But Brecht himself was aware of this danger and took considerable pains, in his notes to the 1955–1956 production version, to make it clear that *The Life of Galileo* was in no way to be taken restrictively as a condemnation of the attitude of the Church, but rather as a condemnation of any institution which suppressed the truth and regarded free research as dangerous. First of all, he demands that actors portraying clerical figures refrain from exaggerating the purely religious reactionary aspects of the roles they play:

> It is important to know that this play will lose much of its effect if the production is directed chiefly against the Catholic Church. Many of the characters wear the vestments of the Church. Actors who might portray these characters as despicable would be wrong. On the other hand, the Church obviously has no right to have the human weaknesses of its members whitewashed. All too often it has encouraged these weaknesses and suppressed exposure of them. But nevertheless the point of this work is not to cry out at the Church, "Hands off science!" Modern science is a legitimate daughter of the Church; it has been emancipated and has turned against its mother.[25]

For it is not simply the Church as a spiritual institution which is under attack here, but rather the Church as a ruling body which suppresses the truth: "In this work the Church, even when it is confronted by free research, functions simply as an authority. Since science was a branch of theology, this was a clerical authority,

[25] *Ibid.*, pp. 206–207.

the last resort of science. But it was also a secular authority, the last resort of politics. The work demonstrates the temporary victory of authority, not just that of the clergy."[26] Brecht goes on in this passage to point out that Galileo never made open utterances against the Church, that the Papal College originally upheld his findings, and that clerics even worked as his colleagues, as the work demonstrates. He does not exonerate the Church from guilt in the suppression of truth and free inquiry, but he does emphasize the fact that the attention of the audience is not to be misdirected away from contemporary authoritarian regimes: "The treatment of the Church simply as an authority certainly does not achieve acquittal for it in the case made by the work for the defenders of free inquiry. It would be quite dubious these days to stamp Galileo's struggle for freedom of research as a purely religious phenomenon. Thereby attention would be directed in the most unfortunate way away from contemporary reactionary authorities of a quite secular kind."[27]

The casual reader of the piece may find it difficult to believe that it can be staged as anything but a scathing criticism of the Church, for the figures as drawn seem explicitly clerical in both garb and attitude, and the work is largely based, as Brecht points out in his notes, upon historical fact which shows the Church in the worst possible light. Yet the figures are by no means so explicitly drawn as they seem at first glance, for three recent productions of the work have succeeded in conveying, at least to members of the audience selected at random, a criticism not exclusively of the Church, but of any absolute authority which suppresses the truth.

Scene Thirteen reveals how contradictory Brecht's dialectic method could be in practice, for he deliberately seeks to suspend what he would call *Spannung auf den Ausgang* (suspense concerning the outcome) by announcing by means of a projection before curtain that Galileo recants his teachings, but then he just as deliberately proceeds to re-create that suspense in the construction of the scene.

26 *Ibid.*, p. 207.
27 *Ibid.*, pp. 208–209.

At curtain, Galileo's assistants and pupils are sitting about in the palace of the Florentine ambassador in Rome awaiting the outcome of the hearing of the Inquisition, and their hopes and fears are themselves dialectical. On the one hand, if Galileo recants, all their research will have gone for naught, for the cause of truth will be set back into the Dark Ages; but if he does not recant, he will surely be burnt, and the mind which, as we know in restrospect, could produce the *Discorsi*, the foundation of modern physics, will be extinguished. The tension of the scene is heightened by the presence of Virginia, kneeling in the background intoning repeated prayers which build to a crescendo as the crucial moment approaches. The dialogue vacillates between reminiscences about the personality of Galileo (i.e., concern for his life) and hope that he will prove intransigent, unshakeable in his faith in truth and reason, until finally an official of the Inquisition enters to announce that Galileo will soon arrive and may need a bed, since he is expected to recant at five that afternoon. The consternation of his disciples is immediate, for despite their sentiments regarding their mentor, it is clear that they expect him to uphold his principles and sacrifice himself as a martyr to the Inquisition. Andrea, now a grown man, is particularly outraged at the news; he shouts the essence of Galileo's findings for all to hear, that the world is not the center of the universe, and even the young monk remarks pointedly that what has been seen cannot be forced out of man's mind.

But here the tension begins to build anew, for five o'clock passes without the tolling of the bell that was to have heralded the public announcement of the recantation, and Galileo's colleagues first begin to hope and then to rejoice that he has stood his ground for the truth. Yet just as their joy reaches its height, suddenly the bell begins to toll, and the voice of a crier intoning the words of Galileo's recantation is heard. Devastated at this turn of events, his colleagues turn to casting aspersions upon the man they have just been praising, and as Galileo enters, reduced to a physical wreck by his twenty-three-day ordeal before the Inquisition, Andrea shouts: "Unhappy the land that has no heroes!" He then proceeds to upbraid Galileo as a wine-guzzler and snail-eater who has sacrificed the truth to save his precious skin, until finally he can stand thinking of such a creature no longer and turns to leave. But Galileo holds him back for a moment, saying: "No, unhappy the land that needs heroes." As the curtain falls, projected upon it is a long quotation from the *Discorsi* which points out that smaller and weaker beings are much more capable of surviving and are indeed proportionately stronger than large creatures. At this point Brecht thus seems to attempt to justify Galileo's recantation as a means to permit him to continue his investigations.

The 1938 original version of the final scene similarly appears to justify the recantation, for in it Galileo is portrayed in a favorable light as an enfeebled old man, bent but not broken by his ordeal, who in his humility retains a certain dignity, if not nobility, and who is still wily enough to complete his *Discorsi* and have them smuggled away under the very nose of the Inquisition which holds him prisoner. As the scene opens, a new figure, Hafner, has arrived, ostensibly to repair the chimney at the estate near Florence where Galileo is imprisoned. Galileo attempts to engage him in a plot to spirit a copy of the nearly completed *Discorsi* out of the country, and the two are almost caught in their conspiracy by a peasant who drops by to deliver a brace of geese as a present from a passer-by who had not given his name. The manuscript is hurriedly hidden in a globe, Hafner exits, and Galileo demonstrates that his sensuality continues as unabated as his intellectual activity by remarking that, although he has just eaten, he wouldn't mind a bit of roast goose. Then he sits down to continue the dictation of the *Discorsi* to Virginia, apparently a hopeless task, since the results must be handed over to the Inquisition to be destroyed. But the monk appointed to supervise this work expresses his distrust of the wily old man, for one manuscript concerning the system of the universe has already appeared in Holland, and sources in Strassburg have reported that a second one is expected. Hence it is obvious that Galileo's work is not as futile as it seems; he is, as his censor calls him, an old fox, and it is to be expected that he will succeed in getting the *Discorsi* out of the country as well. He is interrupted in his work by the arrival of Andrea, on his way to conduct research in Holland, who stops by on the pretext of inquiring after his erstwhile mentor's health at the behest of friends. Galileo welcomes his former pupil with barely restrained emotion, but Andrea pointedly observes that the recantation has taken its toll in science elsewhere, for scholars all over the continent have abandoned their research. He then asks the dismayed Galileo if he recanted, as is generally supposed, in order to gain time to complete his work on the foundation of the new physics. The answer is veiled because of the presence of the supervising monk, but the implication is clear that Galileo had indeed intended to continue research he felt only he could do and that this was his primary concern in recanting, though he realized it would make him seem a coward in the eyes of the scientific world. Sending the monk out on a fool's errand, he then reveals to Andrea that he has sacrificed his eyesight to make a copy of the *Discorsi* supposedly delivered to the Inquisition and that he has once failed to smuggle it away. He then indirectly but intentionally provokes Andrea to take the copy with him to Holland, saying that anyone could manage to steal such a trifle from an old man. Andrea takes the manuscript, saying that at the time Galileo's recantation had seemed like the fall of an indestructible tower, but now that the dust has cleared, he sees that only the upper stories have fallen, that the basic structure remains sound. Galileo expresses his gratification that his assistant has seen that the new age is not so blood-flecked as it had seemed, and he sends him on his way with an admonition to be careful while traveling through Germany with the truth under his coat. To this scene is appended, in all three versions, a short epilogue in which Andrea actually succeeds in spiriting the manuscript across the Swiss border, but this scene was never staged by Brecht, not even in the Laughton production,[28] and it is generally omitted from American productions as well.[29]

What Brecht had originally intended to accomplish in *The Life of Galileo* is made quite clear by his 1938 foreword to the piece, which is especially revealing because, as Elisabeth Hauptmann, editor of *Stücke 8*, points out, Brecht's death followed so closely upon completion of the *Probenarbeit* that he had no time to collect and revise his 1938 notes to the work. It is quite apparent that Brecht sensed that man stood upon the threshold of a new era, from which he was being held back only by the intervention of reactionary *Obrigkeiten*: "It is well known how favorably man can be influenced by the conviction that he stands at the threshold of a new age. His surroundings appear to him then as still quite incomplete, capable of the most gratifying improvements, full of undreamed-of possibilities, as a malleable raw material in his hands. He seems to himself as he might be in the morning, rested, powerful, inventive. Traditional belief is treated as superstition, and what was taken for granted yesterday is subjected to new study. We have been dominated, says man then, but now we shall rule."[30] But he felt that this sensation of a new age could be illusory, and indeed it would be if the hope were not crystallized by some genuine force, for the forces of reaction were so firmly entrenched that they could not be rooted out simply by the passing of today into tomorrow:

> It is a frightful disappointment when man recognizes or thinks he recognizes that he has fallen victim to an illusion, that the old is stronger than the new, that the "facts" are against him rather than for him, that his new era has not come. Then it is not simply as bad as before, but much worse, for he has made all kinds of sacrifices for his plans of things which he now misses; he had dared to go forth, and

[28] Brecht, *Aufbau einer Rolle*, p. 64.

[29] A notable exception was the San Francisco Actors' Workshop production of January, 1963. But even in this otherwise excellent production the scene was felt to detract from the impact of Galileo's self-condemnation.

[30] Brecht, *Stücke 8*, p. 196.

he is now attacked as the old order wreaks vengeance on him. No reactionary is more implacable than the defeated liberal; no elephant is a crueler foe of wild elephants than the tame elephant.

And yet such disappointments can still survive in a new era, an era of great upheaval. They just don't know anything about new eras.[31]

Indeed, he waxes quite pessimistic over the possibilities for a genuine transition into a hopeful new age, yet he does not feel that his work is entirely in vain. He takes pains to point out that he does not busy himself with empty history that occurred 300 years earlier because he has given up on the new era:

> What sort of expression is this: "a new era"? Isn't even this expression hackneyed? Where it is cried at us, it is roared out of hoarse throats. Just now it is barbarianism that deports itself as a "new era." It claims it hopes to last a thousand years.
>
> Should we then hold fast to the old times? Am I already lying abed thinking of the morning past to keep from thinking of the one coming? Do I busy myself with that epoch of blossoming of the arts and science three hundred years ago for that reason? I hope not.
>
> The images of morning and night are misleading. Happy times will not come as morning does after a night's sleep.[32]

Thus it is clear that *The Life of Galileo* was originally intended as a form of *Lehrstück*, to show the way to overcome the reactionary forces which sought to preserve the old order or impose an even more reactionary new order, not by direct confrontation or frontal assault, but by application of *List*. This being the case, it is equally clear that Brecht intended Galileo as a heroic figure, in the peculiar nihilistic sense in which he understood heroism. No longer is the concept of the valorous yet futile gesture or the heroic martyrdom of previous ages valid for him, for such gestures can accomplish nothing against the entrenched forces of reaction, and thus they are empty and useless. Like Galileo, Brecht could never tolerate people

[31] *Ibid.*, pp. 197–198.
[32] *Ibid.*, p. 200.

who suffered for a great cause, for he saw that such suffering was merely the sign of the disappointment and resignation stressed in the previous citation. No, for him the important aspect of any act was its ultimate effect, and he saw the application of what Hegel termed *die List der Vernunft*, the cunning of the reason, as the most effective force which could be brought to bear upon the reactionary forces which seemed to control human destiny.

Hence Galileo seemed to him to embody the characteristics which might enable modern man to undermine the institutions which obstructed the way to the new age. In the first place, he was a scientist, and Brecht had long held an exalted view of the efficacy of science to change the world through materialistic revolution, having even for a while termed his epic theater the "theater of the age of science." But even more appealing must have been the character of the man, for it is historically accurate that Galileo did recant, yet equally accurate that he did complete and disseminate his *Discorsi*. Thus he emerges in the first version of Brecht's play as a hero who gets his way by guile rather than by "heroism"; conscious of his capacity to make a positive and unique contribution to science, he recants what he considers to be an incidental point of truth in order to complete his research, outwit the institution which suppresses his teachings, and make even more fundamental truths available to man. Indeed, the role is convincingly prepared, for such deceit occurs early in the work on a different level when Galileo appropriates the Dutch discovery of the telescope to his own ends. And never in the process is he dehumanized or made into the sort of bloodless figure encountered in the earlier *Lehrstücke*, for throughout the work he retains not only his driving intellectual curiosity, but also his sensual weakness. In short, in the 1938 version of the piece, Galileo plays the game by the ground rules imposed upon him by the Inquisition and still contrives to win by the willfully applied force of his own cunning, which was to Brecht the ultimate form of heroism. Werner Mittenzwei, one of the chief interpreters of Brecht's later works in East Germany, supports this view in his discussion of the final scene:

The whole construction of the scene, as the persecuted, half-blind Galileo hides his book from the spies of the Inquisition, characterizes him as a political figure who here possesses the undivided sympathy of the audience. In this scene Brecht wanted to provide a model for underground work by German antifascists opposed to Hitler's dictatorship. The scene is based entirely on the present, on the playwright's struggle against fascism. Galileo is, even if not with the clarity of the first sketches, still an exemplary figure. His attitude, though restricted to this scene, had been wise and had mobilized him against the power of the ruling class. By his recantation he gained the opportunity to write a decisive work, which his friends then smuggled out of the country to the free world.[33]

Thus in his first treatment of the material Brecht saw Galileo in a positive light, for the entire development of the work up to and including the final scene portrays him as a sympathetic figure.

But while Brecht was engaged in adapting the piece for the 1947 Laughton production in Beverly Hills, the first atomic bombs were dropped on Hiroshima and Nagasaki, and their effect on him was, especially in light of his experience of the inhumanity of the First World War, predictably cataclysmic:

When the first news dispatches reached Los Angeles, we knew that this meant the end of the frightful war, the return of sons and brothers. But the great city fell into astonishing sorrow. The playwright heard bus drivers and fruit market vendors express only fear. It was victory, but it smacked of defeat as well. Then came the secretiveness concerning the source of the gigantic energy on the part of the military and the politicians, which disturbed the intellectuals. The freedom of research and the international community of scientists were silenced by the authorities, who were in turn deeply distrusted.[34]

And since he was at that very time engaged in producing a work concerning the father of modern physics, it seems only natural

---

[33] Werner Mittenzwei, *Bertolt Brecht von der "Maßnahme" zu "Leben des Galilei"* (Berlin: Aufbau Verlag, 1962), p. 277.
[34] Brecht, *Stücke 8*, p. 203.

that the event should be reflected in his treatment of the work, as indeed it was:

> The atomic age made its debut in Hiroshima in the middle of our work. In the space of a day the biography of the founder of modern physics had to be read in a different light. The infernal effect of the great bomb placed the conflict between Galileo and the authorities in a newer, clearer perspective. We had to make only a few revisions—not a single one in the structure. Even in the original the Church had been portrayed as a secular authority, its ideology interchangeable with many another. From the very outset the key point had been the gigantic figure of Galileo with his concept of science in the service of the people.[35]

The words "service of the people" are the key here, for it became Brecht's new intention to show how Galileo had betrayed his tie with the people. While he had formerly seen Galileo's recantation as a means necessary to produce a desired end, the development of modern physics, and where he had previously placed so much faith in science as a means of bettering man's lot, he now became suspicious of the science which had produced a terrifying weapon for the wholesale extermination of human life, and he began to interpret Galileo's recantation as the same sort of abdication of social and moral responsibility on the part of the scientist as that which led to the development and use of the atomic bomb. No longer was he the archetype of the wily modern hero of the people, for he had betrayed the fundamental trust of the scientist and in so doing had betrayed the people themselves:

> Galileo's crime can be regarded as the original sin of modern science. Out of the new astronomy, which interested the newly emergent bourgeois class deeply because it lent support to the revolutionary social currents of the time, he created a sharply defined special art, which, to be sure, was able to develop with relatively little interference pre-

[35] *Ibid.*, p. 201.

cisely because of its "purity," that is, its indifference to the use to which it was put. The atomic bomb is, taken as both a technical and as a social phenomenon, the classic end product of his scientific capacity and his social betrayal.[36]

With this changed perspective on Galileo's role in the history not simply of science, but also of society, Brecht turned again to the task of translation and adaptation, determined to make the "few changes" he referred to above, hoping to shift the emphasis of his work so as to stress Galileo's abdication of his social responsibility. What had been essentially a criticism of a reactionary institution which suppresses the truth and yet is rendered impotent by the cunning of a determined man was now to become a criticism of the man who submits to such suppression, for whatever purpose, and allows himself to be used by such an institution. While there were some few changes within the body of the work—generally consisting of deletion of by-play with minor characters intended to emphasize Galileo's feeling for the people—the bulk of the changes occurred in the concluding scene,[37] the entire emphasis of which was shifted. Where the Galileo of 1938 was a cunning old man who, in spite of near-blindness, enfeeblement, and imprisonment, succeeded in outwitting his captors in conveying the truth to a world held in darkness, the 1947 version (of which the 1955 version is little more than a retranslation) portrays him as a crotchety and capricious old man who regards his drive to research almost as a form of masochism, of weakness of the soul, which he can resist as little as he can resist his sensual appetites and which he carries on without apparent goal or purpose. The entire opening sequence, the unsuccessful conspiracy with Hafner, is omitted entirely; Galileo is simply engaged in research regarding falling bodies when the peasant enters with the geese. When the latter departs, Galileo's daughter urges him to continue dictating his weekly letter to the Archbishop, and,

---

36 *Ibid.*, pp. 204–205.
37 Mittenzwei, *Bertolt Brecht*, p. 277.

though he would rather have her read to him from the works of Horace, he finally agrees to do so. As Miss Rülicke suggests, Brecht's directorial remarks made during the *Probenarbeit* are extremely revealing here, for they show the extent to which his conception of Galileo has changed; no longer is he to be portrayed as a cunning and determined underground fighter for the truth, but simply as a capricious and disagreeable old man who considers himself superior to the recipient of the letter, until finally this joke grows stale in his mouth.[38]

When Andrea enters, Galileo does not welcome him, as he had in the early version, but ponders long over his decision to see his erstwhile pupil, for such figures from the past can only sharpen the gnawing pangs of guilt he already feels concerning his recantation. The dialogue which ensues, in the original version so pointedly led by Galileo to the subject of the completed *Discorsi*, is now halting and fragmentary, interrupted by frequent embarrassed pauses as Galileo learns of the consequences of his cowardice: Descartes has shelved his investigations into the nature of light, the young monk has abandoned physics to return to the bosom of the Church, and research has since languished throughout the world. Here there is a sharp point of difference from the original, for Andrea's question as to the reason for the recantation and Galileo's reply are omitted, and Andrea's bitterness at the cowardice of his teacher is not mitigated by any doubts as to the purpose of his retreat from the truth. At this juncture Galileo sends Virginia away to see after the geese, and, when Andrea asks if he may leave, Galileo reproaches his student for disturbing his peace, since he has to be careful what he says and thinks now that he is under the protection of the Church. While so doing, he casually mentions that he has relapses, and he allows Andrea to draw out of him the admission that he has secretly made a copy of the *Discorsi* to replace the original delivered to the Inquisition. Brecht's directorial remarks of 1955 make it clear that this revelation grows out of nothing but wounded vanity, and it is

[38] Rülicke, "Bemerkungen," pp. 288–290.

only the coincidence of Andrea's visit that chances to bring the *Discorsi* to light at all.[39] The effect on Andrea is kaleidoscopic, for he immediately concludes that Galileo intends him to smuggle the manuscript out of the country, despite the latter's protestations to the contrary, and suddenly he begins to rationalize away the guilt and shame of the recantation. He exclaims that Galileo had been a century ahead of his time in ethical thought, that he had concealed the truth from its enemies, had withdrawn from a pointless political imbroglio in order to gain time to pursue the truth yet further. But Galileo immediately disclaims any such noble motives, pointing out that there is no such thing as a scientific work which can only be written by one man, and further that he recanted because of fear of physical pain from the instruments he had been shown, not because of some plan. At Andrea's expression of incredulity he begins a long and rueful monologue in which he condemns himself as a criminal against science and society alike, who had a chance to make a meaningful contribution to the progress of man, yet who threw that chance away for selfish and cowardly reasons:

> . . . As a scientist I had a unique opportunity. In my time astronomy reached the man on the street. Under these particular circumstances the resoluteness of a single man could have called forth great upheavals. If only I had resisted, if only scientists had something like the Hippocratic Oath of the doctors, a vow to use their knowledge only for the good of mankind! As things stand now, the most anyone can hope for is a race of inventive dwarfs that can be rented out for any purpose. And on top of that, Andrea, I am now convinced that I was never in real danger. For a few years I was just as strong as the authorities. And yet I delivered my knowledge to those in power, to use or not to use, or even to misuse, whatever suited their purpose. I betrayed my vocation. A man who does that can't be tolerated in the ranks of science.[40]

Here Virginia returns with the broiled livers of the geese, and Gali-

[39] *Ibid.*, pp. 277–278.
[40] Brecht, *Stücke 8*, pp. 187–188.

leo turns his full attention to his food, refusing Andrea's hand as he leaves, warning him only to be careful in passing through Germany with the truth under his cloak.

In thus revising the final scene of *The Life of Galileo*, Brecht greatly enriched both the dramatic and philosophical content of his work, but it is quite dubious that he could ever succeed in discrediting and destroying a character so thoroughly and convincingly built throughout the body of the play simply by judicious paring and shaping of the conclusion. Indeed, the fact that the ultimate condemnation of Galileo's action issues from his own mouth, that he acknowledges his complicity in the suppression of the truth, lends a new dimension to the figure, a modern dimension otherwise lacking. Whereas he appears in the first version as an artful and highly successful schemer, in the two later versions he emerges, through recognition of his responsibility to society and the effect of his abdication of that responsibility, as a profoundly more modern figure, one conscious of the guilt shared by the individuals for the injustice wrought by the society of which they are members upon humanity in general. And in the process the work has become more truly dialectic in the literary sense of the word, for it leaves the synthesis up to the spectator. In the original version, with its form of *Happy-End*, the thesis, scientific truth, is opposed by its antithesis, reactionary suppression, which is in turn surmounted by the synthesizing force of individual cunning, so that the truth wins out in the end. Philosophically speaking, the case is closed, the lesson learned. In the Beverly Hills and East Berlin versions, on the other hand, the play does not arrive at a pat conclusion, but rather ultimately poses a question: does reasoned cunning really win out in the end, or does something go awry in the process? Taken in the context of the postwar recriminations concerning the responsibility for the *Nazischreck*, of which the trials of Nürnberg were at best a superficial manifestation, the question is agonizingly fundamental. Or taken in the context of the *Wirtschaftswunder* of the fifties and sixties, it is just as immediate, for those who were responsible for the economic recovery and moral rehabilitation of Germany in the eyes of the western world had generally been opposed to Hitler, yet they were able to save their skins by remaining silent—the so-called *Innere Emigration* is the major literary manifestation of such cunning—and were afterwards able to restore a sense of dignity to their nation. But was there, in that *List* that enabled them to survive, a loss of innocence which soured the sweet taste of ultimate vindication? To what extent were they, by their very silence, responsible for the human anguish which was a direct consequence of the horror which spread into the vacuum left by that silence? Yet could they have accomplished anything but useless martyrdom by outspoken resistance to the Nazis? Were not all who opposed Hilter ruthlessly slaughtered? Isn't the primary human instinct that of self-preservation? These questions cannot be answered, but the fact that they cannot must indicate that the piece is just as dialectical and probably a good deal more effective than Brecht might have hoped.

Yet even more important for an understanding of the truly dialectical effect of *The Life of Galileo*, it has its most subversive effect precisely where, if we were to take Brecht simply as a Communist apologist, we would least expect it, in East Berlin. Friedrich Luft, critic of the West German *Die Welt*, sensed the tension created by the work in his review of its premiere by the Berliner Ensemble:

> Above all one sees a work that, especially when played here in East Berlin, exerts a grippingly revolutionary effect. It concerns the oppressed liberty of the scientific conscience. It demonstrates the dilemma into which Galileo, the brilliant astro-physicist, falls when he has to bear witness to the fact that the old concept of the universe is false and out of date. The new eyes of a new age condemn the scientific beliefs of yesterday as lies.
>
> That's what is seen in this crafty, lucid, often quite warmhearted and frequently poetic sequence of scenes about the man Galileo, who must suffer more than the others because he knows more—who doesn't feel strong enough to be a martyr, and yet, even after he has recanted, turns the tables on those in power. He advances the truth, even if he

must do it in secrecy. At the end Galileo is broken, but he is victorious. He had been forbidden to speak, but his thoughts spoke louder than he.

Now, to hear that precisely in a theater that is situated in a zone where the ruling powers bristle at any change for the more humane is provocative. Professors and students of the East Zone, who will no longer accept the petrified dogma of a long-dead Stalinism, sit in prison. Ulbricht takes any inkling of liberal thought as high treason and persecutes it implacably. To see this *Galileo*, this clever work possessed of so much revolutionary wisdom, at precisely this place, is spooky— it is almost a sort of posthumous political cleansing of Brecht.[41]

While Luft is certainly indulging in a form of anti-eastern polemic of his own in this review, and while he obviously misses much of the point of the work as revised in his all too benign assessment of Galileo, he nevertheless accurately senses the almost unbearably palpable tension produced by the work when it is played in East Berlin. Yet it was no less effective, for example, in an excellent 1966 production by the Goodman Theater in Chicago, particularly when taken in the context of teach-ins and demonstrations against the cruel absurdity of the Viet Nam war. For *The Life of Galileo* is fundamentally dialectic; it poses in the most concrete terms one of the most essential issues of our times, much as it was posed in a direct attack on Brecht by Günter Grass in his work *The Plebeians Rehearse the Uprising*: criticism of those who "cop out," who relive the *Innere Emigration* of the 1930s.

It might be taken for granted that Luft's view of *Leben des Galilei* as a piece subversive to the regime of the German Democratic Republic is not shared by East German critics. Generally speaking, such critics build their interpretation of the work almost exclusively upon Brecht's utterances concerning the social treason committed by Galileo in leading the people into battle for scientific truth and then leaving them in the lurch when the battle became dangerous for him. Käthe Rülicke, for example, in her otherwise incisive analysis

[41] Friedrich Luft, "Brechts *Galileo* von beklemmender Aktualität," *Die Welt* (17 January 1957).

of the development of the final scene, goes so far as to dismiss the character of Galileo as uninteresting: "Thus it is not the 'character' of Galileo that deserves our interest, but his social behavior; as Brecht once said during a rehearsal, 'It is not interesting that a man struggles against himself, but that he battles against others.' Indeed, Brecht almost never mentioned the 'character' of a figure during rehearsals, but rather his way of behaving. He almost never said what a man *was*, but rather what he *did*. And when he sought to characterize a figure, then he referred not to its underlying psychology, but to its social significance. He demonstrated the character of a figure in its *modus operandi*."[42] But while Brecht seldom mentioned "character" specifically during the *Probenarbeit*, preferring to work with the less abstract *Gesten* of the actors (as already noted in Chapter Three), it is certain that a powerful and fascinating portrayal of human character is inherent in the work itself, a portrayal which is not significantly diminished in its power by reading the piece rather than experiencing it on the stage. In short, to dismiss Galileo's character as uninteresting or merely incidental to the political portent of the work is to overlook the one respect in which it is most dialectic in its effect. From the very first scene the two contradictory sides of Galileo's nature have been emphasized: he insists on having the scientific truth, and he insists on having his belly comfortably filled, and he pursues both desires with equal sensuality and vitality. The very gusto with which he lives exudes naive humanity; he contemplates the delights of new discoveries just as he savors the full flavor of an old wine, for both experiences represent to him the essence of human existence. He sees no contradiction in the fact that man is possessed of both an inquiring intellect and sensual desires, for both are simply manifestations of the life force which differentiates man from primate. If at the end of the work (and of his life), contemplating the turning point of his life, he has become less sanguine and now questions the justice of his recantation, he is simply indulging in an age-old human failing, recrimina-

[42] Rülicke, "Bemerkungen," pp. 281–282.

tion concerning the past, which renders him no less appealing to the reader or to the spectator.

Both Martin Esslin and Robert Brustein have suggested that certain characters, notably Azdak of *The Caucasian Chalk Circle* and Mother Courage, were originally conceived of by Brecht as negative, villainous characters, but that they eventually wormed their way into his affection and "got away" from him—that is, they acquired an all too human appeal which prevents them from carrying out the negatively didactic roles originally intended for them.[43] Galileo is certainly another example of such a character who got out of control, the more so because of Brecht's original admiration of him. Once his character was formed in the initial draft of the work, Brecht could no more destroy or discredit him in the final scene by his "social betrayal" than he could, despite countless revisions, prevent audiences from reacting sympathetically to *Mother Courage*. Hence Ionesco's criticism that Brecht's characters are superficial and present only one side of humanity, the social side, must seem empty, for, particularly when played by actors of the stature of Charles Laughton, Ernst Busch, and Helene Weigel, it is the breadth and depth of their human dimensions that delight the spectator and at the same time provoke him to examination of his own character. Indeed, it is noteworthy that both Jacques Lemarchand and Michel Déon, in their reviews of the highly "Brechtian" production of *The Life of Galileo* in French by the Théâtre National Populaire in 1963, rejected the polemic aspects of the work, yet praised it as a study of a contradictory yet eminently credible character.[44]

Werner Mittenzwei, on the other hand, has, even as an East German critic, too much respect for Brecht's ability to create compelling characters to debunk Galileo as readily as does Miss Rülicke, and he

[43] Esslin, *Brecht*, p. 117; and Robert Brustein, *The Theatre of Revolt* (Boston: Little, Brown, 1962), p. 271.

[44] Jacques Lemarchand, "*La vie de Galilée* de Bertolt Brecht au T.N.P.," *Le Figaro Littéraire* (9 February 1963), p. 16; and Michel Déon, "L'ombre du bûcher," *Les Nouvelles Littéraires* (7 February 1963), p. 19.

lavishes particular praise on the power of Brecht's language to portray nuances of character concretely; but he still insists that the work is didactic in both intent and effect. He takes as his target not just the scientists whose criminal negligence led to the production and use of the atomic bomb, but all those intellectuals who once stood by the workers' movement in the revolutionary cause, only later to turn renegade. Taking as his point of departure the juncture in Scene Nine at which Galileo expels a scientific philistine from his house, shouting, "Whoever doesn't know the truth is just an ignoramus. But whoever knows it and calls it a lie is a criminal!"[45] Mittenzwei correctly takes this to be a recurrent *Motiv* in the work. He continues:

> It would be no error to understand this episode, as it was written in Denmark in 1938, as taken from the political struggle of that era, for Brecht's condemnation of renegades had a very particular background. Precisely at the time when *Galileo* was being written, a few intellectuals such as Arthur Koestler, Ernst Glaeser, Fritz Sternberg, and even André Gide, who had previously sympathized with the workers' movement, returned to the fold of the bourgeoisie. The hate and disgust which Brecht loosed upon such renegades is mirrored in the Mucius scene. The condemnation he places in Galileo's lips is Brecht's condemnation of his contemporaries who stabbed the revolutionary workers' movement in the back. Treason found no mercy at the hands of such a dedicated and partisan poet as Brecht.[46]

But to interpret *The Life of Galileo* from such a narrowly polemic point of view is to lose sight of the qualities (praised elsewhere by Mittenzwei before this last word of interpretation of the piece) which raise it to the stature of genuine drama. Indeed, Günther Rohrmoser, a West German critic, raises serious doubts as to whether the work can even be legitimately considered a *Lehrstück*, for he points out weaknesses in its Marxist theory:

[45] Brecht, *Stücke 8*, p. 120.
[46] Mittenzwei, *Bertolt Brecht*, pp. 316–317.

In the failure of Galileo a fundamental error in Marxist historical dialectics is manifested. The materialistic concept of history is fundamentally incapable of producing an ethics of political action. In it no situations are foreseen in which the spontaneous response of the individual is demanded in order to give the movement of history a direction toward a humane *Telos*. Galileo does not betray materialism, but rather his own humanely social inclination, precisely because he is materialistic in a consistent way. Hence the ambiguity in his character in this work. Both the autobiographical material [re. Brecht] and the irresolubility of the question as to how significantly the individual can influence the outcome of an historical process contribute to this ambiguity. The contradiction of official doctrine in which Brecht finds himself in this matter (he is too closely associated with the moral heritage of his late bourgeois origin) stands to the good of the aesthetic quality of the work, but it makes it all but impossible to classify the work specifically.[47]

Indeed, it is precisely this unification of divergent aspects of human nature into an artistic whole in the figure of Galileo that raises the work above the level of polemic drama and expresses a concern that is more fundamentally human than Marxist. In short, Galileo comes on more strongly as a human being than as a scientist; therefore his recantation is seen not restrictively as the social betrayal of the scientist, but rather generally as the weakness of all too human flesh faced with a potent authority.

On the other hand, it is equally clear that Brecht *intended* the work as a criticism of Galileo, as well as of all those, be they scientists, writers, scholars, or politicians, who by their silence allow themselves to be used by corrupt or reactionary regimes. But if such be the case, he is thereby also expressing criticism of his own employment of cunning, for after the workers' uprising of June 17, 1953, it was certainly obvious to him that he was being used as a cultural show-piece by a regime which did not share the interests

<hr />

[47] Günther Rohrmoser, "Brecht: *Das Leben des Galilei*" in Benno von Wiese, ed., *Das deutsche Drama vom Barock bis heute* (Düsseldorf: August Bagel Verlag, 1958), p. 413.

of the working class (cf. the poem cited in Chapter Two, p. 28).
The best evidence that Brecht indeed felt pangs of conscience concerning his own well-being, which had been gained at the expense
of suppressing what must by then have been a fairly strong conviction that the DDR showed little promise of doing anything to improve the lot of the workers, comes to light not in his dramas, but
in his poetry. "Der Radwechsel," the first of three pivotal poems
dating from 1953 to 1956, conveys his impatience at the lack of
progress accomplished in the East Zone after the war: "I sit on the
curbstone./The driver is changing a tire./I'm not happy about
where I come from./I'm not happy about where I'm going./Why
do I watch the tire change/With impatience?"[48] But mere impatience
at the slowness of progress implies neither the direct criticism of
the regime nor the self-criticism found throughout the poem "An
die Nachgeborenen," particularly strongly expressed in the verses
cited below:

> It is true: I still earn my keep.
> But believe me, that is just a coincidence. Nothing
>   I do gives me the right to eat my fill.
> Coincidentally I am protected. (If my luck runs out,
>   I am lost.)
> I am told, "Eat and drink! Be happy that you have!"
> But how can I eat and drink, if
> I tear what I eat from the hands of the starving,
> And someone dying of thirst needs my glass of water?
> And yet I eat and drink.
> I'd like to be wise, too.
> Old books tell us what is wise:
> To keep aloof from the struggle of the world and
> To pass the short time here without fear.
> But to get by without violence,
> To repay evil with good,

[48] Bertolt Brecht, *Gedichte 7* (Frankfurt am Main: Suhrkamp Verlag, 1964),
p. 7.

Not to fulfill, but to forget one's own desires:
That's what's supposed to be wise.
I can't do any of that.
Really, I live in dark times.[49]

The third of these poems, entitled "Böser Morgen," was found in Brecht's *Nachlaß*. Evidently composed at his country house in Bukow, it indicates that his feelings of guilt have even turned the fruits of his own *List* sour in his mouth: "The silver poplar, whose beauty is known all over,/Today an old slut. The lake/A pool of dishwater—don't touch!/The fuschias among the snapdragons vain and paltry./Tonight in a dream I saw fingers pointing at me/As if at a leper; they were worked to the bone/And they were broken./ You don't know! I cried,/Conscious of my guilt."[50]

Hence it appears that *The Life of Galileo* is not simply autobiographical, but actually prophetically so, for when Brecht rewrote the final scene in Hollywood in 1946, he could scarcely have foreseen what was to befall both himself and Germany during the postwar years. When he turned again to the work in order to stage it in East Berlin in 1955, he must have done so with considerable feeling of irony. And while the chief reason for his reevaluation of Galileo, his disapproval of the atomic bomb, coincided with the expressed policy of the Communist Party (at least until Russia became a member of the nuclear club), it was even more fundamentally a manifestation of his own deep-seated feelings, which had long antedated his commitment, feelings which had been conditioned by his own experience of the carnage of war and which were outraged at the prospect of such carnage raised to even more nightmarish proportions. And the drama as a whole, while it was certainly at its inception deeply affected by Brecht's commitment to Communism and enmity toward fascism, emerges from the complex processes of writing, revision, and production not as a polemic, but rather as a

[49] Brecht, *Gedichte 4*, pp. 143–145.
[50] Brecht, *Gedichte 7*, p. 11.

highly confessional work by a stubbornly individualistic writer, a work characterized by deep insights into the complex problems of modern man, who must make his way in an essentially reactionary and oppressive mass society. And it is also a tragedy of modern man, who must live in such a society by connivance and wile, only to discover, having survived and gained a measure of success, that he has defeated his own purpose in the process.

In his play *Exit the King*, Ionesco, like Brecht, turned to a mode of theater different from the plays that had immediately preceded it, but unlike Brecht, he turned away from the relative conventionality of *The Killer* and *Rhinoceros* and even, in structural development, *Amédée*. And again unlike Brecht, he did not move toward a new approach to theater, but rather regressed to the form of theater which had characterized his early works, such as *The Bald Soprano, The Lesson,* and *The Chairs,* and he seems to be continuing in this trend in his latest work at this writing, *Hunger and Thirst.* The middle works of his career had, like *Rhinoceros*, a dynamic dramatic plot and structure; there was exposition, development to a climax, and a resolution of sorts. The early and late works, on the other hand, are essentially static; they are devoid of anything resembling conventional dramatic development or plot. Indeed, with regard to *Exit the King*, it is even difficult to speak of action in the dramatic sense, for the entire development of the play is summed up in the title: the king does indeed die (the title in French is *Le roi se meurt*). And it is not how he dies or why he dies that is of paramount interest, but simply that he dies.

Like the early plays, *Exit the King* consists of one long act in a single setting, the palace of King Bérenger I, and, also like the early works, it employs a small cast of six persons: the king, his two queens, Marguerite and Marie, the court physician (who resembles W. S. Gilbert's Pooh-Bah in that he also serves as surgeon, executioner, bacteriologist, and astrologer), Juliette, the maid, and a senile guard. At curtain the guard is standing alone in the dilapidated throne room of Bérenger's palace, and in rapid succession the other five characters pass quickly across the scene, each announced loudly by the guard; the scene recalls the puppet shows which so delighted Ionesco in his youth. When Queen Marguerite, Bérenger's first wife, returns to the stage, she begins to complain vigorously to Juliette about the slovenly state of the throne room. Juliette complains just as vigorously that she hasn't had time to do "le living room," as she persists in calling it, because there are too many other things needing attention. The guard joins the general chorus of complaint, and it soon becomes apparent that the palace in general is in a sad state: cigarette butts and dust lie everywhere, the heating and plumbing are out of order, there are cracks in the walls and leaks in the roof, and, ominously, the sun has failed to rise, thus defying the king's express command. At this point Queen Marie enters, and the two queens begin a dispute concerning something which they have been expecting, but which they avoid mentioning by name. Whatever it may be, the two are revealed as being entirely different in nature: Marguerite bears striking resemblance to the nagging, anti-romantic virago Madeleine of *Amédée,* while Marie reflects the sensuality and tenderness of the Madeleine of *Victims of Duty* or of the old woman of *The Chairs.* Taken together, the two reflect Ionesco's constant preoccupation with the twofold nature of woman, for never in his works are both sides fused in a single female character.

At any rate, the dispute continues, with Marie insisting that the signs of whatever has been predicted have been mistakenly interpreted. Marguerite will have nothing of such escapism, and she castigates Marie for having indulged the king's fancies and fantasies too long, for having been weak in her tenderness, for having allowed him to waste his time in petty pleasures and neglect the decay of his kingdom. Here it becomes obvious that it is not just the palace, but the entire kingdom which is disintegrating: the fields lie fallow, the dikes have broken and flooded the lowlands, the mountains are sinking, and, inexplicably, acre after acre of the kingdom has been plunging out of sight into immense fissures in the earth. As if that weren't enough, his army has turned craven and lost war after war, the national boundaries have shrunk, and the population has dwindled from nine billion to a thousand old people. When Marie points out that there are forty-five young people as well, Marguerite retorts that even they are old, for, having been captured by the enemy and repatriated at age twenty-five, two days later they are eighty, which is, as she observes, hardly a normal way to grow old.

At this point the court physician enters, announced, as are all entrances, by the guard, to report still further catastrophes: The sun has lost most of its strength, Saturn and Jupiter have collided, and the Milky Way is curdling. When Marie protests her disbelief, he offers her a large telescope and invites her to see for herself (no parody of Brecht's *The Life of Galileo* can be inferred here, since M. Ionesco has expressly stated that he is not acquainted with the play). Moreover, the conditions he has described are not universal, but apply only to Bérenger's kingdom, for right across the border it is spring; the cows are calving twice a day, the trees and grass are growing, and nature is in full bloom. But in Bérenger's kingdom it is November, and everything is dessicated and dying, including his subjects, twenty of whom have been liquified and twelve of whom have lost their heads, this time without the intervention of the physician. But Marguerite either knows of or has expected all of these disasters, since they are signs of what has been predicted.

At this juncture King Bérenger finally makes his appearance, and, while he had seemed fit enough at his first brief entrance (the stage direction indicates that he crosses the stage "with a fairly lively step"), he is now obviously becoming senile. He complains about his health: his legs are stiff, his feet hurt, he has a headache and a pain in the ribs, and he can't sleep. Above all, he is depressed at the incessant rain and angry that the clouds will no longer obey his orders to clear away, and he even has difficulty getting Juliette to go clear away the cobwebs which are proliferating in his chamber.

Suddenly he notices that everybody seems to be staring at him and demands to know the reason. Disregarding Marie's efforts to restrain her, Marguerite tells him why:

MARGUERITE: Sire, we must tell you that you are going to die.

DOCTOR: Alas, yes, your majesty.

KING: But I know that, of course. We all know it. Remind me when it is time. What a quirk you have, Marguerite, of entertaining me with disagreeable things at sunrise.

MARGUERITE: It's already high noon.

KING: It is *not* noon. Ah—yes, it is noon. It doesn't matter. It's morning to me. I haven't eaten anything yet. Send for my breakfast. To tell the truth, I'm not too hungry. Doctor, you've got to give me some pills to stimulate my appetite and stir up my liver. My tongue must be coated, isn't it? (*Shows tongue to doctor.*)

DOCTOR: It's true, your majesty.

KING: My liver's all clogged up. I didn't drink a drop last night, but I've still got a bad taste in my mouth.

DOCTOR: Your majesty, Queen Marguerite speaks the truth. You're going to die.[51]

But Bérenger will hear nothing of such predictions, saying that he'll die when he is ready, in fifty or three hundred years; meanwhile, he tries to turn to the management of his kingdom, or what is left of it. But he cannot, for his ministers have gone off fishing, and Juliette reports that they have fallen into the creek, which has in turn fallen into a fissure in the earth. Nor can they be replaced, for the only subjects left in the kingdom are a few cretins and some hydrocephalic children. As he bemoans the condition of his state, Marguerite interrupts to reassert, with evident relish, her prophecy of his death:

MARGUERITE: You're going to die in an hour and a half. You're going to die at the end of the play.

KING: What are you saying, dear? That's not very funny.

51 Ionesco, *Théâtre IV*, p. 20.

MARGUERITE: You're going to die at the end of the play.

MARIE: My God!

DOCTOR: Yes, sire, you're going to die. You won't have your breakfast tomorrow morning. Nor any dinner tonight. The cook has turned off the gas. He has taken off his apron. He'll fold table-cloths and napkins eternally in the pantry.

MARIE: Don't tell him so fast or so harshly.

KING: Who could give such orders without my consent? I'm fine! You're making fun of me. Lies! (*To Marguerite*) You've always wanted me dead. (*To Marie*) She's always wanted me dead. (*To Marguerite*) I'll die when I please. I am the king. I make the decisions.

DOCTOR: You've lost the power to decide for yourself, your majesty.[52]

Bérenger, thinking that Marguerite and the physician simply want him to abdicate, denounces them for mutinous traitors and commands the guard to arrest them, but he has grown powerless other than to make his increasingly ludicrous inappropriate announcements. At this point Marie enters actively into the dispute, urging the king to assert himself, to exert his will-power, to prove that he *is* still alive and able to manage his affairs. Bérenger attempts to comply, but he cannot, for he has become so feeble that he cannot even stand up unassisted. Struggling to his feet, he immediately falls flat again and again, in the fashion of a grotesque puppet show:

GUARD: Long live the king! (*The king falls down.*) The king is dying.

MARIE: Long live the king!

(*The king picks himself up painfully, with the help of his sceptre.*)

GUARD: Long live the king! (*The king falls down again.*) The king is dead.

MARIE: Long live the king! Long live the king!

MARGUERITE: What a farce!

(*The king picks himself up painfully. Juliette, who has disappeared, reappears.*)

JULIETTE: Long live the king!

(*She disappears again. The king falls down again.*)

[52] *Ibid.*, pp. 22–23.

GUARD: The king is dead.

MARIE: No! Long live the king! Long live the king! Get up! Long live the king!

JULIETTE (*Appearing and disappearing as the king gets up*): Long live the king!

GUARD: Long live the king!

(*This scene must be played as a tragic burlesque, as a puppetshow.*)[53]

Finally, with Marie's help, he succeeds in standing for a few moments, but suddenly he notices that his crown and sceptre have been lost in the struggle, and he commands that they be restored to him; the *guignol* is extended in pantomime as both crown and sceptre fall repeatedly to the floor, and the guard's cry of "Vive le Roi!" sticks in his throat. Finally, commanding Marie to be silent, the physician tries to make Bérenger understand that he has become impotent and is going to die, that his orders are not going to be obeyed any more. To prove that he is still potent, Bérenger shouts a series of orders at the guard, which the latter ignores until they are repeated by Marguerite. Turning then to Marie, who has broken silence to put herself at his command, Bérenger orders her to come and kiss him, to dance, to go to the window, or at least to turn her head, but she is powerless to do anything until Marguerite bids her move. In frustrated fury, Bérenger then orders trees to sprout from the floor, the room to disappear, rain to fall, leaves to grow—all to no avail. In desperation he commands Juliette to enter by the great door, but she enters by the small one, and she leaves while he is still sputtering out his command that she stay. Finally the possibility that he could indeed die dawns on him, and he begins to beg for more time, but suddenly, as in *The Bald Soprano* and *Amédée*, with their clocks gone mad, time has become meaningless. He is, Marguerite reports, now over four hundred years old, yet he insists that he has scarcely started life, having been born only five minutes earlier, ascended the throne but three minutes ago, and only just gotten married. Reminded that he

[53] *Ibid.*, p. 25.

now has but an hour to live, he pleads anew for time, for a chance to take a make-up exam in life, but all his pleas fall on deaf ears, until suddenly, seized by panic, he rushes to the window to shout to his people that he is going to die. But there are no longer any people there to hear him—indeed, even the echo is out of order—and all this display provokes is a clucking of tongues over his lack of dignity in the face of death. Meanwhile his feebleness has returned; his hair has suddenly turned white, and, while he rejects a wheelchair that has been brought, he cannot restrain himself from falling into it, where he is immediately swathed in blankets and hot-water bottles by Juliette. He becomes both increasingly childish and increasingly senile, cursing his parents for the bad joke they have played on him in giving birth to him and not granting him permanent life. Both Marguerite and the physician upbraid him for his craven behavior, reminding him of his courage during his prime, when he came near death in battle thousands of times, and of how he has killed without remorse thousands of others, including the rest of his own family. But he cannot be moved by such reminders, since those deaths had not concerned him.

Beginning to see his fate as inevitable, Bérenger suddenly becomes concerned for the preservation of his memory after his death, betraying the heart of his and Ionesco's concern:

> Without me, without me! They'll laugh, they'll drink, they'll dance on my tomb! I'll never have existed. Oh, let them remember me. Let them cry, let them despair! Let them perpetuate my memory in all of the history books! Let everybody learn my life by heart. Let them all relive it. Let the scholars and students have no other subject but me, my reign, my exploits. Let them burn all other books, let them destroy all other statues and put mine in all public places. My picture in all the ministries, in all sub-prefecture offices, in the offices of fiscal comptrollers, in the hospitals. Let them give my name to all airplanes and ships, to all handcarts and locomotives. Let all other kings, warriors, poets, tenors, and philosophers be forgotten and let only me live on in memory. Only one baptismal name, only one family name for every-

one. Let everyone learn to read by saying my name: B-B-Bérenger. Let me be on all the icons, on the millions of crosses in all the churches. Let all the stained-glass windows be the color of my eyes. Let all rivers trace my face on the plains. May they call my name, pray to me, implore me eternally![54]

To pacify him, the physician offers to have his body embalmed and preserved, only to touch off a new wave of terror, for Bérenger does not want to be embalmed, but to live, to feel warm, loving arms around him, not the coldness of the grave. And yet, though he adamantly refuses to give up life, he has never really experienced it directly, as Marie recognizes, again playing with the concept of time:

MARIE: My dearest, my king, there is no past, there is no future. Tell yourself that there is nothing but the present till the end; everything is present. Be present!

KING: Alas! I'm only present in the past.

MARIE: No!

MARGUERITE: That's it, be clear-headed, Bérenger.

MARIE: Yes, be clear-headed, my dearest king. Don't torment yourself. To exist is a word, to die is a word, phrases, ideas made up by you alone. If you understand that, nothing can harm you. Get a grip on yourself, take yourself in hand, don't lose your perspective, plunge into the ignorance of all other things. You are, now, you are. Don't keep asking the same question always: what's that, what's. . . . The impossibility of an answer is an answer in itself. It is your very being which explodes, which goes out to the world. Plunge into the wonder and amazement without limits, so you can be infinite. Be amazed, be dazzled, everything is strange, indefinable. Thrust aside the bars of your prison, break open its walls, escape from definitions. You'll breathe anew.

DOCTOR: He's suffocating.[55]

And Bérenger is indeed choking, choking to death in his fear of dying. Nothing has meaning for him any more; he cannot even

[54] *Ibid.*, pp. 39–40.
[55] *Ibid.*, pp. 41–42.

understand Marie's joyous reminiscence concerning their courtship, for everything else has become inconsequential next to the realization that he must die. He even goes so far as to wish that all other humans, whom he has just condemned in the previous sentence for being selfish, might die in order that he may live. But then he turns to the countless millions who have died before him, entreating them to teach him how to accept death. The rest of the cast join him in a ritual of supplication to the dead that is almost liturgical in tone, but to no avail, for Bérenger cannot face the extinction of his own being.

Why he cannot becomes apparent in the next phase of development: the others urge him to view life as an exile and death as a return to his homeland, but, appealing as this notion is, Bérenger cannot manage it, for he cannot remember whence he has come. In other words, life is bordered at both ends by lack of consciousness, by lack of self, by a void. In the eyes of the individual, as represented by the king, the world exists only to the extent to which he experiences it, and it seems to him as if he has always existed, as if the world is his exclusively and must perish with him.

But suddenly it occurs to Bérenger that he is still alive, and he determines to get as much as he can out of what remains of his life. He attempts to walk, to move from the spot where he has been rooted, but he is too feeble to do so and falls down repeatedly, recalling the *guignol* of the earlier scene. Unable to move, unable to experience anything of life directly, he turns in desperation to Juliette and begins to pump her concerning her life. He takes vicarious delight in each trivial detail, from her washing the laundry, making the beds, and emptying the chamber pots to her backache, abscessed tooth, and eternal fatigue. He even rejoices over the *pot-au-feu*, the leftover savory stew common to the French proletarian table, but suddenly even the stew seems remote to him, and he begins to doubt that any such thing ever really existed. This doubt is seized upon by Marguerite and the physician as a sign that death is imminent, and the king seems to have ceased his resistance, for to all their condolences and blandishments he can only reply that he is dying. What is to become of the world in the new age that is about to dawn (v. the epigraph of this chapter) is immaterial to him, for he will not be there to experience it. Everything has become a nightmare to him, but then he remembers how Marie used to comfort him, and he begins to reminisce about the little things that they have shared in their life together. Yet when Marie asks if he still loves her, all he can candidly reply is that he has always loved himself. Here Marguerite and the physician intervene, seeking to accelerate the death of the king, only to be interrupted by the guard, who begins to recite, in a long, disjunctive monologue reminiscent of that of Lucky in Beckett's *Waiting for Godot*, the hitherto unknown exploits of his monarch. According to him, Bérenger stole fire from the gods; invented gunpowder, the balloon, the dirigible, the aeroplane, the wheelbarrow, the automobile, the tractor, and the plow; built Rome, New York, Paris, and the Eiffel Tower; and even wrote all the plays of Shakespeare. But to Bérenger all this is a source of wonder, for all he can remember is a little cat he once owned, and he drifts off into a rambling, emotionlessly intoned monologue about his cowardly cat, who finally got out into the world, only to be killed by the neighbor's dog, then to return in a dream transformed into an enormous, ugly, spitting she-cat resembling Marguerite. In short, all his accomplishments are forgotten, overshadowed by the death of a beloved pet, yet even this pet is spectral in form, incorporating as it does the same stifling, anti-romantic spirit which characterizes Marguerite.

At this point the king is wheeled off into the background, and the others begin animatedly to discuss his merits and faults as if he were already dead. At first Marie, Juliette, and the guard defend the king against the attacks of Marguerite and the physician, but gradually they all come to realize that they exist only through Bérenger, who in creating his own microcosm by his act of being has also brought them into being and will cause their extinction by his death. They know without looking that he is still breathing, for they still exist. At this moment Bérenger's heart goes berserk, beating in a thundering crescendo which shakes the palace so that new cracks appear in the walls and one wall collapses. While the others are distracted by this phenomenon, Marie really begins to digest the last observation, realizing that she exists only in Bérenger's mind and faces extinction when he dies:

MARIE: He's forgetting me. At this instant he is forgetting me. I feel that he's abandoning me. I'll be nothing if he forgets me. I won't be able to live if I'm not in his distracted heart. Hold tight! Hold tight! Clench your fists with all your might! Don't let go of me!

JULIETTE: He has no more strength.

MARIE: Hold on! Don't let go of me! I'm the one who keeps you alive! I keep you alive as you keep me alive. Do you understand? Do you understand? If you forget me, if you abandon me, I can't exist any more, I'll be nothing.[56]

Her plea seems to be answered momentarily, for the king's heart begins to beat normally again, and he regains consciousness. But he doesn't appear to recognize anyone around him, least of all Marie, who implores him to recall at least her name. When it becomes obvious that he is moving as a sleep-walker, without perceiving or comprehending anything, Marie suddenly disappears (from this point on Ionesco makes more and more capricious demands of the stage machinery, as the action becomes increasingly *guignolesque*). At the revelation that he has become blind, Marguerite begins exhorting him to look within himself to find the meaning of all this. But all he can see is himself, in everything, behind everything, above everything—in short, everywhere. Finding nothing within himself on which to rely, he turns to the others in despair for help. Juliette and the guard assure him of their eternal devotion to him, but both disappear as they are uttering their vows of fidelity. He turns to the physician to ask whether he is going deaf as well, but the latter exits with profuse apologies, bowing and scraping like an awkward marionette. Shaken by this abandonment en masse, Bérenger turns to

---

[56] *Ibid.*, p. 64.

the only person left, Marguerite, to demand that the others return. But she insists that they cannot, for he has willed them out of existence and cannot now even recall their names. From this point on Marguerite controls the action as she gradually divests the king of every shred of his being, preparing him for extinction. At first Bérenger resists, insisting on the sanctity of his being, but gradually his will weakens, and finally he has no choice but to submit to her ministrations. She starts by casting off the things invisible to the audience that tie him to the world: imaginary fetters, rucksacks, boots, weapons, thorns, seaweed, and ivy that he has been carrying or that have been clinging to him. Then she begins to harass him as a nursemaid would a petulant child, commanding him to stand up straight, to unclench his fingers (in which she discovers his entire kingdom preserved on microfilm, a microcosm of a microcosm, as it were), to cast out fear, and to relinquish his hold on life. To make his way easier she commands the imaginary phantoms, wolves, rats, vipers along the way—the fears of death as the unknown—to cease to exist, and the figures of an old beggar man and a helpful woman with a glass of water—representing the human *caritas* which is his last tie with the world of men—to vanish. She leads him thus to the throne, where she commands him to give her his legs (at each order, he stiffens the member demanded), his fingers, his arms, his chest, his shoulders, and his stomach. When she has taken away the last trace of his humanity, his power of speech, she callously remarks, "That was a useless bit of nonsense, wasn't it? You may take your place."[57] And the long stage direction which closes the piece is quite important to understand the effect desired by Ionesco, to see how near he has come to the sort of stage trickery he had employed in his early works:

> *Queen Marguerite disappears suddenly to the right. The king is seated on his throne. During this last scene the doors, windows, and walls of the throne room have progressively disappeared. This by-play of the set is very important.*

[57] *Ibid.*, p. 74.

Now there is nothing on the stage but the king on his throne, bathed in gray light. Then the king and his throne disappear, too. Finally there is nothing but the gray light.

The disappearance of the windows, doors, walls, king, and throne must be accomplished slowly, progressively, very distinctly. The king seated on his throne must remain visible for a while before sinking into a sort of a vapor.

CURTAIN[58]

Hence it is plain that, in *Exit the King*, Ionesco has abandoned the line of theatrical development he seemed to be following in *Rhinoceros* and his other middle works. In the first place, he has again become quite explicitly confessional, as he was in the early works, and yet the sort of confession implicit in *Exit the King* is considerably more profound than that of early works such as *The Bald Soprano* and *The Lesson*. Both Ionesco and his interpreters have repeatedly observed that such works express his obsessions, but in *Exit the King* he turns to what he has always recognized as the most fundamental of his obsessions, that of death:

> I have always been obsessed with death. Since I was four, since the time I knew I was going to die, anguish never left me. It was as if I understood all at once that there was nothing else to do in life.
>
> Besides, I have always had an impression of the impossibility of communication, of isolation, of encirclement. I write to combat that encirclement. I also write to give vent to my fear of death, my humiliation in the face of death. It is absurd to live in order to die, it is true. This anguish cannot be assessed by the bourgeois or the anti-bourgeois; it comes from too far afield.[59]

Here he touches upon a number of his other obsessions, such as the impossibility of communication and the essential isolation of man, both of which are themes present in *Exit the King*. But the dominant theme of the play, as well as of much of his non-dramatic writing (indeed, he originally returned to Paris from Rumania on a scholar-

---

[58] *Ibid.*

[59] Eugène Ionesco, *Notes et contre-notes* (Paris: Gallimard, 1962), p. 204.

ship to write a dissertation on the theme of death in French literature since Baudelaire),[60] is the inevitability of death and the consequent absurdity which this fact portends for life. In one particularly revealing passage in *Notes and Counter-Notes*, he laments the death of other men of letters and art, such as Camus, Boris Vian, and Gerard Philipe, and goes on to a more personal recollection and the fear it engendered in him: "And then I think of Atlan, who has just died. One of the greatest painters of our times. Constantly we said, 'Ought to see more of you, as soon as possible, without fail.' We'll never meet again. I'll see his paintings again fleetingly; he will be there.

"I am afraid of death. I am afraid to die, doubtless, because without knowing it, I wish to die. Thus what I fear is the wish I have to die."[61] He has frequently given expression elsewhere to such a death-wish, a wish to be shut of the world which dulls his imagination and sense of wonder. He expresses it above all when he looks within himself and finds there, like King Bérenger, only a reflection of the emptiness of the world:

> I look around me, I look within myself, and I murmur: that's impossible, that's too improbable, that's not true, that can't last. And truly it won't last. It is as if I were witnessing the disintegration of this complex of movements and figures, of this semblance of beings and things. In writing my plays, I have the impression that I'm contributing to the acceleration of the process of this disintegration. For all of this has become a painful obsession for me. For once, I'd like to get rid of this world of dreams, this dream of a world, which finally wears down my astonishment so that it fades into habitude and I achieve only boredom, anxiety, and depression.[62]

But then on the other hand, not too much credence should be placed in his expression of a death-wish, for he has written so much about

[60] Richard Coe, *Eugene Ionesco* (Edinburgh: Evergreen Pilot Books, 1961), p. 70.

[61] Ionesco, *Notes et contre-notes*, pp. 213–214.

[62] *Ibid.*, pp. 193–194.

the identity of opposites, particularly the wish and the anti-wish, that one suspects him of playing the philosophical obscurantist. No, it can scarcely be true that Ionesco wishes for death, any more than does Bérenger. It is true that he is obsessed with death in a way that Bérenger is not, at least at the outset of the play, but he is, like Bérenger, tied to life, and, again like Bérenger, the closer death approaches, the more deeply he is bogged down in life, the less prepared he is to die:

> The longer I live, the more I feel attached to life, obviously. I sink more and more into it, I am hung up on it, ensnared in it, taken prisoner by it. I eat and eat and eat: I feel heavy, I doze off into a coma. Once I was a knife blade slicing through the world, passing through existence. The universe now no longer seems astonishing, unaccustomed, unheard of, as it once did. It seems quite "natural" to me. How difficult it will be to tear myself loose! I'm habituated to it, hooked on living. Less and less prepared to die. How painful it will be for me to cut loose all the bonds accumulated during a whole lifetime! And doubtless I won't be here much longer. Most of the course has been run. I ought to start untying all the knots, one by one.[63]

And what is it that keeps him bound so closely to life? Again, like Bérenger, he is acutely aware of the uniqueness, the solitude of his own existence. For reality does not exist for him save through his own consciousness, a consciousness which has already had one finite limit, his birth. And he cannot really conceive of surpassing the other limit, death, for with it his own awareness will be extinguished and with that the world, his microcosm:

> This dream of universal existence, this dream of "me," of "me and the others," which I shall no longer be able to remember. "What did I dream of?" "Who was I?" I often ask myself on awakening with a confused memory of attractive, passionate, *important* things, which are already fleeting as I try to grasp them, sinking into the night of

[63] *Ibid.*, p. 200.

forgetfulness forever, leaving me with nothing but regret at not being able to remember.

Torn away from "reality" by a single blow—I will die. I will no longer remember this theater, this world, my loves, my mother, my wife, my child. "I" will no longer remember. And "I" will no longer be "I."[64]

It must be remarked here that similar obsessions mark Ionesco's later works, particularly *The Aerial Pedestrian* and *Hunger and Thirst*, both of which concern the attempt to escape this oppressive consciousness of existence. In the former, Bérenger, now a playwright, has given up writing because it has become too obsessive and seeks to escape life by flying away from that which enmires him in existence (a similar *motif* exists in *Amédée*, but it is not thought through to a conclusion). But in the end he returns, deeply shaken by the cataclysmic view of the future he has glimpsed, resigned to a finite existence on earth. And in *Hunger and Thirst* Jean attempts a similar escape in a neo-Faustian quest into the great world, the macrocosm, but he finds no release from the cares of existence there; rather, he finds the even deeper terror of infinite existence, infinite in its boredom, pain, and toil. Hence *Exit the King* would seem to be Ionesco's definitive statement on life and especially on death as the terminus of human existence: it is there, waiting for him, ready to extinguish his ego and the universe which he has partly experienced and partly constructed; and the fact that it is there renders everything he does here and now meaningless, absurd. In other words, what Richard Coe has described as the "void at the center of things"[65] could probably better be termed the void at the end of things, for it is this obsession with the inevitable and, for Ionesco, insuperable void at the end of existence which is his fundamental concern and which colors all his works, particularly *Exit the King*.

This obsession does not, however, merely condition the subject matter and thematic content of Ionesco's works; it also exerts con-

[64] *Ibid.*
[65] Coe, *Ionesco*, pp. 61–78.

siderable influence on their form, and again particularly on that of *Exit the King*. As pointed out above, and as critics of this work unanimously agree, it is essentially a static form of drama, and in this respect it comes much closer than *Rhinoceros* or *The Killer* to representing in its form Ionesco's conception of existence. The middle plays were dynamic; they engendered a sense of motion, of something purposeful happening, of action developing to a climax which in turn led to some sort of resolution. But if *Exit the King* may be said to have any action at all, it is only the action of a clock running down to its final tick, for its only purpose is to prepare the death of Bérenger at the final curtain. Yet such development is quite consonant with Ionesco's view of life, for he shares with Beckett the sensation that existence is essentially static. For Bérenger, as for Vladimir and Estragon, for Hamm and Clov, life is not a dynamic experience in which they are engaged as active beings; it is rather something in the middle of which they are stuck, which happens to them as passive objects. They cannot do anything or go anywhere because they do not know where they are, why they are there, or where they are going. They are like the Smiths and the Martins of *The Bald Soprano* or the tutor of *The Lesson*, for they are on a treadmill which takes them nowhere, but upon which they continue to plod away purely as a matter of habit, of form. The chief difference between these early works and *Exit the King* is that they both ended by starting over again from the beginning, as, in essence, does Beckett's *Waiting for Godot*, and are thus open in form, emphasizing the pointless repetition of the formulae of life. But the stark finality of Bérenger's death, accompanied as it is by the disintegration and disappearance of his kingdom and his world, leaving only the eternal gray light, renders *Exit the King* essentially closed in form. Beyond his death there is no repetition, not even of meaningless platitudes; there is simply nothingness. Thus the play serves in form as well as in content to state Ionesco's chief obsession: life is a static form of existence in which we can accomplish nothing significant and beyond which there lies nothing significant.

All this must seem to imply that *Exit the King* is an intensely serious play, but nothing could be further from the truth, for the work represents Ionesco at his comic best and is laden from beginning to end with humor of a very high order. Indeed, the *New Yorker*'s Paris critic, Genêt, describes the first half of the work as straight farce, very comic, and the second half as pure tragedy.[66] But in thus dividing the work into two halves she is describing her own reaction to the play rather than the work itself. Harold Clurman of *The Nation* comes a good deal closer to sensing the true nature of the work in speaking of "alternation between a tongue-in-cheek humor and a more or less real anguish."[67] Actually what both are attempting to describe is neither a division of the play into two dissonant halves nor an alternation between two dissonant moods, but rather a unification of the comic and the tragic (perhaps pathetic would more accurately describe Bérenger's situation) achieved through a constant juxtaposition of the highly risible and the deeply anguished, for just when Bérenger's anguish is the deepest, he appears the most ridiculous. As a matter of fact, in *Exit the King* Ionesco has come closer than in any of his other works to carrying out his frequently stated intention of uniting comedy and tragedy to forge a new kind of drama. In so doing, he has similarly exemplified his theories concerning the identity of opposites, but he has actually accomplished a great deal more. Written or played as straight tragedy, such a play concerning death would be unendurable, just as a straight comedy on the same theme would seem utterly trivial. But in combining the two dramatic effects, in using the risible to comment upon the anguished, and vice versa, he has achieved *Verfremdung* in the most thoroughly Brechtian sense. We are accustomed to equating death, particularly in the drama, with tragedy and associating comedy with human foibles rooted firmly in life. By confronting the spectator with comic aspects of the essentially tragic or pathetic, Ionesco ap-

[66] Genêt, "Letter from Paris," *New Yorker* (12 January 1963), p. 102.
[67] Harold Clurman, Untitled review of *Exit the King*, *The Nation* (19 January 1963), p. 57.

pears to be attempting to force him, as Brecht would have put it, to take a fresh look at his preconceived notions, to think anew in each new situation, to see both life and death in a clearer light. And in so doing, he is also making use of the dialectic approach, again in the Brechtian sense of the word. To the thesis that death is tragic he proposes the antithesis that death is in reality comic, is a bad joke played upon man at the end of his life. The synthesis, that life is hence absurd, he leaves to be drawn by the spectator.

At least, so it works in theory. Unfortunately, what all too many dramatic theorists fail to take into account is the extent to which audiences and individual spectators have been conditioned by life as well as by previous experience and current expectations of drama. Ionesco takes a great deal of pride in the fact that *The Bald Soprano*, like many of his other early works, was a miserable flop at first, but later embarked upon one of the longest runs in the history of the French theater; at last count, it had run over 4000 consecutive performances during a period of over ten years before packed houses (here one might observe that it doesn't take much to pack the Théâtre de la Huchette, which seats only sixty-four persons). Ionesco interprets this and similar reception of some of his other works as a sign of success, yet while it certainly indicates that he has arrived as a dramatist, the question of the philosophical success of the work requires closer examination. To doubt that the play has made any lasting impression upon the audience, one has only to stand outside the Théâtre de la Huchette during the intermission between *The Bald Soprano* and *The Lesson* on a summer night and listen attentively to the reactions of the polyglot audience. Remarks generally turn at first about the truth of the play, the accuracy with which it depicts the total absence of genuine communication in normal social intercourse. That vein exhausted, conversation generally turns to a "safer" topic, for instance, the squalor of the Rue de la Huchette, and then to comparative remarks concerning the dirtiness of the French and Italians as opposed to the cleanliness of the Germans, the Swiss, the Danes, the Dutch, or what have you—in short, remarks every bit as banal, trite, and empty as those which have just been so brilliantly lampooned on the stage. Actually, the response of the early audiences of his works should have been more satisfactory to Ionesco, for at least they recognized that he was making an all-out frontal attack upon their *modus vivendi*. Of course, Ionesco would be the first to disclaim any such notion, for he has repeatedly denied any polemic intention and continues to insist that theater can only be theater, and not some kind of educational institution. Nevertheless, his plays do contain very pointed social criticism, and one wonders to what extent he takes their philosophical content seriously, to what extent he hopes to convey his obsessions and insights into the human condition.

Like *The Bald Soprano, Exit the King* has received rather mixed critical response. Generally speaking, a certain pattern holds true: those critics favorably predisposed to Ionesco have praised the work, while most others have been either perplexed or bored by it. Take, for instance, the reaction of Jacques Lemarchand, critic of *Le Figaro Littéraire* and one of Ionesco's earliest critical defenders:

> With *Exit the King*, Eugene Ionesco uniquely affirms and makes more profound one of the most poignant secrets expressed in one way or another in all of his works; but previously he has dissimulated and camouflaged it, left it up to the spectator to discover. Out of modesty, doubtless, out of fear of being pompous. This method has a great deal of charm, but it also incurs some dangers: it exposes the work to misunderstanding, to misinterpretation, and Eugene Ionesco has already had some bad experiences in that line. But what is most remarkable about *Exit the King*—which I take to be the dramatically strongest work Ionesco has written so far—is that without abandoning anything of his tone or his own personal intentions, Ionesco says clearly and makes understandable to everyone, and in an absolutely new way, that it is painful to die, and that death is waiting patiently for each of us.[68]

[68] Jacques Lemarchand, "*Le roi se meurt* d'Ionesco," *Le Figaro Littéraire* (5 January 1963), p. 16.

Obviously Lemarchand is sensitive to Ionesco's purpose; he has watched him throughout his development as a playwright and is certainly to be numbered among the most knowledgeable and responsive of the interpreters of the *avant-garde* in general. Hence it is no surprise that he detects both the poignant and intensely personal anguish felt by Ionesco in the face of death and the bizarre humor which seems to set him above death. But contrast this reaction with that of the young Scot observed by Roger Gellert, critic of *The New Statesman*, on the occasion of the Edinburgh premiere of the English version of the work:

> "Didn't understand a word of it," said the young chap in the ad-man suit emerging from Edinburgh's Lyceum Theatre. "Not a single bloody word." This criticism, so often and I think so meaninglessly levelled at Ionesco's early work—why demand to understand every detail of another man's world, as long as it's compelling and enriching?—seems an odd one to apply to *Exit the King*, lately given its British premiere in Scotland, and soon to be seen at the Royal Court. Over a span of two hours, without interval, we watch a quaint old tyrant dwindle from defiance into acceptance of death. The play is never obscure; it is beautifully written, in a slightly *démodé* way, and ravishingly interpreted by Alec Guiness.[69]

The reaction of this young man, so condescendingly reported by Gellert, who goes on to give a fairly sensitive evaluation of the work, is highly revealing. For the work is, as Gellert says, never obscure; in fact, it is among the most lucid and clearly pointed plays that Ionesco has written. It is all but inconceivable that an attentive and reasonably literate spectator could fail to get the drift of Ionesco's meaning. Hence the reaction of the "young chap in the ad-man suit" needs closer examination, for in all likelihood he understood much more of the play than he wanted to. He understood enough of it to realize that the essentially bourgeois values upon which he

[69] Roger Gellert, "Quietus," *The New Statesman* (13 September 1963), p. 330.

had heretofore built his existence were under attack, and he rejected the meaning of the play in a purely defensive gesture, refusing to "understand" what must have been for him deeply disturbing thoughts, just as the early Paris audiences of *The Bald Soprano* rejected what this play had to say about their mode of existence. The difference between Gellert's young chap and his compatriots who loudly applauded *The Bald Soprano* in the summer of 1965 is essentially a matter of exposure. By 1965 *The Bald Soprano* had been thoroughly explicated by critics and generally accepted by the public, and seeing it had become an "in" thing to do. In short, as Ionesco himself has recognized, once a thing is known and accepted, it is already out of date; an idea once uttered and understood becomes petrified as a cliché. Presumably, there may come a time, if it has not come already, when the statement of *Exit the King* will be as well explicated and accepted as that of *The Bald Soprano*, when even a young chap in an ad-man suit may enjoy and "understand" a performance of the work, without being deeply affected by it.

Herewith is exposed the principal weakness of any work of literature which simply makes a statement, as, in essence, all of Ionesco's works do, even the most confessional ones. They do so principally because he is obsessed with the view that man is basically passive, at the mercy of the elements, the most important of which is the void which he sees in death. In only two of his works does the hero really seem to exercise his own will in bringing about his fate, and even in *The New Tenant* and *Hunger and Thirst* it is not really the free will that is at work, but simply a peculiar, self-destructive quirk of human nature. The new tenant must be surrounded by his things until they eventually stifle him, and Jean must seek some way out of the feculent existence he faces in his dank basement apartment; both are foredoomed from the outset by the nature of the world and by their own natures. As for the rest, Jacques, Choubert, Amédée, and the four Bérengers, they are simply instruments of an implacable fate, victims of duties imposed on them by society, by marriage, or by their own mortality. None of them have any choice; their fate is dealt out to them peremptorily by some superior and mysterious force over which they have no control and which they do not want to confront in the first place (it is quite significant that both Amédée and the Bérenger of *The Aerial Pedestrian* apologize profusely for the act of levitation that seems to free them from their earth-bound fate; neither wants to fly away, but neither can help it). But if the human condition is seen in such a light, if man is essentially passive, without choice, then the resultant works are without choice; they cannot pose questions concerning the possibilities of human existence, but can only make statements. And once such statements are understood or even accepted and acknowledged, they become just the sort of platitudes which Ionesco is bent on destroying.

To return briefly to the question of dramatic form, Ionesco has repeatedly stated that he hopes to create a new genre of drama by raising the form to the state of paroxysm, where lies the source of both comedy and tragedy. But while *Exit the King* falls short of the sort of paroxysm that characterized the early works and achieves a greater clarity thereby, the question of how dramatic the work is, how suitable it is for the stage, remains open. Even Michel Déon, who otherwise gave the work one of its most sensitive and favorable reviews, felt that it was too long:

> For an hour and twenty-three minutes we experience all the states of mind of the king: incredulity, fear, fury, lack of comprehension, appeal to pity, revolt, denial of death, repudiation, resignation, malice, violence, dissection, and then the slow—too slow—entrance of death, which removes his attributes one by one, his guard (his army), his maid (his court), his mistress (his love), and leaves him alone with his wife, who closes his eyes.
>
> There are some admirable moments in *Exit the King*, and a powerful yet pleasant construction of a barely insane world. There is also plenty of humor, that humor so peculiar to Ionesco, familiar, simple, and easy, yet which grinds all the same and by laughter makes us

conscious of a too seductive madness. There are also tedious passages, and I think above all that the end would gain in intensity if it were shortened.[70]

The English translation by Donald Watson indeed indicates cuts in the original text suggested by Ionesco, apparently prompted by widespread criticism of the length of the work and its tendency to be repetitive, cuts which amount to about a fifth of the original length. Yet even this shortened version, which apparently and unaccountably took longer to perform in Edinburgh, failed to impress English critics as being dramatic. Roger Gellert found the work boring despite its admirable construction, and *The Spectator*'s Clifford Hanley even went so far as to wonder if it were genuinely a play:

> The set, too, which later decays before our eyes, is a nice domineering piece of morbid psychology, and there are fine conjuring tricks by which folk disappear as their functions come to an end. It's a very impressive thing Ionesco has done, but it is not, I think, a play.
>
> Without the high-powered acting talent of this production, *Exit the King* would be an intolerable bore. There's good stuff in it, and death is a fine subject, but the good stuff is stretched thin and the last thirty minutes aged me ten years. Okay, okay, I heard myself muttering, the old boy's good and dead now, why don't we broach the whisky and start the wake? [British critics in general seem to have missed their traditional intermission nip, for three of them mentioned in passing the absence of opportunity for a drink.] But he kept right on dying.
>
> There were jokes in the script, of course. One in particular was the joke in which you create a medieval situation and then throw in something like a zebra crossing [British locution for a pedestrian zone] or a pair of nylons, to paralyse the audience. Ionesco used this crude old gag again and again, without a scruple. I would be ashamed.[71]

These doubts and those of Harold Clurman[72] and even Jacques

[70] Michel Déon, "*Le roi se meurt* d'Ionesco," *Les Nouvelles Littéraires* (10 January 1963), p. 12.

[71] Clifford Hanley, "Long Time Dying," *The Spectator* (6 September 1963), p. 77.

[72] Clurman, Review of *Exit the King*, p. 57.

Lemarchand,[73] both of whom found the piece too long despite the excellence of its construction and its wit, coupled with similar criticisms of Ionesco's longer works, particularly *Hunger and Thirst*, raise the question of whether such a static mode of theater can succeed over the long run. Indeed, it has even been suggested that Ionesco is over-reaching himself in turning to longer, more serious works, that his is essentially a one-act talent. While such a question must surely remain unanswered as long as he continues to write, it nevertheless remains a valid question, and it suggests that his theories regarding pure theater are as *outré* and unworkable as were Brecht's early theories regarding epic theater.

But where does all this leave us with respect to the question of engagement? As was pointed out at the beginning of this chapter, the works selected for examination represent a more confessional than didactic approach to the theater, springing as they do from concerns more basic than mere polemics. Even the titles of the two works seem to invite contrast: Brecht writes of the *life* of Galileo, while Ionesco writes of the *death* of Bérenger. Brecht's Galileo recants because he wants to live, because he cherishes every aspect of life, the sensual as well as the intellectual, and in continuing to live, regardless of his purpose, he contributes to the eventual progress of mankind. But Bérenger is so paralyzed at the realization that he must die that he is impotent to accomplish anything more than a futile plea for his life. Brecht is concerned with life and how it may be lived in modern society, whether it may be lived in decency and dignity without detriment to that society or to the individual. Ionesco, on the other hand, is obsessed with death, with fear of personal extinction to such an extent that he sees the social values of life as meaningless and absurd. Brecht is concerned with freedom in quest of the truth, moral as well as scientific, but Ionesco regards such truth as merely topical, and it pales beside the ultimate truth that man is mortal. Brecht is critical of that which impedes the progress of humanity, while to Ionesco the inevitability of death is so oppres-

[73] Lemarchand, "*Le roi se meurt* d'Ionesco," p. 16.

sive that it renders questions regarding the progress of humanity immaterial and absurd, for the sensation that with him his world will come to an end totally overshadows the real world which exists external to him and will survive him. For Brecht life seems important because of the capacity of man to accomplish something within his lifetime, but Ionesco sees such accomplishments as futile because their fruits lie beyond his existence, beyond the extinction of the self of which he is so aware. Hence the two would seem to occupy opposing positions with regard to the efficacy of human existence.

But do they really? Does Brecht actually take such an optimistic view of the possibilities of human life as the foregoing contrast would seem to indicate? It is obvious that he is concerned with life rather than with death, but what does he see as the likelihood that man can effectively shape his existence? To sense his essential pessimism, a deeper analysis of his Galileo is necessary, and much can be gained by comparison of Galileo with the young comrade of *The Measures Taken*. As was pointed out in the last chapter, the latter was essentially a naive figure with a single purpose: to alleviate human suffering. His selfless compassion was his undoing, for it rendered him immune to party discipline, and he had no choice, at least in his eyes, but to give up his life for the good of the party and, presumably, for the eventual good of humanity. And yet his sacrifice is futile; it accomplishes nothing for the party, for the *Kontrollchor* remains as impassive and dehumanized at the end as it had been at the outset, an authority perhaps even less tolerant than the Catholic Church of the seventeenth century, nor for humanity, for the coolies of Mukden continue to suffer as before, as, indeed, they do even today. Galileo, on the other hand, represents the enlightened Brechtian hero, who has learned to employ *List* to cling to his life and still discover and disseminate the truth. He is still concerned with bettering the lot of mankind, with setting the Italian peasantry free not only from the depredations of physical toil through the application of scientific discovery, but also from the fetters imposed on their minds by undermining the authority which imposes those fetters. But Galileo is frustrated first because both the authority and the oppressed, as embodied in the figures of the young monk and the carnival revelers, resist his good intentions. As a consequence, he is forced to employ cunning to save his life, and such is his nature, as it was Brecht's, that to continue to live means to continue to pursue the truth. But the results of his wiliness, so far as he can perceive them within his own life, are negative: because of his recantation, scientific research in all of Europe languished, and the authority against which he had exerted himself seemed even more deeply entrenched than ever, just as the workers of East Berlin docilely submitted to the DDR, following Brecht's example in the servility of his letter which was quoted by the regime after the 1953 uprising, leaving the regime more firmly entrenched than before. In other words, Galileo's employment of *List* had been as futile in his own eyes as had the sacrifice of the young comrade, as his own self-condemnation in the final scene shows, just as Brecht's employment of cunning had ultimately seemed futile in his own eyes. The rest of Brecht's mature works are characterized by similar failure of cunning, or perhaps self-defeat of cunning would be a better term. Mother Courage loses her children one by one as a direct result of her cunning; Shen-Te's *List* results in the creation of an alter ego who defeats her real intention; in spite of Schweyk's calculated stupidity the war continues; and despite the cunning of the workers the revolution of *The Days of the Commune* fails. In only two of the works from the later period do the central figures remain true to their own natures, *Antigone* and *Coriolan*, both of which are adaptations from models for which *List* would have been an inappropriate quality. Yet even in these two works the protagonists are defeated by their own natures, Antigone by her intransigence and Coriolan by his vanity. Indeed, in only one work does the power of cunning prevail, and there by happy coincidence: in *The Caucasian Chalk Circle* Azdak and Gruscha achieve justice only through the miscarriage of justice which is seen as an exception, a short golden age of near-justice that is not likely to be repeated unless human values change. It is as if an earlier work of Brecht's, "The Song of the Inadequacy of Human Striving," from *Three Penny Opera*, had been prophetic of the statement of his mature works: "Man lives by his head./But his head can't do the job./Try it once: at most a louse/Might live on your head./Because for this life/Man isn't sly enough./He never even notices/All the lies and deceit."[74] But where this song had been satiric in its meaning and effect in *Three Penny Opera*, the same meaning emerges as a perfectly serious effect of the mature works. In short, although they give the appearance of being figures who are actively engaged in shaping their own fates, the central figures of all of Brecht's works are essentially passive, since they are acted upon by elemental forces beyond their control, implacable social forces which seem to offer the protagonist only one choice which will enable him to preserve his existence, but which contrive to subvert his willed actions so that the purpose of his existence is defeated, at least within the experience of the protagonist himself.

Yet this existence still does have a purpose, and it is this purpose which differentiates Brecht's pessimism from that of Ionesco. For while it is true that the Brechtian hero is almost inevitably defeated by the interaction between his own cunning and the social forces which shape his fate, it is the essence of these social forces rather than that of the individual that is shown to be at fault. As Galileo puts it, it is the nation that needs heroes (and thus forces men to turn coward to save their skin) that is unhappy, just as it is the war that forces Mother Courage to employ cunning to preserve her means of eking out an existence yet see her children perish, and as it is the combined misery and greed of the oppressed that brings Shen-Te to invent an alter ego who ruthlessly subverts her good intentions. These are all social institutions which are, at least theoretically speaking, subject to change. And yet they are institutions before which the individual appears to be powerless, for a single voice raised

[74] Brecht, *Stücke 3*, p. 111.

against the monolithic mechanism of mass society is unheard; a single life laid down before the juggernaut of bourgeois conformity is easily snuffed out without effect, without attracting more than momentary notice. In short, as long as society reacts as a mass, as long as the individual surrenders his being to gain security at the cost of his identity, society cannot change. Brecht's mature works make one painfully aware of the human weaknesses of the individual; as Shen-Te puts it, the human being is simply inadequate to be good, absolutely good, in times like these. And yet, in making us aware of our weakness when confronted by an impassive mass culture, he also makes us aware of our individuality, however tenuous it may be, and of our guilt in silently watching injustice, the while paying lip service to justice. Thereby he kindles the hope that, were enough people made aware of their individuality and of the depredations wrought against it by society, they could somehow combine forces and change that society, thereby creating an atmosphere in which man would not have to be a hero or a martyr in order to be good. And this is for him the very essence of the purpose of existence, for it is only through the exertions of the individual that society can be changed. As he points out in his foreword to *The Life of Galileo*, good times will not come as simply as morning comes after a night's sleep; they must be forged by the positive efforts of mankind. The struggle of the individual may seem to be futile, but it is only by such unrelenting struggle, such working against the grain of mass society, that any progress may be made toward a social condition in which the individual is not forced to apply cunning, to go against his own nature, simply in order to survive. And it is only with respect to such a struggle that existence has any purpose at all, even though that purpose cannot be achieved within the life of the individual committed to that struggle.

Ironically, however, Brecht found himself unequal to such a struggle. Sensing the condition of man as he did, he saw no choice but to employ his own *List* in order to survive, no hope for individual heroism to be effective against the institutions of society. And yet, looking back from the height of a successful career, he perceived, as did his Galileo, that he who uses *List* to survive, even if his purpose be to disseminate the truth, inevitably plays into the hands of the regime, of the *Obrigkeit* against which he is surreptitiously working. He is used, as Galileo's recantation was used and as Brecht's letter concerning the 1953 workers' uprising was used, as an example to keep less cunning opponents in check. Thus in a very real sense Brecht saw that his cunning had defeated its own purpose, just as had that of Galileo.

Yet it is precisely this sense of eventual purpose which Ionesco rejects throughout his works, particularly in *Exit the King* and *Hunger and Thirst*. The Bérenger *engagé* of *Rhinoceros* had had such a purpose, as had the Bérenger of *The Killer*: to retain their humanity and identity in the face of just such social institutions as those which concerned Brecht, yet their efforts were futile, resulting in their own extinction. And for the reincarnated Bérenger of *Exit the King*, it is precisely this extinction which renders all else meaningless and absurd. That constellations will be conquered, that new generations will populate the universe, that elixirs of immortality will be brewed, that new stars will appear, that new wisdom will be discovered and new sciences will grow out of the old—all this is immaterial to him, for the only thing that matters is that he is dying and is afraid (cf. the epigraph of this chapter). Nor does the fact that he has contributed to the growth of this miraculous new age make any difference to him:

MARIE: You prepared all of that.

KING: Without meaning to do it.

MARIE: You were a stage, an element, a forerunner. You are part of all the constructions. You count. You will be counted.

KING: I won't be accountable. I'm dying.

MARIE: Everything that was will be, everything that will be is, everything that will be was. You are inscribed forever in the rolls of the universe.

KING: Who'll consult the archives? I'm dying. Let everyone die. No, let

everyone live. No, let everyone die, since my death can't fill the world.
Let everyone die. No, let everyone live.

GUARD: His majesty wants everyone to live.

KING: Let everyone die with me. No, let everyone live after me. No, let
everyone die. No, let everyone live. No, let everyone die, everyone
live, everyone die.[75]

Thus for Bérenger, as for Ionesco, the ultimate truth, that which
overshadows all else and makes the fate of the rest of the world immaterial, is the fact that he must die. The rest of the world may die
with him, survive him, or even be improved because of him; it makes
no difference, for his own existence is the only thing of importance
to him, and that is about to be snuffed out. Beyond this extinction
there is nothingness.

In his latest work at this writing, *Hunger and Thirst,* Ionesco
specifically ridicules Brecht for his belief that something worthwhile
can grow out of human existence, that the disease of mankind is
social. In a long, *guignolesque* scene in the middle of the third act,
a clown named Brechtoll (an obvious play on Brecht's name and
the German word *toll,* crazy, reminiscent as well of Jarry's Dr.
Faustroll) is tormented by imprisonment and denial of food until
he is at the point of doing anything in order to secure food:

BROTHER TARABAS *(to Brechtoll):* Unhappy man! You don't believe in
God! That's why you think men are bad. That's why you've thought up
an impossible human solidarity. This solidarity that you speak of—
what is its cement, if not God?

BRECHTOLL: We don't have any principles. It is the necessities which form
the cement. We'll talk about it after dinner, after dinner, after dinner.[76]

This line, an echo of "Erst kommt das Fressen, dann die Moral,"
of *Three Penny Opera,* is meant as criticism of what Ionesco conceives of as Brecht's fundamental materialism, which he sees as
pointless. As Frère Tarabas later tells Brechtoll: "You believe neither in goodness nor in evil. You don't believe in God. You believe

[75] Ionesco, *Théâtre IV*, p. 55.
[76] *Ibid.*, pp. 149–150.

in soup and in liberty. But I still want to give you that which you can't define: liberty."[77] But the clown figure representing Brecht cannot define liberty, and he is eventually tormented to the point where he renounces his belief in soup and affirms his belief in God, as a contrapuntal development to the torment of a fanatically religious clown figure named Tripp, who finally renounces God in favor of soup. Yet the conversion of each is ultimately pointless, for both are simply shut up in their cages again at the end, their fates to be considered "one of these days."

In other words, there is hope neither in material or social progress nor in belief in God, for ultimately man is shut up in the cage that is life. And life in itself is pointless and infinite servitude, as the conclusion of the piece makes clear. Held in a monastery which he has entered in his Faust-like quest for a better life, Jean, the hero, is told that by enjoying the hospitality of the brothers he has incurred a debt to them which can be made good only by serving them for a certain period of time. Having in the meanwhile refound his wife and daughter, Jean is impatient to return to them and demands to know precisely how many hours he must serve. The answer, which constitutes the end of the drama, is simple yet eloquent: "ACCOUNTANT FRIAR: Number of hours of work owed by our Brother Jean for having been lodged, fed, listened to, and entertained in our monastery: one, three, six, seven, eight, nine, one, seven, three, six, nine, eight, one, seven, three, six, nine, eight, one, seven, three, six, nine, eight. . . ."[78] And so on for a page and a half of closely printed figures, while Jean is driven to a frenzy of work serving the other brothers. In short, at any moment life seems to him to be an interminable form of meaningless servitude. But to return to *Exit the King*, even this servitude is rendered the more absurd by the fact that man must die, must lapse into a void at the end of a pointless existence. In essence, Ionesco thus operates within a closed system

[77] *Ibid.*, p. 151.
[78] *Ibid.*, p. 179.

in which neither life nor death can be meaningful, for the former is pointless, and the latter renders it even more so.

Hence engagement does have a distinct effect upon drama, but it is not the stifling effect which Ionesco claims all committed drama must ultimately suffer. Nor is the polemic intent of the dramatist directly carried out, as is indicated by the embarrassment which *The Measures Taken* and *The Life of Galileo* have caused among Communist critics. What engagement has accomplished, at least in the case of Brecht, is to allay the sense of despair, emptiness, and pointlessness which characterizes the early works, *Baal*, *Drums in the Night*, and particularly *In the Jungle of the Cities*, which presents the pointless struggle between Garga and Shlink as a symbol of life viewed as a gratuitous and meaningless fight to the finish. After his commitment to Communism—and there can be no doubt that Brecht believed in the principles of Marxist dialectic materialism to the end of his days—this human struggle for existence no longer seemed so gratuitous and pointless, for it had acquired a purpose: amelioration of the social condition of humanity. In the early works, human nature was held to lie at the root of human misery, for the characteristics which determined human fate were inherent in the being: lust, greed, passion, perversion, and indifference to the fate of others. In the mature works, these faults are not purely an emanation of human nature, but are socially conditioned, particularly by the depraved, morally bankrupt values of bourgeois capitalist society. This is not to suggest that the essential pessimism of the early works was replaced by a new optimism, for, as Robert Brustein has correctly observed, Brecht responded more to the critical than to the utopian side of Marxism,[79] and he continued to be occupied with the negative aspects of society as he saw it rather than with the possibilities for an improved society. In effect, Brecht's commitment provided him with a social frame of reference within which he could continue to create dramas characterized by the same compelling

[79] Brustein, *Theatre of Revolt*, p. 253.

power of language which had marked his early works, and which ameliorated his essential negativism regarding human nature. But this negativistic despair was by no means completely effaced, for it remained, as Brustein points out, a fundamental aspect of Brecht's works:

> Brecht's Communism, then, is less a substitute for his early Neo-Romanticism [Brustein equates German neo-romanticism with the view that man is at best a helpless thrall victimized by an inhuman world, and at worst a brutal animal who wears the veneer of civilization quite tenuously; he compares Brecht with Büchner and Wedekind in this respect] than a layer superimposed on top of it—his rational ideology emerges as the dialectical counterpart of his irrationalism and despair. Brecht's new commitment permits him to function as an artist, but his political solutions are fashioned for essentially metaphysical problems. To be sure, Brecht's assumptions are now more hopeful and optimistic. Where he once identified evil with fate and assumed it to be fixed, he now identifies it with bourgeois society, and assumes it to be changeable. . . . His despairing belief in Darwinist science (natural selection and determinism) has been replaced by an affirmative belief in Marxist science (class war and revolution)—his despondent feelings about the future of the individual have given way to more cheerful feelings about the future of the collective. Sociological interpretations have grown more important than biological ones; materialistic explanations prevail; and instead of finding everything ruled by blind instinct, Brecht begins to reveal more faith in will and reason. Whatever his expectations of the future, however, Brecht continues to focus on the bleaker aspects of present-day reality. While he refuses to reach tragic conclusions, he is still primarily occupied with tragic conditions. Human deterioration may now be attributed to the social system, but rot still catches his eye, even if it is now called by the name of Capitalism.[80]

Had Brecht been of a more optimistic or utopian bent of mind, he might well have turned to socialist realism, but his fundamental

[80] *Ibid.*, pp. 251–253.

nihilism and despair continued to show through what Brustein refers to as the layer imposed upon them by his commitment.

This newly discovered ideological and sociological stimulus for the drama served first as the basis for the *Lehrstücke* (including *The Measures Taken*) as well as for the more extreme of his theories regarding the capacity of the theater to change the world. But it was eventually assimilated so that it became only one influence among many that shaped the creative process. His commitment seldom exclusively determined the thematic content of his plays, and even when it did, as, for instance, in the reworking of the final scene of *The Life of Galileo* after the explosion of the first atomic bomb, it generally worked in conjunction with his more basic concerns, in this case his hatred of war, and it never permeated the mature works to the extent that they became restrictively polemic.

But above all, Brecht always remained more a dramatist, a man of the theater in the fullest sense of the word, than a polemicist or a politician. Indeed, the tale is still told in the Berliner Ensemble of how, after weeks of *Probenarbeit* on the scene in *Mother Courage* in which the mute Kattrin is shot while trying to save the burghers of Halle from a surprise attack, Frau Weigel is supposed to have finally said reproachfully to her husband, "Brecht, it won't work. In this form the scene can never have an estranging or dialectic effect." To this Brecht is said to have replied with a sigh, "I know, I know. But it's certainly marvelous theater!" Needless to say, the scene stayed in the play, though doubtless Frau Weigel was right; coming as it does just before the brief final scene, it never fails to seize the audience with its pathos and partially negate the effects of all the other *Verfremdung* so artfully contrived in the work. Nor was the recasting of the final scene of *The Life of Galileo* significantly different. While it is certain that Brecht's intention was to take the character he had already created and discredit him as a coward and traitor both to science and to society, some innate sense of theater kept him from tampering with the development of the essential characteristics of the figure he had so carefully built into a credible human being in the early scenes, and the resultant work, particularly as played by the Berliner Ensemble, is if anything better theater than the original version could have been. It is a stronger, more compelling work because it provides a deeper insight into human nature and poses questions which, unfortunately, will probably never pass out of date. In essence, then, Brecht's commitment to Communism provided him not so much with a dogma or a closed system as it did with a sense of balance, a positivistic approach which moderated his earlier nihilism and gave him a sense of discipline, as Bentley, Esslin, Brustein, and Politzer have all recognized. In a real sense, it filled what had been the "void at the center of things" for Brecht, and in so doing, it provided, at least in part, the stimulus for more than a score of dramas, four or five of which must be numbered among the most effective and aesthetically satisfying that have been written in German in this century.

As for Ionesco, it is probably redundant to reiterate here that he remains socially and politically nihilistic, but it is certain that this utter rejection of society and its political games forms a large part of the "void at the center of things" for him. The rest of this void is formed by his own obsession with death as the ultimate absurdity in an otherwise totally absurd existence. As has been repeatedly observed, the process of writing is for Ionesco always intensely personal and confessional, even in his own polemic works. He writes, as he has said, not to change or even necessarily to reflect the world as it is, but to give vent to his own personal feelings, perceptions, and obsessions. And he professes to have no goal outside of creating pure theater, for, as he sees it, theater can only be theater. But such an approach is problematic, and it is fraught with several dangers. In the first place, he has stated repeatedly that he aspires to classicism and universality, yet he seeks to impose his own obsessions upon the spectator, obsessions which are often too intensely personal to be conveyed through the medium of the theater. *Exit the King* may serve as a case in point here, for in trying to convey his obsession with death as the ultimate absurdity of existence, he expressed this perception so explicitly that his point became obvious, and the spectator feels, as French and British critics unanimously felt, that the theme is belabored to the point of overstatement, of boredom. This is not to question the validity of his perception, which is certainly of immense topical importance for literature as well as for philosophy. But it is to question whether such a static form of drama can be a satisfactory vehicle for such a perception.

But even more important is the fact that Ionesco first came to the theater, as he has admitted, or indeed all but boasted, as a dilettante, and because of his philosophical void he remains a dilettante in the original sense of the word, as one who does something purely for its intrinsic delight, with no exterior or extrinsic motive. This fact may well explain why his early shorter works have enjoyed greater success, both critical and popular, than have his later full-scale dramas. To put it baldly, Brecht's commitment to Communism and his total involvement in the theater enabled him to put forth months and even years of concentrated effort in order to bring a work into being, and he would never raise the curtain on a work with which he was less than satisfied (which may well explain why the *Probenarbeit* and production of such minor works as *The Resistible Rise of Arturo Ui* were not undertaken until after his death). His work merely in translation of *The Life of Galileo* with Charles Laughton, for example, spanned the better part of two years, and even such a secondary work as his adaptation of Shakespeare's *Coriolanus* was deemed worth a year and a half of intensive preliminary study by his staff of *Dramaturgen* and eight full months of full-scale *Probenarbeit*. With Ionesco, on the other hand, one frequently feels that the delight he has taken in creating a work has dried up prematurely, that the work has not been systematically thought through and worked out to a successful resolution. There are many of his plays which contain brilliant and delightful scenes or fragments of scenes, but which simply fail to jell as coherent works of theater because the inspiration was not sustained. *Amédée, or How to Get Rid of It* serves well as a case in point here, for its enigmatic ending, in which Amédée simply flies away with the gigantic and grotesque cadaver which has dominated his life, has given Ionesco's critics—not to mention his set designers—no end of trouble. Richard Schechner, generalizing upon a similar act of levitation in *The Aerial Pedestrian*, feels that flying is symbolic of the creative act itself,[81] while George Wellwarth describes it as an antitheatrical burlesque of "Little Eva and her more sublime though no less ridiculous Himmelfahrt,"[82] and Leonard Pronko condemns it as a magical evasion which has sidestepped the problem of resolution rather than face it.[83] In actuality, it is Pronko who comes closest to a correct interpretation, for, queried concerning this scene, Ionesco replied that he had simply grown tired of the gag and couldn't think of any other way to clear the stage of the immense corpse; but he took no little delight in the critical consternation which he had caused.[84] On the other hand, Ionesco himself has expressed more serious doubts concerning the final act of his latest work, *Hunger and Thirst*.

> I like the first act, I like the second, I like the first and even the second part of the third act, but I find the end a bit childish, after the business with the cages [the Brechtoll scene]. And that business with the cages—I don't think it's really bad, but it is quite unsatisfactory, for that which happens everywhere in the world is infinitely more atrocious. Literature can only sugar-coat reality.
>
> The end seems a bit naive to me, but if it is recognized that it presents a theme already treated by several authors who are not exactly unknown, for example by Goethe in *Faust* or by Dante, when he arrives in paradise and meets Beatrice again, then I may feel a bit reassured. On the other hand, that might seem to suggest that the solution rests

---

[81] Richard Schechner, "The Inner and the Outer Reality," *Tulane Drama Review* 7, no. 3 (Spring 1963): 201.

[82] George Wellwarth, *The Theater of Protest and Paradox* (New York: New York University Press, 1964), p. 63.

[83] Leonard Pronko, *Avant-Garde: The Experimental Theater in France* (Berkeley and Los Angeles: University of California Press, 1962), p. 94.

[84] A finding of the writer's interview with Ionesco.

too much on the paradise of bourgeois conjugal love, or on tenderness. It is an almost desperate attempt, naive and ridiculous, to re-establish the power of love.[85]

Thus here again the delight in creating, the inspirational impulse, has not proved enduring enough in itself to sustain the writer to bring the work to such a point of fruition that it satisfies even his own aesthetic demands, even for a work which was to have its French premiere at the Comédie Française. And the dramatic validity of the work has similarly been questioned by others; Jacques Lemarchand, who gave the piece its most sympathetic review, called it a "poem of love and terror," and he even goes so far as to call the first two acts "verses" (*chants*), but he ultimately questions whether it is theater.[86] The reader of this work and of *Exit the King* may well question whether they are truly theatrical as well. There can be no doubt that they are poetic, for there are passages of great power and beauty—it cannot be denied that Ionesco has a compelling way with words—and there are some marvelous theatrical moments, but again the works simply do not come off as theatrical successes because they are too static and too narrowly obsessive. In the end, it is probably this personal obsessiveness which limits most severely the effectiveness of Ionesco's late works, as George Wellwarth recognizes: "In his latest (and probably last) phase, Ionesco has openly become an intensely personal writer. *The King Dies* and *The Aerial Pedestrian* are about Ionesco's preoccupation with his finiteness. Here again the influence of Camus can be discerned. In the future Ionesco must either find some sort of peace in philosophical speculation, as Camus did, or (as he has threatened in *The Aerial Pedestrian*) stop writing altogether."[87] Certainly Wellwarth oversteps the critic's role in suggesting that Ionesco stop writing altogether, just

[85] Claude Morand, interview with Ionesco concerning *Hunger and Thirst*, *Arts* (23 February 1966), p. 17.

[86] Jacques Lemarchand, *"La soif et la faim* d'Ionesco," *Le Figaro Littéraire* (10 March 1966), p. 14.

[87] Wellwarth, *Theater of Protest*, p. 72.

as Kenneth Tynan did in his insistence that Ionesco adopt a positive ideology, for such is the nature of the man that he can do neither. But these two extreme opinions do serve well to illustrate the feeling of many serious critics of theater that Ionesco has, in his personal obsessions with both his fate and pure theater, become too narrow and too static to attain the stature of a major dramatist, which stature no objective critic fails to accord to Brecht. The relative stature of the two is well stated by Jens Bjørneboe in a digressive last paragraph of his review of the Berliner Ensemble's guest performances in Paris in the summer of 1960:

> The only production which could in any way be compared with the level achieved in the East German guest performances was the performance of the two sparkling, nihilistic one-acters by Ionesco in the tiny little Théâtre de la Huchette. Both of these pieces, *The Lesson* and *The Bald Soprano*, have similarly been playing for four weeks now before full houses. The evening really provided, in the finest way, an example of the abstract, unnaturalistic French art of the theater and showed what sort of theater one can really expect in Paris. Nevertheless, they remain in the memory only as a tiny sparkling miniature compared with the massive effect which emanates from the Berliner Ensemble.[88]

In short, in comparison with Brecht, Ionesco remains an important theatrical innovator, but essentially a painter of theatrical miniatures rather than a major dramatist.

This reaction is not based solely on philosophical analysis of the works of the two, though admittedly, by the nature of this study, the preponderance of consideration thus far has turned upon philosophical or even quasi-philosophical points. But at this juncture it is time to lay such considerations aside and have a look at the two from an aesthetic viewpoint, considering the qualitative nature of theatrical experience that is provided by their dramas. It should be

[88] Jens Bjørneboe, "Slutbetraktning over Berliner Ensemble," *Oslo Dagbladet* (5 August 1960), p. 12.

emphasized here that such judgment cannot emerge from textual analysis alone, but must be based upon actual experience of the works in production, for drama can achieve realization as art only upon the stage before an audience. Peter Brook, in his introduction to the English version of *Marat/Sade*, by Peter Weiß, provides a remarkably succinct and effective way of reaching such judgment:

> What's the difference between a poor play and a good one? I think there's a very simple way of comparing them. A play in performance is a series of impressions; little dabs, one after another, fragments of information or feeling in a sequence, which stir the audience's perceptions. A good play sends many such messages, often several at a time, often crowding, jostling, overlapping one another. The intelligence, the feelings, the memory, the imagination are all stirred. In a poor play, the impressions are well spaced out, they lope along in single file, and in the gaps the heart can sleep while the mind wanders to the day's annoyances and thoughts of dinner.
>
> The whole problem of the theatre today is just this: how can we make plays dense in experience? Great philosophical novels are often far longer than thrillers, more content occupies more pages, but great plays and poor plays fill up evenings of pretty comparable length. Shakespeare seems better in performance than anyone else because he gives us more, moment for moment, for our money. This is due to his genius, but also to his technique. The possibilities of free verse on an open stage enabled him to cut the inessential detail and the irrelevant realistic action: in their place he could cram sounds and ideas, thoughts and images which make each instant into a stunning mobile.[89]

It is precisely in its experiential density that the theater of Brecht achieves its fullest measure of success. To put the matter quite bluntly, I have seen productions of eight works by Brecht performed by the Berliner Ensemble; whatever philosophical or aesthetic reservations I may have had in advance about the texts of these works,

[89] Peter Weiß, *The Persecution and Assassination of Jean-Paul Marat as Performed by the Inmates of the Asylum of Charenton Under the Direction of the Marquis de Sade*, intro. by Peter Brook (New York: Atheneum, 1966), p. v.

the productions have never failed to stimulate me, to amaze me, to delight me with the wealth of concrete experience they have provided, with their pure theatricality, with their ability to convey subtle and frequently contradictory nuances of tone and meaning. Probably the most spectacular example of such success is provided by *The Resistible Rise of Arturo Ui*, a work about which I continue to have serious reservations, both philosophical and aesthetic. When I first encountered the text, I dismissed it as utterly hopeless, for on the one hand it seemed philosophically shallow in interpreting Hitler's rise to power in purely Marxist terms, and on the other it struck me as aesthetically weak, smacking of the sophomoric attempts of the currently popular guerila theater to lampoon public figures by making them appear ludicrous. I simply could not conceive of Hitler as a ludicrous figure. But what I was not prepared for, or perhaps am still missing in my reading of the text, was the intensity of malevolent power that emerged from the production, particularly from Ekkehard Schall's portrayal of Ui. And yet it was just this sense of malevolent power so grotesquely applied (to corner the market on cauliflower, of all things!) that was required to demonstrate how perfectly ludicrous—grotesque, brutal, and terrifying, yes, but still ludicrous—Hitler and the movement he represented actually were. This is the sort of dimension Brook is referring to in the passage cited, the experiential density, the interplay of emotion (my memory underscores the reality and magnitude of the horror that resulted from Hitler's usurpation of power), reason (which tells me, as I am experiencing this performance, how utterly absurd it was that nobody managed to untrack the Nazi juggernaut at the outset), and imagination (which invites me to extend the analogy of the work to the contemporary political scene), which, brought into clashing conflict, generate the sparks which distinguish great theater. This is not to say that I consider *The Resistible Rise of Arturo Ui* to be a significant contribution to dramatic literature; I do not because I don't feel that anything less than the polish, verve, style, discipline, and dedication brought to bear on the work by the Berliner Ensemble could save it.

But it is to say again that Brecht's theatrical power cannot be assessed by textual analysis alone, for realized theater is a complex phenomenon that comes at the spectator all at once and will not stand still for rational analysis. And it is to emphasize that I consider such works as *The Life of Galileo, Mother Courage, The Caucasian Chalk Circle, The Good Woman of Setzuan,* and *Three Penny Opera* to be significant contributions to theater, particularly when realized in productions by the Berliner Ensemble.

On the other hand, I have seen six Ionesco productions in Paris, yet I have been satisfied with only one of them as drama, the 1965 production of *The Lesson* at the Théâtre de la Huchette. As for the rest, they struck me without exception as ill-conceived in direction, poorly prepared, and amateurishly staged. In short, they lacked emotional and intellectual intensity, the density of experience cited by Brook as the essential concern of modern drama. The 1965 revival of *The Chairs* by Tsilla Chelton and Jacques Mauclair may serve as a case in point. I was enthusiastic when I first read the piece, and a fairly straightforward American student production came close to realizing the import of the work, but the authentic Ionesco production in Paris came as a disappointment to me. It did so precisely because it failed to provide the density of experience I had expected and had thought to discern in the text. Rather, it seemed to impoverish Ionesco, to diminish the work to the stature of a one-line gag expanded, much in the fashion of a shaggy dog story, to the point of ennui. The chief weakness lay in the broad, burlesque approach to the roles of the old man and the old woman. It strikes me that whatever potential for dramatic intensity exists in the work can only be realized if the two principals appear to take both themselves and their invisible guests perfectly seriously, for both the humor and the pathos of the work are functions of its structure, of the trick ending which renders the immolation of the two absurd. The spectator must be able to believe in their sincerity, must find them and their situation credible, if the final turnabout is to have its effect. When the leading roles are played, as they were in the production in question, which was true to Ionesco's intention (cf. his letter to the director of *The Chairs* cited on p. 95), in a slapstick fashion, in a manner that intimates that the two are in on the gag, the entire production is bound to suffer, to space out its impressions, to lose in density of experience. And such was my impression of not only the production of *The Chairs*, but also of those of *The Bald Soprano*, *Victims of Duty*, *Rhinoceros*, and *Exit the King*, not to mention American productions of *Amédée* and *The Aerial Pedestrian*. They simply failed to convey any sense of urgency or immediacy, any sense that something significant was at issue, any sense of dramatic intensity or economy.

It might be objected, I suppose, that one can scarcely blame Ionesco for such shortcomings, which are probably the fault of poor direction and flawed acting. But I submit that, in managing to bring his dramatic works to a point of genuine and consistent fruition on the stage, Brecht has clearly accomplished the greater achievement of drama as art. I will be the first to admit that his works do not fare as well in the hands of others, that in fact they generally suffer badly when performed in translation on the English-speaking stage. But this observation simply underscores the point I am trying to make, that we miss a great deal of the essential Brecht on this side of the Rhine, and we do so precisely because we too often make the mistake of taking him simply as a radical polemicist, ignoring or failing to discern the quite traditional theatrical discipline that was the basis of his art. And by doing so, we impoverish our experience of him; we sacrifice the potential experiential density which we might realize if we were able to sense his total grasp of theater.

Hence overt political commitment is not, as Ionesco believes, necessarily stifling to art, for, at least in the case of Brecht, it nurtured his creativity by lending him the discipline, the dedication, and the purpose which, combined with his innate talent and sense of theater as well as with his essential artistic honesty, enabled him to produce some of the most powerful dramas of the twentieth century and to exert considerable influence on the development of the modern drama in general. By no stretch of the imagination can he be considered purely a polemic dramatist, for, even when his intention was purely didactic, as in the *Lehrstücke*, his insight led him to prophetic conclusions regarding Communism, and his mature works consistently rise far above polemics. It is true that his commitment left him with some blind spots (*The Round-heads and the Pointed-heads* and *The Resistible Rise of Arturo Ui*, both of which seek to explain the Nazi usurpation of power solely in terms of the machination of capitalism, fail to grasp Hitler's demagogic appeal to the German people), but it did not prevent him from creating works such as *Mother Courage, The Caucasian Chalk Circle, The Good Woman of Setzuan,* and *The Life of Galileo,* which represent considerably more than a Marxist view of man's social condition.

On the other hand, Ionesco has held himself aloof from the taint of any political commitment, or indeed of any external commitment whatsoever, but in so doing he has remained a prisoner of his own obsessions to such an extent that he cannot rise above them. His view of the world is restricted, not *by* some external commitment or engagement, but rather *to* that which he finds within himself, and the resultant works, his late dramas, are as narrowly obsessive as he considers all engaged drama to be.

Ionesco would by no means consider this last remark to be a significant criticism, for he sees himself as unique and solitary, and he seeks to convey this uniqueness and solitude in his dramas. But then, in a very real sense, all human existence is solitary. At conception each of us is genetically unique, and we draw our first breath in the solitude of an alien world. At death, we depart in the same fashion, alone, into an unknown void. Between birth and death the solitary individual experiences either the naive, unrealized loneliness of the extrovert totally projected outward upon society, or, on the other hand, he grasps intuitively the suffering of man as one whose participation in the experience of others is such as to set him apart. Such an individual becomes a sort of a psychic lens through which we ordinary beings are projected and made to focus upon our innermost phantasies and terrors. Creative genius necessarily entails self-knowledge, which in turn engenders loneliness, and as a consequence all great literature is, in the last analysis, literature of loneliness. Both Brecht and Ionesco are essentially thus: lonely, isolated, and nihilistic. But drama, unlike other forms of literature, is not experienced in solitude or isolation, nor is it, in its ultimate form upon the stage, even experienced at leisure. If it is to work, it must somehow bridge the gap posed by the solitude of the author and of the individual spectator; it must be able to seize and move an audience as a collective being. To accomplish this, it must transcend the solitary obsession of its author and find expression in broadly shared human concerns and perceptions. Otherwise it remains poetic, but hardly dramatic. Brecht was able to achieve the dramatic because his fundamental solitude was alleviated by his dedication first to Communism and second to the life of the theater. For Ionesco, it remains unalleviated.

BIBLIOGRAPHY OF WORKS CONSULTED

I. PRIMARY SOURCES

A. *Editions Cited*

Brecht, Bertolt. *Aufbau einer Rolle: Laughtons Galilei*. Berlin: Henschel Verlag, 1962.

——. *Dialoge aus dem Messingkauf*. Frankfurt am Main: Suhrkamp Verlag, 1963.

——. *Gedichte*, 7 vols. Frankfurt am Main: Suhrkamp Verlag, 1964.

——. *Schriften zum Theater*, 7 vols. Frankfurt am Main: Suhrkamp Verlag, 1963.

——. *Stücke*, 12 vols. Frankfurt am Main: Suhrkamp Verlag, 1962.

——. *Versuche*, vols. 1–8. Berlin: Kiepenhauer Verlag, 1930–1933.

——. *Versuche*, vols. 9–15. Frankfurt am Main: Suhrkamp Verlag, 1949–1957.

——. *Werke*, 20 vols. Frankfurt am Main: Suhrkamp Verlag, 1968.

Ionesco, Eugène. "Journal," selections published in *Arts*, 16 March 1966.

——. "Mes pièces ne prétendent pas sauver le monde," *L'Express*, 15 October 1955.

——. *Notes et contre-notes*. Paris: Gallimard, 1962.

——. *Théâtre*, 4 vols. Paris: Gallimard, 1956–1966.

B. *Translations Available*

Brecht, Bertolt. *The Life of Galileo.* Translated by Desmond I. Vesey, in *Plays,* vol. 1. London: Methuen, 1960.

————. *The Measures Taken.* Translated by Eric Bentley, in *The Modern Theater,* vol. 6. Garden City, N.Y.: Doubleday Anchor Books, 1960.

————. *Seven Plays.* Translated and edited by Eric Bentley. New York: Grove Press, 1961.

Ionesco, Eugène. *Notes and Counter Notes.* Translated by Donald Watson. New York: Grove Press, 1964.

————. *Plays,* 6 vols. Translated by Donald Watson. London: J. Calder, 1958–1965.

II. SECONDARY SOURCES

A. *Books*

Abel, Lionel. *Metatheatre: A New View of Dramatic Form.* New York: Hill and Wang, 1963.

Adorno, Theodor W. *Noten zur Literatur,* vol. 3. Frankfurt am Main: Suhrkamp Verlag, 1963.

Artaud, Antonin. *The Theater and Its Double.* Translated by Mary C. Richards. New York: Grove Press, 1958.

Beigbeder, Marc. *Le Théâtre en France depuis la liberation.* Paris: Bordas, 1959.

Benjamin, Walter. *Schriften,* 2 vols. Frankfurt am Main: Suhrkamp Verlag, 1955.

Bentley, Eric. *The Dramatic Event.* Boston: Beacon Press, 1954.

————. *The Life of the Drama.* New York: Atheneum, 1965.

————. *The Playwright as Thinker.* Cleveland: Meridian Books, 1946.

————. *What Is Theater?* Boston: Beacon Press, 1956.

Berlau, Ruth, ed. *Theaterarbeit: Sechs Aufführungen des Berliner Ensembles.* Frankfurt am Main: Suhrkamp Verlag, 1961.

Brustein, Robert. *The Theatre of Revolt.* Boston: Little, Brown, 1962.

Coe, Richard. *Eugene Ionesco.* Edinburgh: Evergreen Pilot Books, 1961.

Demetz, Peter, ed. *Brecht: A Collection of Critical Essays.* Englewood Cliffs, N.J.: Prentice-Hall, 1962.

Desuché, Jacques. *Bertolt Brecht.* Paris: Presses Universitaires de France, 1963.

Dhomme, Sylvain. *La mise en scène contemporaine d'André Antoine à Bertolt Brecht.* Paris: Fernand Nathan, 1959.

Dort, Bernard. *Lecture de Brecht.* Paris: Éditions du Seuil, 1960.

Esslin, Martin. *Brecht: The Man and His Work*. Garden City, N.Y.: Doubleday Anchor Books, 1960.

———. *The Theatre of the Absurd*. Garden City, N.Y.: Doubleday Anchor Books, 1961.

Franzen, Erich. *Formen des modernen Dramas*. Munich: C. H. Beck Verlag, 1961.

Geißler, Rolf. *Zur Interpretation des modernen Dramas: Brecht, Dürrenmatt, Frisch*. Frankfurt am Main: Verlag Moritz Diesterweg, 1962.

Glaubert, Barbara. "Bertolt Brechts Amerikabild in drei seiner Stücke." Master's thesis, University of Colorado, August, 1961.

Gray, Ronald. *Brecht*. London: Oliver and Boyd, 1961.

Grimm, Reinhold. *Bertolt Brecht: Die Struktur seines Werkes*. Nuremberg: Verlag Hans Carl, 1962.

———. *Bertolt Brecht und die Weltliteratur*. Nuremberg: Verlag Hans Carl, 1961.

Grossvogel, David I. *Four Playwrights and a Postscript*. Ithaca, N.Y.: Cornell University Press, 1962.

Hecht, Werner. *Brechts Weg zum epischen Theater*. Berlin: Henschel Verlag, 1962.

Hinck, Walter. *Die Dramaturgie des späten Brecht*. Göttingen: Vandenhoeck und Rupprecht, 1962.

Hoffman, Stanley. *In Search of France*. Cambridge: Harvard University Press, 1963.

Ihering, Herbert. *Bertolt Brecht*. Berlin: Rembrandt Verlag, 1959.

Jäggi, Willy, and Hans Oesch, eds. *Das Ärgernis Brecht*. Basel: Basilius Presse, 1961.

Kaufmann, Hans. *Bertolt Brecht: Geschichtsdrama und Parabelstücke*. Berlin: Rütten und Loening, 1962.

Kesting, Marianne. *Bertolt Brecht in Selbstzeugnissen und Bilddokumenten*. Hamburg: Rohwolt Verlag, 1959.

———. *Panorama des zeitgenössischen Theaters*. Munich: Piper Verlag, 1962.

Klotz, Volker. *Bertolt Brecht: Versuch über das Werk*. Darmstadt: Gentner Verlag, 1957.

Mann, Otto. *B. B.: Maß oder Mythos?* Heidelberg: W. Rothe Verlag, 1958.

Mayer, Hans. *Bertolt Brecht und die Tradition*. Pfullingen: Verlag Günther Neske, 1961.

Mittenzwei, Werner. *Bertolt Brecht von der "Maßnahme" zu "Leben des Galilei."* Berlin: Aufbau Verlag, 1962.

Müller, Andre. *Kreuzzug gegen Brecht*. Berlin: Aufbau Verlag, 1962.

Pronko, Leonard. *Avant-Garde: The Experimental Theater in France*. Berkeley and Los Angeles: University of California Press, 1962.

Rühle, Jürgen. *Gefesseltes Theater*. Munich: Deutscher Taschenbuch Verlag, 1963.

———. *Literatur und Revolution*. Munich: Knaur Verlag, 1963.

Schumacher, Ernst. *Die dramatischen Versuche Bertolt Brechts, 1918–1933*. Berlin: Rütten und Loening, 1955.

Schwartz, George, and Philip W. Bishop. *Moments of Discovery: The Origins of Science*, 2 vols. New York: Basic Books, 1958.

Sénart, Philippe. *Ionesco*. Paris: Éditions Universitaires, 1964.

Serrau, Geneviève. *Bertolt Brecht, Dramaturge*. Paris: L'Arche, 1955.

Steiner, George. *The Death of Tragedy*. New York: Hill and Wang, 1961.

Sternberg, Fritz. *Der Dichter und die Ratio: Erinnerungen an Bertolt Brecht*. Göttingen: Sachse und Pohl Verlag, 1963.

Strelka, Joseph. *Brecht, Horvath, und Dürrenmatt: Wege und Abwege des modernen Dramas*. Vienna: Forum Verlag, 1962.

Strindberg, August. *Six Plays*. Translated by Elisabeth Sprigge. Garden City, N.Y.: Doubleday Anchor Books, 1955.

Szondi, Peter. *Theorie des modernen Dramas*. Frankfurt am Main: Suhrkamp Verlag, 1956.

Tertz, Abram [pseud.]. *On Socialist Realism*. Translated by George Dennis. New York: Pantheon Books, 1960.

Trilling, Lionel. *The Liberal Imagination*. Garden City, N.Y.: Doubleday Anchor Books, 1953.

Valentin, Karl. *Gesammelte Werke*. Munich: Piper Verlag, 1961.

Weideli, Walter. *Bertolt Brecht*. Paris: Éditions Universitaires, 1961.

Wellwarth, George. *The Theater of Protest and Paradox*. New York: New York University Press, 1964.

Willett, John. *Brecht on Theatre*. New York: Hill and Wang, 1964.

———. *The Theatre of Bertolt Brecht*. London: Methuen, 1959.

Wintzen, René. *Bertolt Brecht*. Paris: Éditions Pierre Seghers, 1954.

B. *Signed Articles*

Ahrendt, Hannah. "What Is Permitted to Jove," *New Yorker*, 5 November 1966.

d'Amico, Fedele. "Gangster und Naziismus," *Neues Deutschland*, 16 December 1959.

Benedictus, David. "We Came, We Saw, We Concurred," *The Spectator*, 20 August 1965.

Bjørneboe, Jens. "Slutbetraktning over Berliner Ensemble," *Oslo Dagbladet*, 5 August 1960.

Bryden, Ronald. "The Brechts of the Apostles," *The New Statesman*, 20 August 1965.

Clurman, Harold. *"Rhinoceros,"* *The Nation*, 28 January 1961.

————. Untitled review of *Exit the King, The Nation,* 19 January 1963.

Déon, Michel. "L'ombre du bûcher," *Les Nouvelles Littéraires,* 7 February 1963.

————. *"Le roi se meurt* d'Ionesco," *Les Nouvelles Litteraires,* 10 January 1963.

Dussane [pseud.]. *"Rhinocéros,"* Mercure de France 338, no. 1159 (March 1960).

Esslin, Martin. "Brecht, the Absurd, and the Future," *Tulane Drama Review* 7, no. 4 (Summer 1963).

Gauthier, Jean-Jacques. "À l'Odéon: *Rhinocéros* d'Eugène Ionesco," *Le Figaro,* 26 January 1960.

Gellert, Roger. "Quietus," *The New Statesman,* 13 September 1963.

Genêt. "Letter from Paris," *New Yorker,* 12 January 1963.

Gilliat, Penelope. "Brecht and Company," *The Observer,* 15 August 1965.

Grimm, Reinhold. "Brecht, Ionesco, und das moderne Theater," *German Life and Letters* 13 (April 1960).

————. "Ideologische Tragödie und Tragödie der Ideologie," *Interpretationen 2: Deutsche Dramen von Gryphius bis Brecht.* Frankfurt am Main: Fischer Bücherei, 1965.

Hanley, Clifford. "Long Time Dying," *The Spectator,* 6 September 1963.

Hewes, Henry. "Rhinoceros on the Loose," *Saturday Review,* 26 January 1961.

Hobson, Harold. "Brecht for Grown-ups," *The Times* (London), 19 August 1965.

Kingston, Jeremy. Untitled review, *Punch,* 18 August 1965.

Kurella, Alfred. "Ein Versuch mit nicht ganz tauglichen Mitteln," *Literatur der Weltrevolution* 4 (1931).

Lemarchand, Jacques. *"Rhinocéros* d'Ionesco à l'Odéon," *Le Figaro Littéraire,* 27 January 1960.

————. *"Le roi se meurt* d'Ionesco," *Le Figaro Littéraire,* 5 January 1960.

————. *"La soif et la faim* d'Ionesco," *Le Figaro Littéraire,* 10 March 1966.

————. *"La vie de Galilée* de Bertolt Brecht au T.N.P.," *Le Figaro Littéraire,* 9 February 1963.

Luft, Friedrich. "Brechts *Galileo Galilei* von beklemmender Aktualität," *Die Welt,* 17 January 1957.

Lüthy, Herbert. "Vom armen Bert Brecht," *Der Monat,* no. 44 (May 1952).

Marcabru, Pierre. "Un rhinocéros à qui Barrault a coupé les cornes," *Arts,* 27 January 1960.

————. "Un rhinocéros chasse l'autre: Bouquet remplace Barrault: Une pièce rénait," *Arts,* 11 January 1961.

Marcel, Gabriel. "Une mesure pour rien," *Les Nouvelles Littéraires,* 10 March 1966.

Moran, Claude. Interview with Ionesco concerning *La soif et la faim, Arts*, 23 February 1966.

Poirot-Delpech, Bertrand. *"Rhinocéros* d'Eugène Ionesco au Théâtre de France," *Le Monde,* 24 January 1960.

Politzer, Heinz. "How Epic Is Bertolt Brecht's Epic Theatre?" in Travis Bogard and William Oliver (eds.), *Modern Drama: Essays in Criticism.* New York: Oxford University Press, 1965.

Rohrmoser, Günther. "Brecht: *Das Leben des Galilei,*" in Benno von Wiese (ed.), *Das deutsche Drama von Barock bis heute.* Düsseldorf: August Bagel Verlag, 1958.

Roy, Claude. *"Le roi se meurt* d'Ionesco," *La Nouvelle Revue Française,* no. 122 (February 1963).

————. "L'utilité de ne pas comprendre: *Le Galilée* de Brecht," *La Nouvelle Revue Française,* no. 124 (April 1963).

Sandier, Gilles. "Shakespeare, Lorca, Ionesco," *Arts,* 15 March 1966.

Sarraute, Claude. "Propos de *Rhinocéros,*" *Le Monde,* 19 January 1960.

Saurel, Renée. "Saint Ionesco, l'anti-Brecht," *Les Temps Modernes,* no. 158 (Spring 1959).

Schechner, Richard. "The Inner and the Outer Reality," *Tulane Drama Review* 7, no. 3 (Spring 1963).

————. *"TDR* Comment," *Tulane Drama Review* 7, no. 4 (Summer 1963).

Scheer, Maximilian. "Brechts *Galilei* in den Kölner Kammerspielen," *Berliner Tägliche Rundschau,* 26 May 1955.

Thieme, Karl. "Des Teufels Gebetbuch," *Hochland* 29, no. 5 (February 1932).

Tynan, Kenneth. "Ionesco and the Phantom," *The Observer,* 6 July 1958.

————. "Ionesco: Man of Destiny?" *The Observer,* 22 June 1958.

Welles, Orson. "The Artist and the Critic," *The Observer,* 13 July 1958.

c. *Unsigned Reviews and Articles*

Unsigned review. "Brechts *Die Maßnahme,*" *Die Linkskurve,* 24 January 1931.

Unsigned article. "Ionesco's *Rhinoceros,*" *New York Times,* 3 November 1960.

Unsigned review. "Nashorn marschiert," *Der Spiegel,* 11 November 1959.

d. *Special Editions of Periodicals*

Benmussa, Simone, ed. *Ionesco: Les rhinocéros au theatre. Cahiers de la compagnie Madeleine Renaud—Jean-Louis Barrault,* February, 1960. (Special issue devoted to Ionesco.)

Cahiers des Saisons, no. 15 (Winter 1959). (Special issue devoted to Ionesco).

Europe: Revue Mensuelle, nos. 133–134 (January–February 1957). (Special issue devoted to Brecht.)

Huchel, Peter, ed. *Sinn und Form: Sonderheft Bertolt Brecht, 1949*. Berlin: Rütten und Loening, 1949.

———. *Sinn und Form: Zweites Sonderheft Bertolt Brecht, 1957*. Berlin: Rütten und Loening, 1957.

INDEX

Actor: as demonstrator of role, 71–73, 104

Ammer, K. L.: translator of ballads of Villon, 154

Anthony, Joseph, 120–121, 130, 133

Anti-theater, 7, 53

Aristotelian theater, 103, 149, 163

Atomic bomb, 23, 177; Brecht's reaction to, 179, 190; end product of Galileo's recantation, 179

Barrault, Jean-Louis, 129–130, 133, 136

Beckett, Samuel: *Endgame,* 88, 207; *Waiting for Godot,* 200, 207

Benjamin, Walter, 69, 73, 148

Berliner Ensemble, 3–4, 45, 46, 59–62, 81, 82–85, 183–184, 230, 231–233

Bouquet, Michel, 133–134

Bourgeoisie, 19, 20, 23, 25, 27, 31, 32, 39, 62–64, 108, 109–110, 123, 124, 130, 135, 137, 141, 143, 223; political apathy of, 23, 35

Brecht-Archiv, 26, 47, 48

Brecht, Bertolt: abhorrence of war, 27–28, 49–50; accused of plagiarism, 154; antiromantic spirit, 30, 141; avoidance of empathetic acting, 74, 95, 103–104, 135; commitment to Communism, 8, 25, 37–38, 47, 50, 68, 190, 223, 225–226; criticism of own works, 30–32; criticism of Soviet art, 39, 41, 81; destruction of theatrical illusion, 30, 65, 70–72, 75; dialectical thought process, 34, 45, 68, 78–79; didacticism, 38–39, 50, 69; as a director, 55–62 *passim,* 81–85; distrust of bourgeoisie, 28, 31, 35; eastern criticism of, 26, 39, 108–112; employment of cunning, 41–45, 47, 116–117; exile, 39, 155, 187; Galileo as parallel, 150, 154–155, 165–166, 175–176, 188, 190, 217; illusion of new era, 174–175; importance of naiveté, 81, 88; innate sense of theater, 55, 61, 225; lack of capacity for enthusiasm, 29, 32; and Marxism, 33–36, 39, 48, 66; misunderstanding of theories by critics, 52–53, 54–55, 58, 77, 80–81; *Nachlaß,* 26, 190; need for external discipline, 6, 37–38, 115, 117, 223, 226, 234,